Tex
RiTTER

Tex Ritter, 1905-1974.

Tex RiTTER

America's Most Beloved Cowboy

By

Bill O'Neal

EAKIN PRESS ★ Austin, Texas

Published in the United States of America
By Eakin Press
A Division of Sunbelt Media, Inc.
P.O. Drawer 90159
Austin, Texas 78709
e-mail: eakinpub@sig.net
www.eakinpress.com

Unless otherwise credited, the photographs in
this book are courtesy of the Tex Ritter Museum.

Library of Congress Cataloging-in-Publication Data

O'Neal, Bill, 1942–
    Tex Ritter : America's most beloved cowboy / by Bill O'Neal—
1st ed.
      p.   cm.
    Discography: p.
    Includes bibliographic references (p.   ) and index.
    ISBN 1-57168-249-X
    1. Ritter, Tex.   2. Singers—United States—Biography. I. Title.
ML420.R62054 1998
791.43'028'092—dc21
[B]   97-28565
                                                 CIP
                                                 MN

For Tommie Ritter Smith—
founder of the Tex Ritter Museum
and keeper of the flame.

iv

Contents

Acknowledgments

This book would not exist without the vision and efforts of Tommie Ritter Smith. A relative of Tex Ritter, Tommie has served for many years as director of the Panola County Chamber of Commerce. With herculean exertions Tommie organized and opened the Tex Ritter Museum in the Chamber of Commerce building at Carthage, Texas. Tourists have flocked to this excellent museum, and there have been repeated requests for a book about Tex Ritter. The only previous biography, *The Tex Ritter Story*, was written by Ritter's friend and business partner, Johnny Bond, shortly after Ritter's death in 1974, but that book has long been out of print. Tommie approached me about writing a new biography, and she generously offered to share the wealth of files, scrapbooks, photographs, phonograph records, and miscellaneous artifacts collected for the museum. Throughout this project Tommie has suggested people to contact, provided introductions and phone numbers, and responded resourcefully to my repeated inquiries and requests. Tommie has done more than any other individual to perpetuate the memory and history of Tex Ritter.

In July 1997 a Tex Ritter exhibit was opened at the Grand Ole Opry Museum. John and Tom Ritter, sons of Tex, appeared at the ceremony and at an Opry performance recognizing their father. Tommie Ritter Smith organized a bus tour to Nashville for these events, and I was privileged to be a part of the group. She arranged for me to meet and interview John and Tom Ritter, as well as numerous other individuals who had known and worked with Tex. For three days my wife and I researched in Nashville, working at the Country Music Hall of Fame, interviewing, and travelng to sites important in the life of Tex Ritter.

I am indebted to Tom Ritter for tirelessly fielding my requests for information about his father and mother. Tom's insights and recollections have been invaluable to my understanding and accumulation of knowledge about his parents. I also am deeply grateful to John Ritter for taking the time from a busy evening at the Grand Ole Opry to grant me a delightful interview backstage.

In Nashville I was privileged to meet Joe Allison and Les Leverett, who were closely associated with Tex for many years. Allison regaled me with Tex Ritter stories, while Leverett graciously granted permission for me to use his superb photographs. I was treated courteously and informatively by staff members at the Country Music Hall of Fame. In addition to the exhibition on Tex Ritter, the Hall of Fame Library and Media Center maintains a vertical file on Tex, with newspaper clippings, album covers, photos, and similar materials.

Through the auspices of the East Texas Historical Association, I was awarded a research grant from the Ottis Lock Endowment. This grant was provided to facilitate my research of an East Texas native who made a significant impact on the field of entertainment. I am indebted to Dr. Archie P. McDonald, executive director of the association and a noted historian of Western films, for helping me to obtain this grant. I am privileged to be a member of the association, and I am most appreciative of the generous support of the Lock Endowment.

Earl Cariker, a lifelong resident of Panola County and a highly respected educator, has conducted interviews with childhood friends of Tex Ritter, and he has investigated and mapped the site of Murvaul, the vanished hamlet that was the family home of the Ritters. Earl was assisted in these activities by Donnie Pitchford, instructor of TV video productions at Carthage High School and a wizard with video equipment and similar technology. Earl and Donnie demonstrated and loaned me video and audio tapes that they had prepared, and Earl enthusiastically tracked down obscure items of information which had stymied me. Lincoln King, history and journalism teacher at Gary High School, has achieved national renown for his folk publication, *Loblolly.* Years ago for *Loblolly,* Lincoln and his students compiled a fund of interviews and information about Tex Ritter's early life, and he generously located and shared those articles with me. Linda Haynie, librarian at Carthage High School, industriously explored the resources of her library on my behalf.

At Panola College in Carthage, the staff at M. P. Baker Library granted me their customary cheerful assistance. Christi Ferguson and head librarian Phyllis Reed were espeically helpful with interlibrary loan procurements. Brenda Allums, head of Panola's journalism department, was a newspaper reporter in Port Arthur when Tex Ritter was buried nearby, and she shared with me recollections of the time she spent with the family. Another Panola colleague, retired instructor J. R. Brannon, was related by marriage to Tex, and he told me about the entertainer's visits to the home of his brother, David Ritter.

At the Old Jail Museum and Genealogical Library in Carthage, Lelia Belle LaGrone and Jo Wedgeworth resourcefully unearthed information about the Ritter family. Two other longtime Carthage friends, Bev Brown and Jerry Hanszen, told me about contacts they and their relatives had experienced with Tex.

Another friend, Gail Beil of Marshall, Texas, was a member of the First Methodist Church of North Hollywood during the early 1960s, when the Ritters also were members and Tex sang in the choir. Chris Smith, my nephew and a doctoral student in history at the University of Houston, aided me in researching Tex Ritter's activities in Houston during the late 1920s, especially at KPRC. Following a performance of the Light Crust Dough Boys, venerable musicians Smokey Montgomery and John Walden related to me their professional experiences with Tex.

At Beaumont's South Park Middle School, formerly South Park High School, librarians Deborah Wozniak and Mabel Broussard graciously assisted me in locating information about Woodward Ritter, Class of '22. Kevin Coil, assistant manager of Oak Bluff Memorial Park in Port Neches, guided me to Tex Ritter's gravesite. Ken Ritter, nephew of Tex and former mayor of Beaumont, generously shared his recollections with me on two occasions. Dr. Ralph Wooster, noted historian and author from Lamar University in Beaumont, told me about an encounter with Tex during the 1940s.

My friend Red Underhill of Jacksonville, Florida, has graciously volunteered to help me with several past projects, and once again he came to my aid. While working for the Acuff-Rose Publishing Company of Nashville during the 1960s, Red became well acquainted with Tex, and he recounted several experiences to me. Bobby Fluker of Corsicana, Texas, is an extremely knowledgeable historian of B Westerns and country music. Bobby encountered Tex at personal appearances and Dorothy Ritter at B Western conventions, and he related to me a number of intriguing anecdotes and reflections.

The Registrar's Office at the University of Texas responded promptly to my request for a copy of Woodward M. Ritter's transcript. Equally helpful was the interlibrary loan staff of UT's Main Library, sending me copies of the university's annuals from the 1920s. I also appreciate the efforts of the Registrar's Office at Northwestern University.

My wife Karon accompanied me on research trips, shot photographs, helped me with interviews, and tirelessly transformed my penciled manuscript into a computerized printout and diskettes. I also drew upon her musical expertise, as well as the loving encouragement and support which make it possible for me to complete a book-length project.

Sincerely Tex Ritter

A GRAND NATIONAL STAR

America's Most Beloved Cowboy

The same movie publicity machine that dubbed Roy Rogers "King of the Cowboys" also labeled Tex Ritter "America's Most Beloved Cowboy." After half a century Rogers still enjoys permanent identity as King of the Cowboys, and with equal loyalty a generation of movie fans, as well as a legion of Ritter's friends and colleagues, came to regard the versatile entertainer as nothing less than America's Most Beloved Cowboy.

Throughout a diverse career which spanned more than four decades, Tex Ritter displayed a gift for making friends that was as great as his singular talent for making music. Audiences responded to the obvious pleasure he took in entertaining, while friends and acquaintances found him to be sociable and generous. No country artist ever displayed a wider range of accomplishments. With lengthy stays in America's greatest entertainment capitals—New York, Hollywood, and Nashville—Tex Ritter found success in early radio, on Broadway, in scores of Western movies, in a recording career that covered hundreds of songs and narrations, as a songwriter, on television, and as a road performer in countless appearances across the United States and abroad. While Gene Autry and other singing cowboys had little or no acting experience when starting their movie work, Tex had spent years as a stage and radio performer before coming to Hollywood. Of the singing cowboys, only Gene Autry and Roy Rogers starred in more Western films than Tex Ritter, and Ritter's ten years as a movie star gave him a national exposure that was invaluable to his later career as a country artist.

Unlike many other of today's city-bred "country" performers, Tex Ritter was born and reared on a farm in one of America's poorest and most rural counties. But he managed to acquire more than five years of university training, giving him one of the best formal educations of any country artist of his generation. He developed a love for folk music, with a special interest in Western songs and cowboy ballads that disregarded popular musical trends. Indeed, after starring in sixty Western movies, and after vigorously performing and recording cowboy tunes, Tex Ritter was one of the artists most responsible for the transformation of country music from its hillbilly roots to country and western. Keenly conscious of his Western image, Tex always wore Western suits, Stetsons and boots, and even had his tuxedos tailored to a Western cut. He so disliked the old-fashioned hillbilly image of country music that he tried unsuccessfully to come up with another title for his great hit, "Hillbilly Heaven." Although Tex was an avid collector and performer of folk music, after some folk singers acquired a hippie-like identity he refused to permit himself to be publicized as a folk singer.

Following a long and happy bachelorhood, Tex met the love of his life on a movie set. He and his vivacious bride were married for thirty-three years, without a hint of scandal and despite long absences necessitated by his ceaseless touring schedule. The lure of the road was irresistible, compelling him to maintain a nomadic travel pace until he died. In the course of taking his music to every corner of the land, Tex developed a deep appreciation for America, a love for her people and principles that was strongly reflected in his recordings and performances. Tex had a lifelong passion for politics, and his sense of patriotism eventually propelled him into a race for the U.S. Senate. He twice won election as president of the Country Music Association, and his peers selected him as one of the first members of the CMA Hall of Fame. Tex Ritter enjoyed honors, rich travel and work experiences, a host of friends and fans, and a loving family.

"I've had a good life. I've been lucky," reflected Tex to a reporter, just before an outdoor show in 1967. "I've gotten to see a lot of America and the world, which might not have been possible had I not been in show business . . . . For the last thirty years, I've tried to follow a philosophy. I've looked for the beauty in America. It's everywhere. You might not see it, but it's there. There's beauty in nature. There's beauty in people. Look for that beauty. . . ."

He looked for that beauty throughout a long and varied career, and he found it over and over in the warm reaction of fans to the talent and dedication of a performer who loved his art and shared it tirelessly. Tex Ritter did indeed have a good life.

"Tex was always a cowboy"

Tex Ritter was born and raised in a backwoods hamlet in one of the poorest counties in Texas. Panola County was organized in 1846, but pioneer settlers from the United States began slipping across the Louisiana border into this region of Mexican Texas in the 1820s. Tex Ritter's great-grandfather, Everett J. Ritter, came to Texas in 1831 in search of land. Born in Alabama in 1810, Everett migrated to Tennessee and married Anna Goodwin of that

state when they both were eighteen. The Land Act of 1820 offered western settlers eighty acres for $100, but if a pioneer were willing to venture into Mexican Texas, he could obtain 4,605 acres—a labor (177 acres) for farming and a league (4,428 acres) for stock-raising. Everett left his wife with her family and traveled to Texas, obtaining a league and a labor in the heavily forested area that would become Panola County.

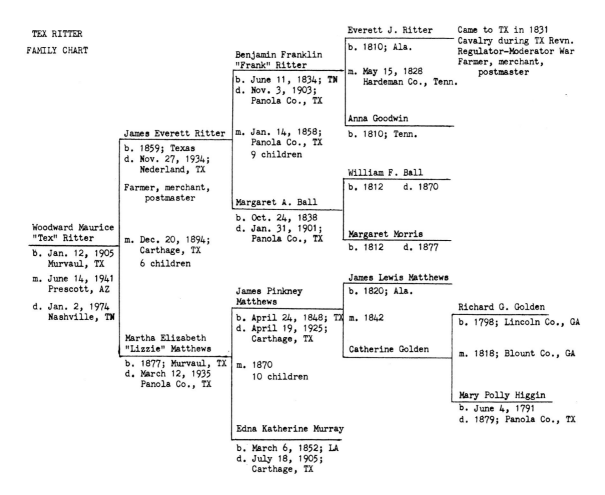

TEX RITTER
FAMILY CHART

Everett J. Ritter — Came to TX in 1831; Cavalry during TX Revn.; Regulator-Moderator War; Farmer, merchant, postmaster
b. 1810; Ala.
m. May 15, 1828 Hardeman Co., Tenn.

Anna Goodwin
b. 1810; Tenn.

Benjamin Franklin "Frank" Ritter
b. June 11, 1834; TN
d. Nov. 3, 1903; Panola Co., TX
m. Jan. 14, 1858; Panola Co., TX
9 children

William F. Ball
b. 1812   d. 1870

Margaret Morris
b. 1812   d. 1877

Margaret A. Ball
b. Oct. 24, 1838
d. Jan. 31, 1901; Panola Co., TX

James Everett Ritter
b. 1859; Texas
d. Nov. 27, 1934; Nederland, TX
Farmer, merchant, postmaster
m. Dec. 20, 1894; Carthage, TX
6 children

James Lewis Matthews
b. 1820; Ala.
m. 1842

Richard G. Golden
b. 1798; Lincoln Co., GA
m. 1818; Blount Co., GA

Mary Polly Higgin
b. June 4, 1791
d. 1879; Panola Co., TX

Catherine Golden

James Pinkney Matthews
b. April 24, 1848; TX
d. April 19, 1925; Carthage, TX
m. 1870
10 children

Woodward Maurice "Tex" Ritter
b. Jan. 12, 1905 Murvaul, TX
m. June 14, 1941 Prescott, AZ
d. Jan. 2, 1974 Nashville, TN

Martha Elizabeth "Lizzie" Matthews
b. 1877; Murvaul, TX
d. March 12, 1935 Panola Co., TX

Edna Katherine Murray
b. March 6, 1852; LA
d. July 18, 1905; Carthage, TX

Everett returned to Tennessee periodically, and the couple's first two children were born there: William A. in 1833, and Benjamin Franklin (future grandfather of Tex) on June 11, 1834. During the Texas Revolution, Everett enlisted in Captain Hooper's cavalry company at San Augustine. Following the Mexican defeat at San Jacinto in 1836, Everett brought his family to his Texas property, where seven more children were born. When the region was wracked by the bloody Regulator-Moderator War during the 1840s, Everett was included in a list of "doomed citizens" which was posted by the feudist Regulators in June 1844. But he survived to raise cotton and operate a general store, where he served as postmaster of the community known as Murvaul. Murvaul Creek, named after a Caddo chief, ran just south of the hamlet where a growing number of the Ritter clan lived, along with the Matthews and other families.

During the Civil War, Everett Ritter's oldest son, William, joined the regiment of Texas Lancers. He was killed at the Battle of Mansfield in 1864, leaving a wife and four children. Benjamin Franklin "Frank" Ritter married in Panola County in 1858, when he was twenty-three. His nineteen-year-old bride, Margaret Ball, had come to Texas from Georgia with her family. Frank and Margaret farmed and were active in a nearby Methodist church. The first of their seven children, James Everett, was born in 1859.

James (Jim) Ritter was a thirty-two-year-old widower without children when he married Ella Matthews in December 1891. She was a third-generation Texan whose father, James Pinkney Matthews, soon would be elected sheriff of Panola County, and later county clerk. Sadly, Ella soon died. As frequently happened under such circumstances, Jim Ritter wed his sister-in-law, seventeen-year-old Martha Elizabeth "Lizzie" Matthews. They were married on December 20, 1894, by Judge Thomas Hull.

Jim owned about 400 acres of land south and east of Murvaul. During this period the Gulf, Colorado and Santa Fe Railroad built a north-south line through the village, and proposed to name their depot site Ritterville. The Ritter families declined the honor, preferring to stick with the old Murvaul label. Jim and Lizzie lived in a four-room frame house just east of the railroad tracks. Bisected by an open hall or "dog-trot," the house faced west with a roofed porch across

Frank and Margaret Ritter and their seven sons (daughters Sally and Lula are not pictured). Jim, the first-born, is seated next to his mother; he would become Tex Ritter's father.

the entire front. Jim raised cotton, corn, peanuts, hogs and cattle on his acreage, and he operated the general store, handed down by his grandfather, just across the railroad tracks. For two years, from February 1901 to February 1903, Jim served as postmaster of Murvaul. He permitted a school to be erected on land a short distance east of his house. Later, when Gulf Oil built a pipeline through the neighborhood, Jim was hired to look after the pump station constructed northeast of the Ritter home.

"Mother was very ambitious for us and father was very strict," recalled Ola Mae Bee Ritter, daughter of Jim and Lizzie. The Ritters' first child, Diamond Edna Margaret Ritter, also was elaborately named. She was born in 1896, and Ola Mae came along the next year. The first son, David Hobson, was born in 1898. Another daughter, Lucille, was born in 1901, and the fifth child, Booty A., made his appearance in 1902. Howard Hardin, a playmate and schoolmate of the Ritter children, remembered their parents as good neighbors and community lead-

The Ritter home had four rooms, two on each side of the "dog-trot."

ers: "Mr. Ritter and Miz Lizzie was mighty fine folks."

Jim and Lizzie's youngest child, Woodward Maurice, was born on January 12, 1905. He was called "Woodard" until he was in his twenties, when New Yorkers dubbed him "Tex" because of his drawl. (When Tex was thirty-one, Hollywood publicists subtracted two years from his age to keep the budding cowboy star in his twenties. The publicists' 1907 birthdate became generally accepted, and has caused confusion for more than six decades.)

"Tex was always a cowboy," recalled a Ritter cousin, Mrs. H. M. Dry. "He liked to ride stick horses, and he always liked dogs and cats. In other words, he liked animals. Uncle Jim had an old gray horse called Marvin that Tex and his brother used to ride."

How did a farm boy from the piney woods of East Texas, far from ranching country, become infatuated with cowboys? Woodard's boyhood was the heyday of melodramatic, visually striking William S. Hart and other Western stars of the silent screen. The nearest movie house was on the courthouse square in Carthage. But Carthage, twelve miles away by wagon road, was not frequented by Murvaul residents, who usually traveled to Gary, less than three miles to the south. Gary, with a population of only a few hundred, never boasted a theater. Woodard once went with his family on the train to Longview, where he would have had a chance to attend a movie.

If Woodard had little opportunity during the impressionable years of boyhood to watch cowboy movies, he could read. Tex was a life-

Jim and Lizzie Ritter and their growing family, probably late in 1901. Daughters Diamond (left) and Ola are in front, while the baby apparently is the third daughter, Lucille, born on March 27, 1901.

long reader whose large library eventually contained an impressive collection of Western literature. Zane Grey began publishing frontier romances about the time that Woodard Ritter was born. Grey's most memorable novel, *Riders of the Purple Sage*, was released in 1912, and thereafter the prolific author enjoyed enormous popularity and sales. Boys of Woodard's generation were captivated by the West through Zane Grey's books, just as countless youngsters of the nineteenth century were drawn to the cowboy world through dime novels.

Theodore Roosevelt, who had written vividly about his adventures as a Western rancher and hunter, was in the White House when Woodard Ritter was born. Automobiles were a rare sight to Murvaul residents, but a passenger train from Longview passed through each morning headed south for Beaumont, then rumbled back toward Longview in the afternoons. There were no radios, but Murvaul was on a rural telephone system, with ten or twelve families on each "party line." A distinctive ring, a long and a short or perhaps two longs and a short, identified the desired party, but nothing stopped other parties from listening to shouted conversations over the wall-mounted crank phones. The frame and log houses of Murvaul had no running water or electricity. Dark homes were illuminated by kerosene lamps. Wells provided drinking water, and outhouses handled sewage in Murvaul. Baths were taken in washtubs with water heated on wood stoves. Cutting firewood for heating and cooking was a constant chore. Baths were a lot of trouble, but barefooted children were expected at least to wash their feet every night.

The women of Murvaul cooked over wood-burning ranges. Milch cows yielded milk and butter. Hens laid eggs, and fried chicken and chicken pie were staples. Everyone had a vegetable garden and a smokehouse. Hogs were fattened, then killed and butchered on a frigid "hog killin' day." The casings were cleaned, then stuffed sausage was made and smoked in the smokehouse. The Ritters and many other families grew sugar cane to make ribbon cane syrup. When fruit peddlers occasionally passed through the area, families bought apples by the sack and bananas by the bunch.

Flour, salt and sugar, along with whatever other items a family did not make for themselves, were purchased from the two or three general stores which lined the west side of the tracks at different times. The Murvaul depot also was on the west side of the railroad, and the post office was operated in one of the stores. A sawmill was

Wood(w)ard

When Tex Ritter was born, in 1905, Panola County did not yet issue birth certificates. Births were recorded in a large ledger, the *Panola County Birth Record Book*, Volume I. There were spaces to list the date, name, gender, parents, and attending physician, if any. The names were not provided for a great many infants, including a male baby born to the Ritters on January 12, 1905. Although the boy was called "Woodard," he listed his name on various records as Woodward Maurice Ritter. In 1942, probably to establish his age for Selective Service early in World War II, Tex obtained from Panola County an official birth certificate, spelling his name "Woodward." But the name came from his mother's family, and on at least one old gravestone (in the Buncombe Cemetery, near Murvaul), the name is spelled "Woodard." In the absence of a 1905 birth certificate, it is quite possible that his mother intended for his name to be spelled the same way it was pronounced. When Woodard was in his twenties, New Yorkers began to call him "Tex," which *was* spelled the same way it was pronounced!

built in the southern part of the community, just east of the tracks. West of the railroad a cotton gin, one of 30,000 in Texas, processed the only cash crop produced by Murvaul-area families. Although East Texas was part of the Southern Bible Belt, there were no churches in Murvaul. Murvaul families attended churches in Gary or Buncombe, although Sunday services sometimes were conducted by one denomination or another in the Murvaul schoolhouse. When a Baptist "revival" meeting was held, everyone joined in, and when the Methodists conducted a revival, everyone went to the Methodist church. The Ritter family regarded themselves as Methodists. "We were reared with a very religious background," declared one of the Ritter sisters, Ola.

Since there were no churches in Murvaul, community life centered on the school, located only a couple of hundred yards east of the Ritter home. The story-and-a-half frame structure measured about thirty feet by sixty feet. The large schoolroom downstairs was topped by a smaller room under the roof which served as a meeting hall for the local Woodmen of the World. But the school population eventually exceeded seventy pupils in grades one through eight, and the WOW moved out as the upper grades were installed upstairs. The two teachers usually were men, although women sometimes taught at Murvaul. During most terms at least one of the teachers took room and board at the nearby Ritter house.

The countryside was thick with farm houses, and most children walked to school. In the mornings teachers rang the school bell to assem-

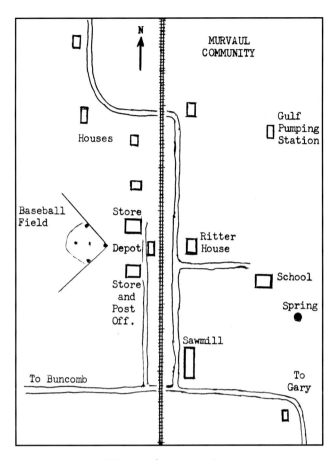

N

MURVAUL
COMMUNITY

Houses

Gulf
Pumping
Station

Baseball
Field

Store

Depot

Ritter
House

Store
and
Post
Off.

School

Spring

Sawmill

To Buncomb

To
Gary

Murvaul community.

ble the students in two lines, one for boys and one for girls. A few minutes later the bell rang again, and the two lines filed inside. Booty Ritter, Woodard's older brother, habitually dawdled until the second bell sounded, then sprinted from his house to the end of the line as the boys passed through the double doors.

Inside the boys sat on one side of the room and the girls on the other. The gender

segregation extended outside, where two water buckets sat beside the entrance—one for the boys and one for the girls. Of course, the children drank from a common dipper. The buckets were refilled from a spring located about fifty yards southeast of the school. Above the spring Jim Ritter had a barn and a horse and cow lot, but students did not "remember anybody ever dying" from tainted water. Girls had an outhouse, but boys went into the woods.

During recess and lunchtime, students drank directly from the spring, which is about the only thing besides the railroad bed that remains today of Murvaul. Students brought their lunches in syrup buckets or brown bags. Lunch staples were biscuits, boiled eggs, sausage, sweet potatoes, and cookies. A shoe polish bottle or other small container held ribbon cane syrup for the biscuits. As students sat eating around the schoolground, hogs sometimes emerged from nearby woods to snatch up the lunch bags. During recess the little girls, like other generations of East Texas girls before and since, arranged pine straw into "play houses"—room outlines with door openings—and the girls would bring broken glass from home for "windows." The boys played ball, marbles, and "flying jennies." A flying jenny was a long pole placed across a tree stump, "and they tried to see how fast that they could make it go around and around and around," reminisced Grace Gray, a pupil at the old school. "They would sit on the ends of the pole and sometimes would fall off when it went around."

In the classroom older students helped beginning pupils with their work, an effective

Two teachers, forty-four pupils, and two dolls at the Murvaul school, probably during the 1911-12 term, when Woodard Ritter was in the first grade. Little Woodard peers intently at the camera from the front row, sixth from the left.

method of instructing a large number of children and of reviewing the lessons of earlier years for students in the higher grades. Homework emphasized spelling and recitation. On Fridays there was a spelling bee, and even as a youngster Woodard excelled, often outspelling older students. "He was a shrewd little boy," admired an older classmate, Omar Thomas.

On Friday nights the community sometimes gathered at the school for a spelling bee, which included adults, and to watch the students recite their lessons. On one of these occasions Woodard memorized a recitation about a man selling his wares on a passenger train. When Woodard called out, "Razors!" he suddenly forgot his script. Trying to remember his next line, he repeated, "Razors! Razors! Razors!"

"Sit down up there," his older brother, Booty, helpfully called out from the audience, "you forgot it."

But Woodard suddenly recalled his lines and continued the recital. Parents and students in the audience laughed, assuming that the pause and Booty's loud taunt were part of the act. It was Woodard's first taste of an audience response to comedy, and in time he would master the technique for stage shows.

Woodard enjoyed his school recitations. As a boy he came to admire the speechmaking of political candidates. His sister, Ola, reminisced that "one of our happy pastimes as children was going to all-day political meetings during election years to hear different speakers." Politics was a popular spectator sport of rural America, and Texas held elections every other year. Rival candidates stumped every community in the county, and everyone came to what was as much a social event as a political function. Jim Ritter exercised considerable influence in the neighborhood, while Lizzie's relatives had held several county offices. Visiting candidates, centers of attention to expectant audiences, were deferential to Woodard's parents. Woodard also was exposed to the courtroom dramatics of trial lawyers at the ornate red brick courthouse in Carthage. Trials provided dramatic entertainment that brought country people to town. "I enjoyed watching the lawyers," Tex later recalled, "and I was impressed with the way they handled things." It was known around Murvaul that Woodard "told all the family that he was going to be a lawyer when he grew up."

Impressed by the orations of politicians and lawyers, Woodard often went outdoors to practice making speeches to imaginary audiences. When the Ritter children were sent to the fields to chop or pick cotton, Woodard usually skipped away to stand on a stump and practice speeches. Ola Ritter remembered going to the field one day where her brothers had gone to work, only to find the older boys "throwing clods of dirt at Tex, trying to get him out of the fence corner to work. But Tex would just sit in the fence corner and poke weeds and sticks in the ground—for people—and get up and make political speeches to them."

On another occasion Ola's boyfriend "was driving along the road in his buggy and heard this loud speech. It was Tex standing on a stump in the sugar cane patch. When Tex finished, the boy friend clapped his hands real loud and Tex was embarrassed." But not embarrassed enough to stop. A neighbor named Pate, hunting a cow in the woods, spotted young Woodard Ritter standing on a stump practicing a recitation. "Mr. Pate thought it was so good that he began to clap his hands," related a cousin, Mrs. H. M. Dry. "This frightened Tex, and he fell over backwards in the pond."

When not falling into ponds, Woodard went swimming in them with his brothers. When the boys were left at home by their parents, usually during visits to relatives, they were ordered not to go swimming. "But if we did something like that, and we did, my father would always say, 'I owe you a whipping,'" reminisced Tex. "So we would go with that over our heads. Then when he would get his razor strap out he whipped us all and you knew you'd been whipped."

Prowling the woods near his house with a shotgun, Woodard developed a passion for hunting. A lifelong sports fan, during his boyhood Woodard played baseball on the field west of the stores in Murvaul. He also was exposed to music at church and at home, although his participation was limited. In Murvaul there was virtually no opportunity to hear popular songs of the day, so everyone sang mostly hymns and gospel music, along with folk tunes. "We always had crowds at our home on Sundays for song festivals," said Ola. "Our mother played the organ." Not many rural households could afford a piano, but a little harmonium or pump organ was possible for families like the Ritters. Singing around the pump organ was a favorite activity of the Ritter clan.

"My family sang a lot," affirmed Tex. "My two older brothers were very good singers. There again it was mostly church music, but usually they wouldn't let me sing with them because I couldn't sing well enough. I remember once my mother said it would be nice if her boys would sing so we got up in front of the fireplace and sang about half a song and the others stopped and said, 'Mama, would you make him sit down?'"

Tex reflected wistfully upon the limited music of his early years. "When I was a boy it was a rather Victorian society, but when my father was a boy every young man would ride horseback for thirty or forty miles and dance all night into Sunday. By the time I came along it was taboo—the Baptists and Methodists stopped it."

But the Baptists and Methodists hosted singing schools during the summers. Music publishing companies would send out itinerant music teachers to conduct singing schools and to hawk paperback hymnals. Ola Ritter regarded the summer singing schools among the most enjoyable experiences of childhood. Tex recalled one singing school which lasted for three weeks. From the post-Civil War period through the early decades of the twentieth century, itinerant singing instructors taught the "shape note" method of music. This simple system featured notes of basic shapes: square, circle, diamond, and triangle. During the heyday of singing schools, there probably were more Texans who could read music—shape note music—than could read words. The four-note emphasis encouraged the teaching of four-part harmony. Gospel quartets, featuring a first tenor, second tenor, baritone and bass, often were brought in to climax a long singing school. The Stamps-Baxter Company of Dallas worked East Texas, and Tex remembered V. O. Stamps, who formed the famous Stamps Quartet, as a singing teacher.

During his boyhood Tex was influenced by a middle-aged black farmhand named Robert Williams. A lay preacher, Williams sang and practiced his sermons while he worked. Tex listened avidly, and one of the folk ballads he learned, "Boll Weevil," would become a popular part of his performing repertoire. He also went with his uncle, Tom Ritter, to Williams' church services. "Looking back over my life-time," recalled Tex, "I think I heard some of the best sermons I ever heard from him, and I'd sing the song the way that I remembered he would sing it to us."

Ola Ritter remembered that "singing and speeches were the thing, and they both rubbed off on Tex." He aspired to be a lawyer, and continued delivering pleas to an invisible jury and political speeches to make-believe crowds of voters. But the boy also absorbed the music around him. His family sang enthusiastically, his mother played the organ, and he heard powerful church hymns, besides learning the rudiments of music at summer singing schools. He soaked up the religious music and the folk ballads of an isolated country region, and these musical influences would ferment actively in a somewhat unpromising vessel.

Early in 1917, when twelve-year-old Woodard was in the sixth grade, the Murvaul school burned to the ground. On cold mornings one of the Ritter brothers was expected to light the wood-burning stove before other students arrived. "One such morning, Woodard had the job," cousin J. Rex Ritter related to Johnny Bond. "He must have loaded the stove pretty good and the extra firewood must have been too close because on our way to school we were astounded to see the schoolhouse going up in flames." Other schoolmates did not remember that Woodard might have been the accidental culprit, but it was a certainty that the Murvaul school was a bed of coals.

Murvaul schoolchildren finished the term at Gary, a two-and-a-half-mile walk along the railroad tracks. The schoolhouse was a two-story frame building that still stands. The Ritter children apparently stayed with relatives in Gary during the week. A new Murvaul school was soon constructed, but because a great many Murvaul students lived on farms to the north, the new school was built two miles north of the little community. Most of the Ritter children had left school by this time, and Jim and Lizzie had decided to send Woodard and Lucille to the large brick school in Carthage.

The county seat provided a complete program of eleven grades, while Murvaul offered only eight grades. Lucille wanted to graduate from high school, and Woodard's goal of a law

The two-story Gary school was built in 1911. Woodard Ritter finished the sixth grade here in 1917, after the Murvaul school burned.

degree demanded the best academic preparation within reach. For that reason, the family rented a house in Carthage. The old Murvaul community, with the school gone and the Jim Ritter family departed, began a rapid decline.

After twelve years in an isolated if secure environment, the horizons of Woodard Ritter began to expand.

C & W in Texas

In 1923, almost two decades after Tex Ritter was born in a Panola County farmhouse, James Travis Reeves was born in another Panola County farmhouse. Later known as Gentleman Jim Reeves, he was posthumuously inducted into the Country Music Hall of Fame in 1967, three years after Tex Ritter's induction. Thus Panola County is the only county in the United States to have produced two members of the CMA Hall of Fame.

But Tex Ritter and Jim Reeves are only two of an impressive parade of native Texans who made significant contributions to country music. Marion Try Slaughter, born in Marion County, Texas, was the first artist to record popular country music, and he became known as "Vernon Dalhart," a performing name he adapted from two West Texas towns. Bob Wills and His Texas Playboys created a sensation with western swing. Gene Autry, from Tioga, Texas, became the movies' first singing cowboy, as well as an immensely popular recording star. Country giant Ernest Tubb, the "Texas Troubadour," was born on a farm in Ellis County, Texas.

One of country's greatest songwriters, Cindy Walker, is from Mexia, Texas. Buck Owens, responsible for the Bakersfield Sound and star of *Hee Haw*, was from Sherman, and CMA Hall of Famer Lefty Frizell was from Corsicana. Tex Ritter gave important boosts to the careers of fellow Texans Hank Thompson and Barbara Mandrell. Larry Gatlin and Tanya Tucker both were born in Seminole. The incomparable George Jones called Saratoga home, while Willie Nelson hailed from Abbott. Other notable Texas artists include Waylon Jennings (from Littlefield), Kenny Rogers (Houston), Roger Miller (Fort Worth), Jimmy Dean (Plainview), Mac Davis (Lubbock), Linda Davis (Panola County), Michael Martin Murphy (Dallas), Ray Price (Perryville), Johnny Horton (Tyler), and Clint Black (Houston). Cowboy music originated in Texas because cowboys originated in Texas. Country music was not transplanted to Texas—C & W has deep roots in the Lone Star State.

Country Goes to Town

In 1917 the twelve-year-old country boy began a more cosmopolitan life. For the next three years Woodard Ritter would attend school in a county seat town. Then he would finish his final two grades at a city high school, before entering the University of Texas at the state capital. During his years of adolescence and early manhood, Ritter was exposed to a prodigious array of new experiences, but his transformation never erased his rural roots.

Carthage was a metropolis compared to the unincorporated village of Murvaul, with its handful of modest structures and tiny population. Although there were no paved streets in Carthage, automobiles chugged through town. Around the courthouse square were brick commercial buildings, several of them two stories tall. Carthage boasted two banks, a variety of stores, four churches, fraternal organizations, half a dozen garages, five doctors, nine lawyers, and a population that had grown to nearly 2,000. A two-story brick opera house built in the 1890s showed silent films, while the one-story Victory Theater was erected on the east side of the square. Woodard now had ready access to the exciting films of William S. Hart, Tom Mix, and other Western stars, which stirred his growing fascination with the cowboy culture of the Old West.

He also found stimulation at the three-story brick school a few blocks northwest of the square. Woodard attended the seventh, eighth, and ninth grades at the Carthage school, which accommodated 250-300 pupils during his tenure. The seventh-graders were called "preps," eighth-graders were "fish," and ninth-graders were sophomores. After Woodard's seventh-grade year, his class enjoyed graduation exercises into high school.

Beginning in 1913, a school annual was

Woodard Ritter attended Carthage High School from 1917 to 1920.

produced every four years. Unfortunately for posterity, the future Tex Ritter attended school in Carthage during the three years between the 1917 and 1921 annuals, so details of his CHS career are inexact. But for Woodard, as well as his sister Lucille, Carthage High School definitely offered a rich variety of classroom and extracurricular activities. In addition to English, math, history, and other basics, the high school offered subjects such as "Expression" and "Piano and Violin." The Carthage High School Orchestra was nicknamed the "Jazz Hounds of CHS," and there also was a Mandolin Club. The boys' and girls' basketball teams played on an outside court with wooden backboards. Each year there was a senior play, a junior play, and a minstrel show. About 100 students were enrolled in high school, and all of them participated in the CHS Literary Society. Also, CHS hosted the county meet of the Interscholastic League contests, which featured debate, declamation, spelling, and essay. As a CHS student, Woodard, who had practiced speechmaking since boyhood, excelled at declamation. He won the district and regional meets, and earned a trip to the state meet at the University of Texas in Austin, a school which made a deep impression on the aspiring student. After his sophomore year at Carthage High School, his family would make a move that would further improve Woodard's hope of studying law at a quality university.

Woodard Ritter's grandfather, J. P. Matthews, served as county clerk and as sheriff out of the Panola County Courthouse, built in the 1880s. Hanging out at the courthouse, Woodard was captivated by the drama of the courtroom and determined to become a lawyer, an ambition reinforced by his mother.

Woodard's oldest sisters, Diamond and Ola, had married in 1912 and 1913 respectively. Ola had been courted by Walter McCauley, an Ohioan who had been sent by Gulf Oil to Panola County. Little Woodard, descended from Texas Confederates, told his mother that his sister simply could not "marry a Blue Belly Yankee," and the boy sometimes threw clods at McCauley. Despite the passionate opposition of her eight-year-old brother, Ola wed Walter, and soon the couple was transferred to Nederland, about 175 miles due south near the Gulf Coast. Walter performed shift work, and when he worked nights Ola liked to have one of her brothers come to stay with her. Several times Woodard made the train trip to Nederland, and when school was in session he would attend classes, beginning at the age of

ten. Ola pointed out that "Mother thought he was too smart for the little country school in Murvaul and the teacher agreed."

Founded just before the turn of the century by immigrants from Holland, Nederland meant "lowland" in Dutch. The settlers were dairymen and rice farmers, but in 1901 a great oil gusher came in nearby at Spindletop, just south of Beaumont. Founded in the 1830s, Beaumont already boasted a population of nearly 10,000 when the spectacular oil discovery stimulated further growth. By 1920, Beaumont, located only nine miles northwest of Nederland, was a bustling city of 40,000. When Woodard visited his sister, there were theaters in Beaumont showing Western films, along with many other experiences for the country boy. He played and went to school with children different from his rural East Texas playmates. "A lot of them were Dutch kids," recalled Tex, "descendants of the people that founded the town and a lot of them were Cajun kids." The other boys liked silent Western stars Tom Mix or Buck Jones or William S. Hart, but Tex preferred Hoot Gibson, who later became Ritter's "dear friend," because of the comedy he injected into his films. "The rest of them were so solemn to me," Tex later reflected. "So I decided I'd have a few laughs in my pictures and I liked that about Hoot."

The central part of South Park High School was built in 1908, with additions in 1911 and 1915. The wing at right housed a second-floor auditorium where Woodard Ritter performed in school plays.

In 1920 Jim and Lizzie joined their daughter in Nederland. Jim had maintained a Gulf pump station at Murvaul for years, and now he went to work full-time for the oil company as a machinist. David Ritter, now in his twenties, stayed in Panola County, but the rest of the family made a two-story frame house on Nederland Avenue their home. A good secondary school, Beaumont's South Park High,

Popular and deeply involved in school activities, Woodard Ritter was elected senior class president at South Park High School.

One of only two returning lettermen from the 1921-22 basketball team, Ritter (fourth from left) was a stalwart at forward.

was located only a few miles from Nederland. An interurban line offered easy transportation, and Woodard Ritter spent his junior and senior years at South Park, with the intention of preparing himself for university work.

As a junior at South Park High in 1920-21, Woodard joined the debate team and the Philomathian Literary Society. He was chosen as the male lead—Chester Phelps, bridegroom—in the junior play, *The Terrified Bridegroom*. Now grown tall and lean, he also made the varsity basketball and baseball teams. With all of these activities, he maintained a B average with a full class load.

His senior year brought an even fuller slate of sports and debate and drama, including a

featured role in the senior play, *It Pays to Advertise*. Woodard played on a fourteen-man football squad, which won four of seven games. He was one of just two returning lettermen on the basketball team, which managed only one victory in eight games. Woodard was selected as one of seven student and faculty members of the school's Athletic Council. He was sergeant-at-arms of the Philomathian Literary Society, and he also joined the Spanish Club and the Boy's Glee Club. Genial and popular, he was elected senior class president. "He debates, he declaims, he's a first-class actor," proclaimed the senior class poem. "But he's known everywhere by his loud, funny laughter." He smiled and laughed easily, and his deep laughter would prove infectious to those around him throughout his life. "As for laughing, there is no one to be compared with him," stated the high school yearbook beside his senior class photo. "If he were as good a bluffer in classes as he is in debating, we know that he would have won the honors of any class." Yet he still compiled a B average with a full course of study. When he graduated in 1922, he had taken a wide variety of high school classes, including two years of Spanish and two of Latin.

By this time the outgoing Woodard readily broke into song. "About the time we left East Texas my voice started changing," he reminisced. His voice became deep and powerful. He sang a rich baritone, but could range down to a resonant bass. Although untrained musi-

As a participant in football, basketball, and baseball at South Park High, Ritter was a natural choice for the Athletic Council.

During his senior year Ritter (eighth from left in the rear) was sergeant-at-arms of the Philomathian Society.

cally, he had developed phrasing and expression through debate, declamation, and dramatics. He began to sing at Nederland's First United Methodist Church and with Loveless Theriot's barbershop quartet. He loved to sing, and in college he would eagerly pursue opportunities to develop the musical talent that had been unsuspected during his younger years.

His family always had supported his ambition to become a lawyer. Lizzie Ritter, staunchly religious, wanted her son to attend a church school, such as Southern Methodist University in Dallas or Baylor in Waco. But Woodard had his sights set on the University of Texas. A

The most prominent building on the UT campus during the 1920s was Old Main.

cousin, Rex Ritter, was about to enter his junior year as an engineering major there, and he promised to "look after" Woodard. Lizzie gave in, and Woodard entered the University of Texas in the fall of 1922.

The University of Texas had opened in Austin in 1883 with 221 students. The first structure that went up on the original forty-acre campus was the Main Building, eventually known as Old Main. Located north of the impressive State Capitol, the campus was dotted with mesquite and live oak trees and was dominated by the four-story Old Main. Other facilities were steadily added to the growing campus, including the three-story Law Building in 1908. Three years later the handsome Library Building went up just southwest of Old Main. Enrollment at the university rose to more than 2,200 students by the outbreak of World War I, then nearly doubled within the next few years. In 1921, a year before Woodard Ritter enrolled, the board of regents voted to move the campus to a 444-acre site on the Colorado River, but alumni protests kept the campus on the "Forty Acres." Adjacent property began to be acquired for expansion, and temporary frame structures were erected all over the campus. These simple frame buildings were dubbed "shackeresque" architecture, and included a ramshackle gymnasium. Many students roomed at boardinghouses near the campus, including Rex Ritter, who arranged for his young cousin to stay at his house.

When Woodard Ritter arrived for the fall semester of 1922, the student body numbered well over 4,000 and the campus throbbed with the excitement of a growing university. Staffed primarily with scholars from quality eastern universities, the University of Texas was the finest educational institution in the Lone Star State.

During the spring semester of Woodard's freshman year, in May 1923, the university staged a three-day celebration of its fortieth anniversary. Also in 1923, oil was discovered on University of Texas lands in West Texas. The discovery well was the Santa Rita #1, and

As a UT freshman, Woodard Ritter (middle row, third from left) joined the Pre-Law Association. But he soon became more interested in the Glee Club.

revenues from the great oilfield soon would trigger a building program on the campus, while permanently enriching the university. The campus was bordered on the west by Guadalupe Street, called "The Drag"—three blocks of cafes, hamburger stands, and drug stores where students driving "flivvers" could order malted milks, cherry Cokes, and "java" by curb service. Stronger drinks, during this Prohibition era, could be obtained on the outskirts of Austin at "road houses," where college students could dance the Charleston to the soaring music of Dixieland jazz bands. On Saturday nights at the Women's Gymnasium a dance known as the "Gymjam" was held. Woodard usually did not have the twenty-five cents' admission, but he hung around near the door hoping to intercept an exiting co-ed. During Woodard's sophomore year, Memorial Stadium opened with a 28-10 Longhorn loss to the Baylor Bears, but at the stadium dedication, on Thanksgiving Day of 1924, Texas defeated arch-rival Texas A&M, 7-0.

The population of Austin was nearly 34,000, and the capital city grew steadily during the 1920s. Austin was bounded on the south by the Colorado River; below the river stood only the isolated buildings of St. Edward's University. Above the river Austin was a compact city, with gracious old houses on tree-studded hills throughout the picturesque townsite. The massive State Capitol, completed in 1888, boasted the tallest dome of any other state capitol (the dome atop the U. S. Capitol is seven feet taller, but a fourteen-foot statue was placed atop the Texas dome). The business section centered around Congress Avenue, stretching from the Capitol south to the Colorado

Freshman classes met in large lecture halls, and college men wore coats and ties.

River. There were tall commercial buildings and banks and hotels, and the Austin Street Railway System provided trolley transportation throughout the city. Barton Springs and the Deep Eddy area on the Colorado River were popular spots for young men and women clad in the full coverage swimsuits of the 1920s. Downtown, the superb Majestic Theater had been showing silent films since 1915, while the newest movie house, the Queen, opened nearby in 1921, the year before Woodard Ritter moved to Austin.

To earn money for college Woodard worked one summer at a steel construction job, and during other years for the Pure Oil Company at Beaumont. A fall from an oil derrick produced neck and back injuries which would bother him in later years. During his first two years at the university he washed dishes at the Scottish Rite women's dormitory and worked at the university library. Then he tried selling life insurance. After peddling policies "to every relative I had," he started after his friends. "When I noticed my classmates beginning to duck behind the corners

The Law Building at UT. Although a pre-law major, Ritter earned his greatest education in music.

of the administration building every time they saw me, I lost heart and gave it up."

Ritter was loaded with a heavy freshman schedule. He dropped a physics class his first semester, and in the spring term he withdrew from a math course. Otherwise Ritter performed well as a beginning college student. During his first two years he eagerly took four courses in public speaking, but his grades would prove that "chemistry, physics and math—they left me cold." As a freshman he joined the Pre-Law Association, and despite his "frosh" status he easily associated with the junior friends of his cousin Rex. "Tex was always a social animal," admired Rex. In their rooming house Woodard sang happily from an old songbook, and he often locked himself in the bathroom to practice speeches. When his speechmaking went on too long, of course, anyone who needed to use the bathroom was forced to pound on the locked door. One of his housemates recalled that everyone knew when Woodard returned to the house, because he loudly practiced his scales as he ascended the stairway to his second-floor room. "He would hit the first note of the scale on the first step and climb the scale as he went up the steps," said John Gray, Woodard's old partner on the South Park High debate team. "He always descended the stairs in the same manner."

By his sophomore year, the enthusiastic young singer had joined the University Glee Club, touted as the "Greatest Male Chorus in the Southwest." The stated purpose of the Glee Club was "to give the people of Texas, during its periodic tours, high

class musical programs worthy of being rendered in the name of the University." In addition to on-campus concerts, the Glee Club traveled to cities and towns across the state, and sometimes out of state. Each fall as many as 150 men auditioned for about thirty-two Glee Club positions. Twenty-four members of the Glee Club made the tours, and Ritter soon became a traveling singer—an activity which he would follow for the rest of his life. During his years with the Glee Club he journeyed as far as Canada and Mexico City, along with trips to New York City and Chicago. For an East Texas country boy the trips to famous cities and foreign lands offered adventure and excitement, and he developed a boundless appetite for travel. As though the Glee Club did not provide enough extracurricular activity, Ritter also joined the Oratorio Society, and he sang bass in a popular quartet.

The frequent trips interfered with his studies, but Ritter invariably gave musical travels priority over course work. During his freshman and sophomore years, Ritter successfully handled a heavy course load, and he spent the summer of 1924 in Austin, taking five courses. But in his junior year, 1924-25, the Glee Club made more than twenty out-of-town appearances, including three "extended tours." Ritter took only nine courses during the year, making four D's and an F, and dropping analytic geometry with an F. The next year, while serving as president of the Glee Club, he took ten law courses, but made five F's, three D's, and two C's. During his fifth year, 1926-27, he tried to

The 1924-25 Men's Glee Club, "The Greatest Male Chorus in the Southwest," scheduled more than twenty out-of-town appearances before audiences which totaled at least 25,000. Ritter (third row, fifth from left) began to acquire a taste for the lifestyle of a traveling performer.

The Oratorio Society was founded in 1925 by Oscar Fox for men, women, and faculty members. Ritter (fifth from the right in the rear) joined the Society, which first performed on the All-University radio program. Ritter began to realize the possibilities of the new medium.

recover academically, signing up for a dozen courses (none from the law department). Reflecting on a physics class he failed that year, Ritter remembered that he missed labs because of his trips. "They gave me a zero," he said with a note of surprise. "They didn't care if you were singing in Lubbock."

But the future singing star received a superb education in the field that was to mean the most to his career. In 1925 Ritter and a few other members of the Glee Club "staged a coup," maneuvering to replace their conductor in favor of Oscar J. Fox, one of three notable men who, according to Ritter, "encouraged me to sing and . . . helped direct my career." Fox was born in 1879 on a ranch in Burnet County, northwest of Austin, and he would have a life-long interest in cowboy music. His family provided musical training in San Antonio, then sent the teenager to Zurich, Switzerland, to study piano, violin, and choral direction for three years. There were two more years of study in New York City before Fox went to Galveston as choirmaster of the First Presbyterian Church. In 1904 he moved to San Antonio as choirmaster of the First Presbyterian Church, and he also conducted the San Antonio Choir Club. Fox worked with the great collector of cowboy songs, John A. Lomax, composing music for the ballads Lomax collected. Fox came to the University of Texas in 1925 to direct the men's and women's Glee Clubs and the Choral Society. He also organized the Oratorio Society, a choral group of sixty members from the faculty and student body, and Ritter joined as one of

the key singers. Ritter received instruction in voice, guitar, trumpet, and sight reading from Fox, and the young musician was fascinated by his mentor's work with Lomax in Western music.

Lomax was born in Mississippi in 1867, but two years later the family moved by covered wagon to Texas. They settled on a farm near Meridian alongside a branch of the Chisholm Trail, and Lomax grew up listening to cowboy ballads and other folk songs. He went to school and began teaching, finally graduating from the University of Texas in 1897. Lomax married and began to teach English at the Agricultural and Mechanical College of Texas. In 1906 he received a scholarship for graduate work at Harvard University, where he was encouraged to systematically collect Western songs. Partially funded by Harvard fellowships, Lomax ran ads in Western newspapers and traveled widely in search of old-timers with musical memories. Ultimately he traveled 200,000 miles while collecting folk music. His first collection, *Cowboy Songs and Other Frontier Ballads*, was published in 1910. That same year he was named secretary of the University of Texas Alumni Association, a position he held through Woodard Ritter's first three years at the university. Ritter naturally gravitated to the foremost collector of cowboy songs, who urged Woodard to compile his own collection. From Lomax, Ritter learned oral history at its purest, listening to the words and inflections of cow country songs from venerable ranch people. Lomax also probably was instrumental in bringing his friend and collaborator, Oscar Fox, to the University of Texas from San Antonio.

Lomax was one of the founders of the Texas Folklore Society, and in 1922 J. Frank Dobie became secretary-editor of the organization, a position he would hold for more than two decades. Dobie was born on a South Texas ranch in 1888, and his ranching heritage exerted a lifelong influence on his personality and interests. In 1906 Dobie enrolled in Southwestern University at Georgetown, where he met his future wife and where he was encouraged as a writer. After receiving an M. A. from Columbia University, he joined the English faculty at the University of Texas in 1914. Dobie served as an artilleryman during World War I, returned to the university, then left again to manage his uncle's ranch. After a year of ranch work he rejoined the UT English Department in 1921, the year before Ritter enrolled. From 1923 to 1925 Dobie served as chairman of the English Department at Oklahoma A&M. Returning again to the University of Texas, the charming Dobie was present during Ritter's final three years on campus.

Dobie worked to preserve the culture and traditions of Texas and the Southwest, collecting and publishing folk tales just as John A. Lomax was collecting and publishing cowboy songs.

After becoming a star, Ritter emphasized that "Dobie played a large part in making me what I am today." Greatly impressed by the charismatic Dobie, Ritter emulated his habit of pipe smoking. Like most other young men—and "flappers"—of his era, Ritter smoked cigarettes, but, like Dobie, he also developed a lifelong

The Men's Glee Club in 1926-27, Ritter's final year as a member. He is in the front row at far right. The Club was invited to present Oscar Fox's cowboy songs in Chicago at the Convention of Federated Music Clubs.

affection for pipes. Reportedly, while accompanying Dobie on a research trip, Ritter collected the folk song "Rye Whiskey," which later became his first hit record and a permanent part of his performing repertoire.

Dobie and Lomax encouraged Ritter's fascination with the Old West and urged him to compile a portfolio of cowboy songs and folk ballads. Fox provided voice training, along with performance and travel opportunities with the Glee Club, and he saw that his pupil worked to master the guitar. He developed a program of Western songs for the Glee Club and included a scene in which Ritter soloed on some of these

ballads. Ritter's mentors helped him put together a lecture-music program on "The American Cowboy and His Songs," then arranged for him to deliver the program on campus and around Austin. Dobie, Lomax and Fox, legendary figures in preserving and teaching the customs and music of the West, found an eager disciple in Ritter. Inspired and instructed by these three men, Ritter would spend the rest of his life transmitting Western music and traditions through his great variety of entertainment activities. He would focus his career on the Old West, and in later years, when public interest in frontier culture waned, he doggedly continued down the trail he had found at the University of Texas, like a loyal cowboy remaining true to a vanishing way of life.

At the end of his fifth year at the University of Texas, Ritter had not yet completed a law degree, but he continued to move inexorably toward his true calling. A traveling troupe of J. J. and Lee Shubert brought the operetta *Maryland, My Maryland* to the old Hancock Opera House, built in 1896 by Austin Mayor Louis Hancock. By the 1920s college students who did not have the price of admission had learned to climb the fire escape and slip inside the balcony door. Ritter had mastered this form of entry, and reportedly he attended every Austin performance of *Maryland, My Maryland*. After visiting backstage with the actors, Ritter was offered a role in the male chorus. Badly infected with the showbiz virus, he packed his belongings and went on the road with the show.

The Shubert brothers were the largest theater owners in New York City and the most active producers in America. During the first half of the twentieth century, the Shuberts produced more than 500 plays on Broadway, with an emphasis on musicals, which were quite profitable when successful. Traveling with a Shubert road show gave Ritter a taste of professional show business.

After the show ended, Ritter returned to Texas and obtained an appointment as choir director of Houston's Third Presbyterian Church for $25 a week. Then he managed to land a thirty-minute program of cowboy music over radio station KPRC in Houston on Saturday mornings.

Radio had become a sensation across the United States during the 1920s. The invention of the vacuum tube made possible free home entertainment, and the manufacture and sale of radio sets soared. The first station in Texas was WRR of Dallas in 1920, and within two years twenty-five stations were operating across the state. KPRC began broadcasting in May 1925. Early programming centered around live musical performances. Entertainers on local programs were not paid, but musicians found irresistible the opportunity to entertain a large radio audience. Radio exposure also frequently led to paid performances. Ritter filled his Saturday half hours with Western music from his growing portfolio of cowboy songs, interspersed with introductory explanations. He became radio's first cowboy balladeer, a role he later would resume on the airways of New York City.

But the old ambition of becoming a lawyer had not yet disappeared. "Singing was always just a hobby," said Tex of his feelings at this juncture. "I never thought about anybody get-ting paid for it, or making a living at it." Still hoping to complete his studies, he recalled, "I wanted to get some money so I wouldn't have to work while I was going to law school." An oil company offered a job in Venezuela, but he decided to study voice and try for other show business work in New York. His brother-in-law, Walter McCauley, was a Northerner and "had always told me that a year or two in the East would be good for a Texas boy because it moved a little faster and gave you a different outlook." Of course, this "Texas boy" now was twenty-three and had spent five years at the University of Texas. Exposed to quality instruction and to numerous broadening experiences, the maturing young man confidently determined to seek "a different outlook."

Soon after making his decision, Ritter encountered a boyhood schoolmate, Howard Hardin, in a cafe in Center, thirty miles south of Carthage. Hardin asked if he was going to Murvaul for a visit.

"No," replied Ritter. "I'm going to New York."

Lullaby of Broadway

In 1928 Woodard Ritter, by some accounts touring with a small Western band, lugged his clothes, guitar, portfolio of Western songs, and a suitcase full of books to America's biggest city. New York in the 1920s was the busiest port in the world, and was the unchallenged center of the American economy, ranking first in industrial production, wholesale trade, and bank deposits. The Empire City boasted the largest concentration of bankers, lawyers, architects, advertising executives, industrial designers, and corporate officials on the continent.

New York was as dominant culturally as in business and finance. Broadway was the focus of American theater, with eighty theaters producing more than 250 shows each year, including a record 268 productions in 1927. Many of the country's foremost writers lived and worked in Manhattan, while artists congregated in Greenwich Village. There were more than eighty colleges and universities in greater New York, along with scores of museums and the Metropolitan Opera. Although the movie industry had shifted to Hollywood, New York became the home of America's new radio networks and of the recording business. Madison Square Garden was the most famous indoor sports arena in the nation, and Babe Ruth and Lou Gehrig broke in Yankee Stadium during the 1920s.

Madison Square Garden, Broadway, radio programs, recording studios, colleges—all of these would become performing venues for the young man from Texas. When Ritter arrived at New York, the city pulsated with creative energy and the challenge of limitless opportunity. City streets teemed with a diverse and ambitious population. Newcomers were awed by towering skyscrapers. In 1928 the Woolworth Building (792

feet) was New York's tallest, but within two years the slender Chrysler Building (1,048 feet) was completed, and in 1931 the Empire State Building (102 stories and 1,250 feet) became the city's most famous skyscraper. New York's subway system was the most extensive in the world, and noisy elevated railways also helped to move millions of rapid-transit passengers daily. A hub of railroad traffic was Grand Central Station, an enormous terminal complex. The Statue of Liberty and the Brooklyn Bridge and Coney Island were only a few of the sites which would attract newcomers like Woodard Ritter. Although Prohibition supposedly was in effect, liquor was readily obtained at New York's illegal "speakeasies," which numbered more than double the total of the city's pre-Prohibition bars.

Ritter arrived at New York with $30, and soon was reduced to selling his books in order to buy food. He spent the "summer singing my cowboy songs," sometimes for a meal in Greenwich Village "emporiums." He found a little work, mostly private parties, which sometimes were birthday celebrations for children of the wealthy. But his luck was about to change. In a subway he encountered an acquaintance from the University of Texas who was about to visit home and who loaned Ritter his apartment. By summer's end, Ritter had landed a role in the chorus of *The New Moon*, a romantic musical comedy by Oscar Hammerstein.

Billed as W. M. Rytter, he probably got into the show through one of his contacts from *Maryland, My Maryland. The New Moon* opened in New York's Imperial Theater on September 19, 1928. *The New Moon* was set in eighteenth-century New Orleans, and Ritter was part of a large chorus of courtiers, ladies, servants, sailors, and pirates. The brightly cos- tumed male chorus helped sing the rousing "Stouthearted Men," along with "Softly as in a Mountain Sunrise" and "Lover Come Back to Me." With 509 performances on Broadway, *The New Moon* was the last operetta of its era to enjoy a long run.

Ritter's deep voice was a strong addition to the chorus, although his thick Texas drawl pre- cluded any speaking part in the sophisticated operetta. Indeed, his pronounced accent quick- ly earned him the sobriquet "Tex." For a time he persisted in using "Woodard Ritter" in billings, but the tall Texan soon became perma- nently branded as Tex Ritter.

A formal pose, in about 1930, during Tex Ritter's early years in New York.

Although Ritter did not constantly work in the low-paying chorus job, he was part of the cast when *The New Moon* went on the road. The show ran for more than two months in Chicago late in 1929. Tex wangled an appear- ance there at Northwestern University as "The Singing Lecturer." Impressed with the campus, he impulsively enrolled in Northwestern's law

school. Still harboring the old ambition of becoming a lawyer, he attended classes during the day and performed in the evenings. When the show moved to Milwaukee in January 1930, Ritter tried to commute to his classes. But the show shifted to the Shubert Theater in Indianapolis for a week late in January, then on to the Shubert Rialto Theater in St. Louis for two more weeks. Forced to miss final exams at Northwestern, Ritter wrote his professor with an explanation, along with vague hopes of re- entering "in the summer." But Tex Ritter con- tinued to find show business opportunities, and he never returned to the classroom as a student. The longtime goal of a law degree faded before the bright lights of the entertainment world. The closest Ritter would come to a courtroom was in 1944 and 1945, when he played fron- tier lawyer Tex Haines in eight movies.

As the tour of *The New Moon* continued in the spring of 1930, Ritter said, "I got to playing poker with the boys in the show and sometimes I'd lose my week's salary to one or another of them." When the tour ended, he returned to New York with two road shows and a chorus part in a Broadway hit to his professional credit.

Looking for more work, Tex soon heard of a Western show with cowboy songs that was being assembled by the Theatre Guild. *Green Grow the Lilacs* was set in pioneer Oklahoma (in 1943 the Theatre Guild would rework it into the enormous hit *Oklahoma!*). Playwright Lynn Riggs had grown up on a ranch near Claremore, Oklahoma, and he incorporated cowboy tunes and ranch lore into his "Folk-Play." Hired as an actress-singer and music consultant was Margaret Larkin, who had grown up on a ranch near Las Vegas, New Mexico. The cowboy and folk songs of *Green Grow the Lilacs* were the type of music Ritter had studied and collected at the University of Texas. When he auditioned, the drawl that had produced the nickname "Tex" and that had rendered impossible a speaking role in *The New Moon* now proved to be an invaluable asset. At the audition in the fall of 1931 he read lines with a natural twang, then sang cowboy tunes in his matchless style. Margaret Larkin emphatically stated, "This boy's authentic."

Also authentic were several rodeo cowboys who auditioned. The World's Championship Rodeo had just closed at Madison Square

Garden, and a casting call had been announced for cowboys who could sing and play guitars, banjos, or fiddles. Among the rodeo performers chosen for *Green Grow the Lilacs* were Everett Cheetham and Hank Worden, who would become lifelong friends of Tex Ritter.

Along with Lynn Riggs and Margaret Larkin, Tex contributed to the musical authenticity which proved to be such an appealing part of *Green Grow the Lilacs*. Tex—still billed as "Woodward Ritter"—was cast as Cord Elam, and as the understudy for Curly McClain, the male lead part. During three musical interludes between scenes Ritter's character led the other cowboys and cowgirls in singing such cowboy standards as "Git Along Little Dogies," "Goodbye Old Paint," and "Bury Me Not on the Lone Prairie." In Scene Four Ritter soloed on the classic "The Old Chisholm Trail." Tex was costumed in fancy stitched cowboy boots, checkered shirt, red bandanna, and light felt hat.

The innovative set of Green Grow the Lilacs. *The cabin would be wheeled around to show the interior of the main room and the exterior of the side room.*

Tex, facing his black-hatted pal Hank Worden, on Broadway in Green Grow the Lilacs.

Following rehearsals the show first opened at the Tremont Theater in Boston on December 8, 1930. During the two-week Boston run it was decided that James Patterson, originally hired to play Curly McClain, did not fit the role. The show returned to New York for fine tuning and Franchot Tone was engaged to play Curly. Tone was a fine young actor with handsome features, a slender physique, and a cultivated

voice—but he was not at all convincing as a Westerner. He proved as durable as a cowboy, however, never missing a single performance. June Walker, the female lead, let her understudy play the role of Laurey Williams several times. But Tex Ritter had to be content with the part of Cord Elam, since Tone would not step aside even for a matinee performance.

On January 5, 1931, *Green Grow the Lilacs* opened for a week at Philadelphia's Garrick Theater. Another brief engagement, in Washington, D.C., began on January 19, 1931, and there also was a performance at Baltimore's Ford Theater. Opening night on Broadway was January 26 at the Guild Theater. The price of tickets ranged from $2.50 down to a mere seventy-five cents. The program offered New York patrons an explanation of such cowpoke terms as "Dogies" and "Mavericks" and "Shivaree." The set featured a rustic, turn-of-the-century farmhouse interior.

"The whole affair is likable," remarked one reviewer. The reviews were favorable, and there was special praise for the "old songs born and reared humbly in the West." Tex smiled happily throughout his performance, responding to the audience and obviously enjoying his work.

Tex, Everett Cheetham, and Hank Worden rented an apartment a couple of blocks from the Guild Theater. An assistant stage manager soon was invited into the apartment, and the bachelor quartet hired a cook. Tex collected steady paychecks as *Green Grow the Lilacs* ran for eight weeks on Broadway.

The company then took *Green Grow the Lilacs* on the road, with a week each in Cleveland, Pittsburgh, St. Louis, Milwaukee, and Minneapolis, then three weeks in Chicago. Tex and Everett Cheetham roomed together. Tex was one of the hits of the show with his exuberant performance of cowboy music, while the banjo-playing Cheetham atttracted special attention with his rendition of his own composition, "Blood on the Saddle."

Tex in his costume from Green Grow the Lilacs.

Before the show left Chicago, Tex and Everett received an inquiry from an advertising firm to audition for radio work. The audition was conducted at NBC studios in Chicago, and the two performers were offered attractive radio contracts, to begin within a few weeks. They eagerly signed, because after its Chicago engagement, *Green Grow the Lilacs* was scheduled for only one more week, in Detroit.

During twenty-three weeks on Broadway and on the road, *Green Grow the Lilacs* ran for 205 performances. Tex was deeply gratified with a long run as a featured performer in a popular show. He had a grand time onstage, as well as a great deal of fun at various dinners and parties after performances. With a radio contract in his pocket, his career was definitely on the rise.

Tex and Everett traveled by train back to New York, where Cheetham had stored his 1930 Model-A Ford during the roadshow. They then drove to Chicago, only to learn that their radio work would be performed in NBC's New York studios. Cheetham sold his Ford, and the two friends returned by train to New York, where they were installed at the Roosevelt Hotel. At NBC they made rehearsal tapes, then went on the air. Tex performed his songs and dialogue capably, but Cheetham admitted to Johnny Bond that the microphone "scared me to death." After a couple of weeks both Cheetham and Tex were canceled by NBC. Cheetham returned by train to Sheridan, Wyoming, while Tex decided to visit Texas.

After seeing his family in Nederland, Tex went to Austin. During this trip he spent time with J. Frank Dobie, John A. Lomax, and Oscar Fox. Inevitably he toyed with the notion of trying to finish law studies at the University of Texas. But by the summer of 1931 the country had been mired in the Great Depression for nearly two years. Money for another year or more of college would be more difficult than ever to raise. Besides, Tex had enjoyed an impressive measure of success in the entertainment world, as his university mentors probably pointed out.

By the fall of 1931 Ritter was back in New York. But Broadway was suffering from the double impact of the depression and of talking movies. While many of the best playwrights and most promising young players defected to Hollywood, the number of Broadway productions and ticket prices dropped steadily. Tex could not find theater work, so he again sang for his supper at Greenwich Village, where his staggering rendition of "Rye Whiskey" was a hit. He regularly made the rounds of theatrical and radio agencies, but landed only a few radio commercials. When Tex and another out-of-work actor, Russell Swan, were reduced to splitting a donut and a cup of coffee, "I was pretty hungry, real hungry," Tex recalled. At

Thanksgiving he found only ten cents in his pocket.

"That time I took my dime down to a restaurant and ordered french fries and poured ketchup all over them," he reminisced. "This Greek that ran the joint gave me hell for using so much of his ketchup."

That Christmas, Tex "didn't have anything." But the new year would bring a turn of fortune. Although 1932 was the worst year of the depression, Tex won the role of "Sage Brush Charlie" in *The Roundup*, a revival of a 1907 romantic comedy which had made a star of Fatty Arbuckle. In 1907 *The Roundup* had run for 155 performances. This updated version would include Western music during the interludes between the four acts, a device adapted from *Green Grow the Lilacs*. Tex Ritter was placed in the cast so that he could sing and play the type of cowboy ballads that had been such a popular feature of *Green Grow the Lilacs*.

The Roundup opened at New York's Majestic Theater on March 7, 1932. The reviewer for the *New York Herald-Tribune* wrote that "Tex Ritter is excellent as a bronco buster," while the critic for the *New York Evening Post* found that Tex "has an exceptionally winning personality." Aside from Tex, however, *The Roundup* did not fare well with reviewers. The best seats in the house cost only one dollar, and seats for the Wednesday, Thursday and Friday matinees cost just seventy-five cents. But crowds did not materialize, and *The Roundup* folded after a short run.

With Broadway as well as Wall Street suffering, Tex could not find another theatrical role. Aware that the American Record Corporation was producing Western recordings by radio singer Gene Autry, Tex approached Art Satherly, head of ABC's hillbilly division. Satherly had seen Tex in *Green Grow the Lilacs*, and he let the singer record "The Cowboy's Christmas Ball." Tex accompanied himself on the guitar. The song was recorded on October 31, 1932, but was never released.

Tex began to appear on the radio at this time, however, prompting Satherly to offer him a flat fee of $100 for a recording session on March 15, 1933. Again accompanying himself with his guitar, Tex recorded four sides, standard for a recording session. "A-Ridin' Old Paint" and "Everyday in the Saddle" were not

issued. But "Rye Whiskey, Rye Whiskey" and "Goodbye Old Paint" became his first record release.

Satherly advised Tex that the catchy "Rye Whiskey, Rye Whiskey," with his unique delivery, could prove to be a bread and butter number for him. Tex already had seen favorable response to "Rye Whiskey, Rye Whiskey" among different types of audiences, and the tune indeed proved to be a staple throughout his performing career. The folk song "Rye Whiskey, Rye Whiskey" originally was called "Jack O'Diamond, Jack O'Diamond" after the opening line, but Tex changed that to the more descriptive name.

Within a month, on April 14, 1933, Satherly produced another session, this time hiring a fiddler to blend with Ritter's guitar. Tex re-recorded "A-Ridin' Old Paint" and "Everyday in the Saddle," and this version of the songs was released. But there were no more sessions for the American Record Corporation, which later became Columbia Records.

Almost two years would pass before Tex would record for another company, but in the meantime his career accelerated impressively. In the fall of 1932 he was hired by radio station WOR to headline *The Lone Star Rangers*, New York's first Western-oriented program. Tex sang cowboy ballads and told tales of the Wild West, and his stint on *The Lone Star Rangers* would lead to other radio assignments.

By this time there were 600 broadcast stations across the United States. The first radio network, NBC, was formed in 1926. Within two years CBS began broadcasting, while the Mutual Broadcasting System would be organized in 1934 (ABC was not founded until 1943). During the depression year of 1932, three million radio sets were manufactured, a total which doubled in 1935. Advertising agencies found radio to be a gold mine, and broadcasting became heavily commercialized. While musical performances dominated early programming, by the 1930s listeners also enjoyed a variety of dramatic and comedy shows, as well as the beginnings of news and sports broadcasts. Networks competed for the talent of popular singers and comedians: CBS boasted Bing Crosby, Kate Smith, Jack Benny, Fred Allen, and Burns and Allen, while NBC countered with Rudy Vallee, Eddie Cantor, Al Jolson, and Ed Wynn. NBC began broadcasting *Amos 'n Andy* in 1929, and the nightly fifteen-minute comedy quickly became the most popular program on the air. Housewives enjoyed daytime fifteen-minute soap operas, while juvenile programs were scheduled for early evenings and Saturdays. In New York actors with rich voices performed on numerous programs, sometimes proceeding from one studio to another during a workday. Often these actors performed multiple roles on a single show, changing their voices for different characters. They stood in front of bulky microphones, holding their scripts behind the mike to avoid paper noise. When the script moved to another page, each actor discarded a sheet, and by the end of a program the floor was littered with script pages.

The cast of the WHN Barn Dance, *at the Roxie Theater in New York. Tex stands at far left, waving his hat.*

This rapidly expanding New York broadcasting scene would markedly add to Tex Ritter's identity as an entertainer. He had become radio's first cowboy balladeer at KPRC in Houston in 1928, and in 1931 he had a brief flirtation with NBC. Starring in *The Lone Star Rangers* in 1932 introduced Tex to New York audiences as a Western character. His deep, strong voice was ideal for radio, and he began to be hired for commercials as well as for acting-singing roles.

In 1932 CBS aired a juvenile show called *Bobby Benson's Adventures*, sponsored by Heckers H-O Cereals. "Bobby Benson," although only a youngster, owned the H-Bar-O Ranch (named after the cereal, of course) in the Big Bend country of Texas. Supporting characters included Bobby's foreman, "Tex Mason," along with an Indian ranch hand named "Harka," and a teller of tall tales, "Windy Wales." When Tex was hired to play Tex Mason, the character of another yarnspinner, "Diogenes Dodwaddle," was created for Ritter. Ritter changed his voice for these two diverse characters, then altered his voice again to play various small roles. *Bobby Benson's Adventures* ran five times a week over CBS, and when H-O Cereals canceled their sponsorship, the name of the show was changed to *Bobby Benson and the B-Bar-B Riders*.

Ritter's work on *Bobby Benson's Adventures*

led to numerous other radio shows. *Tex Ritter's Campfire* played to juvenile audiences over WHN in 1933, and he also performed as emcee and featured singer for the *WHN Barn Dance* on Saturday nights, which was New York's response to the Barn Dance craze that swept across the country. Also in 1933, WINS created a children's cowboy show, *Cowboy Tom's Round-up*. The title role was played by George Martin as an old-timer who told tales about the Old West. Ritter was hired for the part of "Tex," the romantic interest who frequently sang cowboy ballads. There also were two Indian characters, "Chief Shunatona" and "Shookum." In addition to his duties as co-star and singer, Tex helped write the program. Playing for fifteen minutes each weekday afternoon, *Cowboy Tom's Round-up* quickly became the most popular juvenile program in New York. A songbook promptly was prepared for sale to fans, *Cowboy Tom's Round-up Book, Published for His Thousands of Radio Listeners*. The program ran for three years, 1933-1936, including network broadcasts by NBC.

The success of *Cowboy Tom's Round-up* generated roles for Tex on a variety of other shows. Like other successful radio actors, he appeared concurrently on as many as three programs. Tex had a role on *Maverick Jim* over WOR, and he was heard on *The Gibson Family*, *Terry and Ted*, *Court of Human Relations*, and *Cafe of the Red Dagger*. *The Eno Crime Club*, sponsored by Eno "Effervescent" Salts, made

Cowboy Tom's Round-up Book *featured the four characters on the cover: Cowboy Tom (at left), Chief Shunatona, Tex, and Shookum (bottom).*

Cowboy Tom, Chief Shunatona, and Tex in a publicity still for Cowboy Tom's Round-up.

its CBS debut in 1931. There were interconnecting thirty-minute mystery episodes on Tuesday and Wednesday nights, and the central character was "Spencer Dean—the Manhunter." Tex landed a role on *The Eno Crime Club*, and he also played on *The Lux Radio Theatre*, a CBS drama which ran on Sunday nights at 9:00. Another long-running program which afforded work for Tex was *Death Valley Days*, a series of true Western adventures which was first heard on NBC in 1930. The last network show which provided a role for Tex was the immensely popular *Gang Busters*, a hard-hitting crime show that became a Wednesday night fixture over CBS in 1936.

Passages

In 1934-35, while Tex was making a name for himself on the New York radio scene, his parents passed away within a few months of each other. At the age of seventy-five, Jim Ritter died in Nederland on November 27, 1934. Married for four decades, Lizzie was lonely and ailing after Jim's death. She visited relatives in Panola County, where she died on March 12, 1935, at just fifty-seven years of age. Although he had lost his mother and father, throughout the remainder of his life Tex traveled to Texas to visit his siblings and other relatives.

Late in 1934 Tex found work in another Broadway show. *Mother Lode* was a musical romance set in San Francisco during the gold rush. Early in *Mother Lode* Tex played a character called "Red Dog," then changed costumes and appeared in later scenes in an unnamed part. *Mother Lode* was directed by Melvyn Douglas, a talented actor who also played a role. After rehearsals and a trial run out of town, *Mother Lode* opened at New York's Cort Theater on December 12, 1934. The play did not work with New York audiences, and closed on December 29. But *Mother Lode* proved to be a successful road-show, touring for two years.

Tex decided not to follow the show. He stayed in New York, continuing with *Cowboy Tom's Round-up* and other radio work. Recent successes also resulted in another recording contract, with Decca Records. Decca had been formed in mid-1934, and,

Another publicity shot for Cowboy Tom's Round-up.

Tex, behind the microphone at center, helping to entertain children for WINS, the station which broadcast Cowboy Tom's Round-up.

searching for artists, signed Tex late in December 1934. His first session at Decca's New York studio was on January 21, 1935, with David Kapp as producer. Accompanied only by his guitar, Tex sang "Sam Hall," which enjoyed modest popularity, and "Get Along Little Dogies."

David Kapp, who would produce each of Ritter's seven Decca sessions, called Tex back into the studio a couple of weeks later, on February 5. The customary four numbers were recorded: "Thirty Three Years in Prison," "Lady Killin' Cowboy," "I'm A Do-Right Cowboy," and "Bill the Bar Fly." The latter three songs were written by the prolific composer Buck Nation, who provided accompa-

niment on guitar and whose band provided more depth with steel guitar, fiddle, and harmonica.

Later in the year, on October 16, 1935, Kapp produced a session in Chicago. Accompanied by a guitar, fiddle, harmonica, bass, and steel guitar, Tex cut "Nobody's Darling But Mine" and "My Brown Eyed Texas Rose," along with "Boots and Saddles" and "The Oregon Trail." Kapp brought Tex back to Chicago for a session on April 17, 1936. Backed up by a guitar, fiddle, and steel guitar, Tex recorded "Answer to Nobody's Darling But Mine," "A Melody From the Sky," "The Hills of Old Wyoming," and "We'll Rest at the End of the Trail." None of the Ritter records sold well for Decca, but Tex was given a movie contract later in 1936, and David Kapp would continue to arrange recording sessions in Hollywood.

Exposure on radio led to invitations for "The Singing Lecturer" to present "The Texas Cowboy and His Songs" at New York University and other area colleges. Tex gave private

Dogie or Doggy?

During the 1930s it was considered chic in the East to embrace the culture of the Old West, but Easterners did not always enjoy full comprehension, as Tex Ritter discovered after performing at a theater in Virginia. The theater owner introduced Tex to a local woman who had heard him over the radio.

"Mr. Ritter," she queried, "I've been meaning to ask you a question for a long time. I used to hear you sing that song about 'Get Along Little Doggy' and I told my husband that no man with such a nice voice would ever make a dog run all the way from Texas to Wyoming."

During the 1930s Tex Ritter became a well-known radio and stage personality in New York.

guitar lessons to young fans. He also worked as a featured singer at the World's Championship Rodeo. The famous indoor arena opened in 1879 in a converted railroad station on Madison Square at 26th Street. This structure later was replaced by a larger building on the same site. In 1925 the third Madison Square Garden was erected uptown at Eighth Avenue and 50th Street. But this time the World's Championship Rodeo, promoted by "Colonel" William T. Johnson of San Antonio and offering large purses, became a major event of the rodeo circuit. Madison Square Garden had hosted Wild West shows since the late 1800s, and large crowds trooped to the World's Championsip Rodeo. In 1936, for example, nearly 250,000 spectators

attended the Madison Square Garden Rodeo during nineteen days in October. Each fall the rodeo brought Hank Worden and Everett Cheetham to New York, and for nearly a month they stayed at the apartment of their old pal, Tex Ritter.

Ritter's apartment also was the site of regular poker games with a radio crowd which included announcer Harry VonZell, actor-emcee Warren Hull, who later would become famous on *Strike It Rich*, Curtis Arnall, who played Buck Rogers and who initiated the title role of the popular soap opera *Pepper Young's Family*, busy actor Andre Baruch, popular bandleader Russ Morgan, cartoonist Dow Walling, and Frank Readick, star of *The Shadow*. The only woman was actress Anne Elstner, who would star as *Stella Dallas* during the entire nineteen-year run of the soap opera. Anne and Tex appeared together on *Maverick Jim* and other radio shows. She and her husband, Jack Matthews, sometimes hosted the poker group, and Jack always insisted that Tex perform "Rye Whiskey." Tex, Anne, and Jack became lifelong friends, and in later years Ritter visited their home when his tours brought him near.

"She played poker like a man," admired Tex. "We usually played once a week and I usually lost. I was a little reckless. When I'd win I'd usually win pretty big because I used to bluff a lot. But I'd usually get caught, and then I'd lose a lot."

By 1936 Tex also had become friends with the owner of the Wallpack Center Dude Ranch in New Jersey. "It wasn't a terribly authentic dude ranch," reminisced Tex, but it offered New Yorkers a nearby outdoor haven where they could ride horseback. Tex began going out to New Jersey on weekends, helping with the horses and trail rides, and singing cowboy ballads to add Western flavor. He always enjoyed a chance to entertain, and "there were a few pretty little unattached girls who were always coming out there," he recalled happily. Tex spent his weekends singing and riding and flirting with girls, and the modest dude ranch would provide the setting for Ritter's next big show business opportunity.

Hooray for Hollywood

When Tex Ritter came to Hollywood in 1936 to star in B Westerns, such films formed a staple of the motion picture industry. There were eight major studios which filmed A movies, features that were eighty to ninety minutes in length (and sometimes longer). B movies were shorter features, about fifty-five to sixty-five minutes, and were used for double bills. An A film would provide the feature attraction of a double bill, while the lower half was filled by a B movie (although sometimes a double bill was made up of two B features). Major studios maintained B units to produce Westerns, mysteries, and other short features, and a number of small "independent" studios concentrated their total efforts on B movies.

During the silent film era, Broncho Billy Anderson, William S. Hart, Fred Thomson, hard-riding Ken Maynard, flamboyant Tom Mix, and a host of lesser cowboy heroes churned out Western movies by the hundreds. The historic West of cattle drives and outlaws and gunfighters had only recently passed into history, and young audiences thrilled to the screen adventures of heroic celluloid cowboys sporting six-guns and big hats. The emphasis was on action: chases, fistfights, shootouts. The Western, with its sweeping scenery and galloping horses, was perfect for the big screen. Motion pictures needed movement, and Westerns *moved*. The pianos of silent film theaters banged out musical accompaniment which added to the excitement. Tom Mix, Ken Maynard, Hoot Gibson, and other screen cowboys had been rodeo and Wild West show performers; they were impressive figures on horseback, and since the films were silent it did not matter that most Western stars could not handle dialogue.

In the late 1920s, however, the movie industry was faced with the difficult and expensive transition to sound. Then the film business, as well as the rest of the economy, had to grapple with the Great Depression. At the end of the decade of the Roaring Twenties, there were 23,000 movie theaters across the United States, with a weekly attendance of 80 million (total U.S. population was 122 million). But after five depression years, 4,000 theaters had closed their doors and weekly attendance sagged to 55 million. In 1928 Hollywood released 834 A and B features; two years later, the total of releases had dropped to 595. In order to lure audiences back, double bills—two for the price of one—were relied upon, and by the mid-1940s four out of five theaters were running double features. Features customarily were changed three times per week: Sunday-Monday, Tuesday-Wednesday, Thursday-Friday-Saturday. A theater could use 300 features per year. There was an enormous demand for product, and by 1935 the total number of Hollywood features had climbed back to 766.

Westerns remained the most popular motion picture genre. During the mid-1930s, Hollywood filmed about 300 B Westerns per year. For three decades Westerns had been produced by the hundreds, and as the formula began to grow stale, the musical tradition of the singing cowboy seemed to offer fresh possibilities. Early sound Westerns, in the interest of economy, had not inserted background music. But the dialogue was simple and clichéd, and most cowboy stars delivered their lines awkwardly. Although fans came to Westerns for action, not acting, the action seemed flat without the exciting musical strains provided by

Hollywood

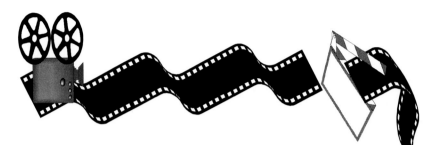

Hollywood, destined to become the glamorous capital of the motion picture industry, was settled in the 1880s and named by the wife of a real estate developer. By 1909 Hollywood, located among lemon groves and hills a few miles north of Los Angeles, was a residential suburb of 4,000. Within four years the population nearly doubled, because motion pictures began to be filmed in this region of varied scenery and dependable sunshine. The first movie company headquartered in Hollywood in 1911, and within a decade more than a score of studios were producing silent films there.

As the population exploded, commercial buildings and luxury hotels went up along Hollywood Boulevard. Movie stars built splendid mansions. During the 1920s four palatial movie houses were erected: Grauman's Egyptian Theatre, Grauman's Chinese Theatre, Warner Brothers Theater, and the Hollywood Pantages. These ornate theaters hosted numerous movie premieres, which attracted legions of fans. Tourists also delighted in the movie-making which constantly took place on the streets of Hollywood. Streets were roped off to stage automobile accidents or store robberies. Banks were looted on Saturdays, Sundays, and bank holidays. Passersby were enlisted on the streets to take part in crowd scenes.

The Great Depression and talking pictures rocked Holllywood at the same time. But the advent of "talkies" captivated the public more than ever, and by the time Tex Ritter arrived in Hollywood, the atmosphere in the movie capital was electric with excitement and glamor and opportunity.

silent theater pianists. Ken Maynard tried short musical interludes in some of his films, and so did young John Wayne. Wayne's singing voice had to be dubbed, and his experiment as "Singin' Sandy" proved brief. Maynard engaged Gene Autry, a Chicago radio star, to deliver musical numbers in his movies.

After appearing twice with Maynard in 1934, the following year Autry starred in *The Phantom Empire*, a science fiction serial with a Western setting. The role was intended for Maynard, but the cantankerous star was replaced by Autry. Although Gene was physically unimpressive and uncomfortable as an actor, he was pleasant and sang well, and audiences responded in large numbers. Soon he sang his way through *Tumbling Tumbleweeds*, the first of a series of musical Westerns which established Autry as a major box-office attrac-

tion. Gene Autry was a screen phenomenon of 1935, and alert producers began to scout for other potential singing cowboys.

One man who sensed the new trend in Westerns was thirty-nine-year-old Ed Finney, advertising chief for recently organized Grand National Pictures. Grand National was the latest studio on "Poverty Row," the Hollywood neighborhood where independent producers of B movies centered their filming activities. Film executive Edward L. Alperson opportunistically signed James Cagney, who was involved in a contract dispute with Warner Brothers, and Grand National launched its operations in 1936 with one of Hollywood's premier stars as headliner. Finney, a fifteen-year veteran of the movie business, agreed to head advertising and publicity for the new company, on the condition that he would be allowed to produce a series of

On weekends Tex (at right) often helped out at a New Jersey dude ranch, where he was discovered by Ed Finney of Grand National Pictures.

Westerns. For his "Range Rider" series he wanted to introduce a singing cowboy.

Grand National maintained offices on Sixth Avenue in New York City, where Finney was headquartered. Finney had heard Tex on the radio show *Cowboy Tom's Round-up*, and he encountered Ritter when he went horseback riding at the Wallpack Center Dude Ranch in nearby New Jersey. Tex later recalled seeing Finney on three consecutive weekends. Finney listened to Tex sing cowboy ballads at the dude ranch and watched him handle horses on the trail rides. He noted Ritter's tall, rangy physique, his Texas drawl, and his easy smile. While at the ranch, Finney discussed with Ritter his plans for a new singing cowboy, and Tex eagerly agreed to make a screen test. Tex signed a personal services contract with Finney, rather than with Grand National. The movie executive shrewdly reasoned that if Tex Ritter clicked as a star, then Ed Finney would direct and profit from his career.

Finney hoped to film a screen test with Tex and a horse in the wilds of Central Park, but arrangements could not be finalized. Next Finney turned to a friend, Eddie Senz, a make-up man from Paramount, which was filming a feature on a nearby lot. Finney was allowed brief access to a tavern set which resembled a saloon. Tex squinted noticeably before the unaccustomed glare of klieg lights, but Finney clambered atop a stool and directed his protegé to look up at him. Tex then was filmed singing a song and reading dialogue. He had performed both of these tasks professionally for several years, and he looked good in his cowboy duds.

But he was somewhat awkward in his first appearance on film, and there was a mixed reaction to the screen test at Grand National. It was critical, however, for the new company to produce motion pictures. Finney persuaded Alperson to order a series of eight Range Rider features starring Tex Ritter. B Westerns usually were produced in a series of six or seven or eight features; by using the same actors, director, producer, crew, and even locations, a great deal of money and time could be saved on each film. Ed Finney, investing his own funds in the Tex Ritter project, organized a production unit called Boots and Saddles to film the Range Rider series. The series was modestly budgeted at $8,000 to $12,000 per film. From this budget Tex would be paid $2,000 for each movie. B Westerns could be expected to earn at least $50,000, which provided solid profits with minimal investment for the studio. As producer, Ed Finney put together the Boots and Saddles unit, while assembling a cast and commissioning a script for the first Tex Ritter film, *Song of the Gringo.*

When Tex arrived in California to film Song of the Gringo, *Grand National welcomed their new star with a musical group, veteran villain Glenn Strange (third from the right), leading lady Joan Woodbury, the first White Flash, and John P. McCarthy (holding dog), who wrote and would direct Ritter's first movie.*

In August Tex packed up, said his goodbyes in New York, then boarded a TWA plane at the airport in Newark, New Jersey. The coast-to-coast ticket cost Grand National $160, and Tex arrived at Glendale Arport on Tuesday, August 18, 1936. Grand National had arranged a reception: a white horse was waiting with an ornate saddle; a small Western band was there; and the entourage included leading lady Joan Woodbury, veteran character actor Glenn Strange, and John P. McCarthy, who wrote the screenplay for and would direct *Song of the Gringo*. Tex was dressed in Western attire, and Grand National publicists sent out stories and photos touting the arrival of their new Western star.

Early publicity photo for Grand National's new singing cowboy.

Tex was installed in Hollywood's Knickerbocker Hotel, but soon Grand National moved him to an apartment. Filming on *Song of the Gringo* was scheduled to start just ten days after Tex reached Hollywood. Tex was busy at Grand National offices, working with publicity, wardrobe, and makeup people. His name was appropriate for a cowboy star, but the publicity department did not want juvenile fans to know that Tex was older than thirty. His birthdate was moved from 1905 to 1907, so that he could be described as twenty-nine. Soon Grand National publicists referred to his age as twenty-eight, and Tex happily remained in his late twenties for years.

While performing on radio, Tex had delivered dialogue by reading from a script into a microphone. As a movie actor he would have to memorize his lines, but there was no difficulty, because for more than a decade he had memorized and performed song lyrics, and, of course, he had appeared in extended stage productions.

Two of the songs in the film would be Tex Ritter standards, "Rye Whiskey" and "Sam Hall." Tex wrote "My Sweet Chiquita" for the movie, and "Out on the Lone Prairie" was the best of three other songs that were included in *Song of the Gringo*. Tex and backup musicians recorded these songs on a sound stage before filming began. Filmmakers already had learned that a far cleaner sound could be recorded inside, and Tex would learn to lip sync the lyrics while riding his horse or performing some other activity.

When a new star was introduced, special care was taken with the first film of a series in order to make a favorable impression on audiences—then production values usually were cut in later series features. This pattern was repeated with Tex Ritter. *Song of the Gringo* featured solid production values, including an impressive fandango scene with striking costumes and elaborate choreography. Finney also put together an experienced cast to support his novice star.

Dark-haired leading lady Joan Woodbury already had played opposite Western stars William Boyd (Hopalong Cassidy) and Tim McCoy. Sidekick Fuzzy Knight was an old vaudevillian who had reached Broadway before coming to Hollywood a few years earlier. The sheriff was played by Monte Blue, whose first film was D. W. Griffith's 1915 classic *The Birth of a Nation*. The bad guys were led by lantern-jawed Warner Richmond, who had begun in silent films and, in recent years, had played a villain against such Western stars as Gene Autry, John Wayne, Bob Steele, and Johnny Mack Brown. Towering, moustachioed Glenn Strange had been a heavyweight boxer and a stunt man, and he later would earn television recognition as Sam the bartender on *Gunsmoke*.

Tex was mounted astride a big, white stallion dubbed White Flash.

The horse was rented, as was the sound stage at Talisman Studios and the exterior set, at Monogram Ranch in Newhall, just outside the Los Angeles city limits. Independent companies usually rented studio facilities, equipment, costumes, crews, and almost everything else it took to make a film. All of these things were readily available in Hollywood, with the result that scenes filmed by independent companies could reflect the same technical competence as those shot by major studios, even though the independents did not have to produce the massive capital outlays of the majors.

The Grand National clock, with its hands whirling excitedly, opened and closed Tex Ritter's movies.

The first day of filming on *Song of the Gringo* was at Newhall Ranch, and when Tex mounted his horse, the big white animal spooked and began bucking. Glenn Strange hinted to Johnny Bond that one of the practical jokers on the set slipped a burr under the saddle blanket. Not expecting to rodeo, Tex went flying through the air onto a pile of horse manure. Everyone on the set howled with

laughter, but Tex grinned good-naturedly and said something about doing better "if I had one of my old plow horses from down home."

Director John P. McCarthy stuck to his schedule, and filming was finished within the allotted five days. The five-day shooting schedule that was common for B Westerns required precise planning, a great many camera setups during a day—sometimes 100 or more—and long workdays. Major features were filmed at a more studied pace, but B crews had to work rapidly. Although some B Westerns were filmed in three or four days, the result was an obvious "quickie," while a few series movies enjoyed the luxury of a two-week shooting schedule. Gary Cooper said that a two-week Western was considered an "epic," but the Tex Ritter films were scheduled for five days.

One of the cast members was Al Jennings, an old-time Oklahoma outlaw and convict who incongruously played a judge. Jennings coached Tex, who was issued a fancy two-gun rig, on fine points of the fast draw and gunhandling. But Tex was not given much instruction in screen fisticuffs; the big fight scene between Tex and "Cherokee" (Warner Richmond) was unconvincing. Tex also was awkward and uncertain onscreen, which could only have been expected by hurrying a rookie actor through his first film. In his initial scene he posed as an outlaw, complete with a scruffy beard. Even after he was revealed as a good guy, his small hat and the rest of his outfit were undistinguished. But Tex sang well, and the shortcomings of his screen persona would be rapidly remedied.

The final cut of *Song of the Gringo* was sixty-two minutes, and the film was released on November 22, 1936. Reviews were good. The *Hollywood Reporter* observed that *"Song of the Gringo* has given a little more production value than an indie of this type," and the *Film Daily* considered the film "above average outdoor film drama." Various sources proclaimed Tex the "newest bet in prairie warbling" and "a sensational new cowboy singing star."

"This young star is going places," said V. A. Maurin, owner of the Fox Theater in Houma, Louisiana. "Everybody likes him and wants to know when we are going to play the next picture. Give us more like these."

The next picture was *Headin' for the Rio Grande*, and it was released less than a month

Song of the Gringo *(1936) was the first Tex Ritter film. Sidekick Fuzzy Knight looks over the star's left shoulder, and glaring from far right is lantern-jawed villain Warner Richmond—a bad guy since silent movie days.*

after *Song of the Gringo.* The director was Robert N. Bradbury, father of B Western star Bob Steele. A veteran director of Westerns, Bradbury worked on four more films in the first Range Rider series. Another old pro, Gus Peterson, was the cameraman for the first ten Tex Ritter movies.

In his second film, Headin' for the Rio Grande *(1936), Tex felt the gun barrel of Charles King, one of the busiest of all Western villains. Another veteran bad guy, Warner Richmond, looks on from the right.*

Returning to the cast to work with Tex were jut-jawed Warner Richmond and William Desmond. Syd Saylor was the new sidekick, and Tex wangled a small part for one-time

Keystone Kop Snub Pollard, who had been a boyhood favorite of Ritter's as a silent screen comedian. The new leading lady was pretty Eleanor Stewart in her first starring role. She caught on quickly, working as a leading lady in Westerns for the next nine years. She played opposite Bob Steele, Ken Maynard and Hopalong Cassidy, as well as several lesser cowboy stars.

Joining Warner Richmond in opposing Tex Ritter's hero were veteran heavies Earl Dwire,

Tex and sidekick Syd Saylor in Headin' for the Rio Grande.

Bud Osborne, and Charles King. Each of these reliable character actors started in films during the silent era, then became familiar faces—usually as bad guys—in the B Westerns of the 1930s. Movie fans knew what to expect from B Westerns: a staunch hero, a damsel in distress, galloping horses, fistfights, gunplay, and villains for the hero to vanquish. Men like Richmond, Dwire, Osborne, and King played villains in one film after another, and when they appeared onscreen knowledgeable fans instantly recognized them as bad guys. Throughout his career as a cowboy star, Tex would benefit from the consistent presence of quality villains.

In *Headin' for the Rio Grande* villains Richmond, Dwire, and King run a gang which preys on cattle drivers, offering "protection" and, if refused, shooting up the crew and driving off the herd. Tex adds the proper flavor by yipping his way through a couple of cowboy songs, while handling his dialogue with much

In Headin' for the Rio Grande *Tex serenaded Eleanor Stewart. Early in his film career Tex had a different leading lady in every movie.*

Among the arduous duties of a cowboy star were appearances with such beauties as Barbara Moffett, "Miss California Cowgirl." She was screen tested by Ed Finney "for the role of leading lady opposite Ritter in a forthcoming western film," but the proposed team failed to materialize.

greater ease. Two-gun Tex shoots the revolvers from the hands of three different bad guys, and engages in the first of scores of rousing fist-fights with Charlie King. There are two cattle stampedes, and in the last one Earl Dwire is trampled to death.

For the third Tex Ritter movie, *Arizona Days*, the cast and crew traveled to Arizona for location shooting near Wilcox. Although a Western about Arizona certainly should include scenes from Arizona, it was not common for B Westerns to indulge in the expense of filming very far from Hollywood. There usually was the atmosphere of a camping trip when on location, but the *Arizona Days* company soon returned to California. More outdoor scenes were shot at Chatham Ranch just outside Los Angeles, then filming ended on a rented sound stage at the International lot.

Perhaps to save a little expense for the Arizona trip, pretty Eleanor Stewart was limited to just one costume. There were several familiar faces in the cast: William Desmond had appeared in all three Ritter movies; Glenn Strange returned, and so did Earl Dwire, Snub Pollard, and Syd Saylor, who tried to generate humor by pumping a trombone. In one of the five musical numbers Shorty Holmes, living up to his reputation as "the harmonica maestro," played two harmonicas at once—one with his mouth and the other with his nose!

Tex co-wrote three of the songs for *Arizona Days*, and he had co-written three of the songs

for *Headin' for the Rio Grande*. The movie numbers were published as sheet music, and Ritter's Decca producer, David Kapp, made arrangements to record the most promising movie tunes. Tex left on his first promotional tour, through the South. Shortly after Ed Finney had signed Tex to a movie contract, the producer engaged the William Morris Agency to book Ritter's first public appearance tour through neighborhood theaters in Virginia, Tennessee, and the Carolinas. The greatest popularity enjoyed by B Westerns was in the rural South, as well as the rural West and Midwest. Personal appearance tours attracted fans to theaters which would exhibit Tex Ritter movies, promoting both the star and specific films. Seeing their hero in person, hearing him sing and talk, walking up and handing him a scrap of paper for an autograph—such an experience generated a sense of personal identification and an intense loyalty among young fans. Tex proved to have a taste for the road, interacting easily with audiences and entertaining tirelessly—and building a fan base which would sustain him throughout his career.

Following the tour Tex spent Thanksgiving with his family in Nederland. Back in Hollywood, on December 2, 1936, he took his guitar and music to Melrose Studios in Los Angeles for a recording session. He was backed by a steel guitar, fiddle, accordion, and bass. Two numbers from each of his first three movies were recorded: "Out on the Lone Prairie," "My Sweet Chiquita" (which was not released), "Headin' for the Rio Grande," "Jailhouse Lament," "High, Wide and Handsome," and "Arizona Days."

Two and a half weeks later, on December 20, *Headin' for the Rio Grande* was released to solid reaction. By the end of 1936 Tex had filmed three movies, completed his first promotional tour, and recorded music from his films. Soon he would begin work on *Trouble in Texas*, destined to be one of his best films, and he was scheduled for another personal appearance tour. After just four months in Hollywood, Tex Ritter had experienced a major career leap, and 1937 promised more excitement and fame.

The Sidekicks

One of the essentials of an entertaining story is comic relief, which was provided in Western movies of the 1930s and 1940s by the heroes' sidekicks. Gene Autry and Roy Rogers were teamed with the best Western sidekicks in the business, Smiley Burnette and Gabby Hayes. Indeed, a primary reason for the success of Autry and Rogers was the audience appeal of the musically gifted and rubber-faced Burnette and the gruff, bewhiskered Hayes.

Tex Ritter never appeared in a film with either Smiley Burnette or Gabby Hayes. He tried a great number of sidekicks, sometimes two in a single movie, but they proved mostly to be a succession of second- and third-rate buffoons who added little to the Ritter film image. A principal reason that the Tex Ritter movies never achieved the success of Gene Autry or Roy Rogers films was the mediocre roster of his sidekicks.

In Ritter's first film, in 1936, his comic companion was Fuzzy Knight, who also was a talented musician. As a teenager Knight worked as a tent show minstrel, then went on to vaudeville and Broadway before coming to Hollywood in the 1930s. He appeared in more than 100 Westerns as a sidekick, most effectively in twenty-eight films with Johnny Mack Brown. When Tex went to Universal in 1942 as a co-star with Johnny Mack Brown, he was reunited with Knight. In their ten Universal films Fuzzy played such characters as Happy T. Snodgrass (*Deep in the Heart of Texas*), Glow-Worm (*Marshal of Gunsmoke*), and Banjo Bonner (*Oklahoma Raiders*). Knight sometimes sang in these movies, and in *Arizona Trail* Tex and Fuzzy warbled a duet. Fuzzy sang well, but the comedy he provided in eleven films with Tex was ordinary at best.

Arizona Days (1937) was the third starring film for Tex, and the second—and last—time that Syd Saylor would ride as his sidekick.

In the second and third Ritter movies the sidekick was Syd Saylor, whose trademark was a bobbing Adam's apple. In 1935 Saylor played Lullaby Joslin, the sidekick in the Three Mesquiteers series, but he was dropped after one film in favor of Max Terhune, who would become one of the most popular of all Western sidekicks. In 1944 Max worked with Tex and Charles Starrett in *Cowboy Canteen*, but it was the only time the able ventriloquist-comedian appeared opposite Ritter.

Syd Saylor and his Adam's apple departed after only two Tex Ritter films. By that time Snub Pollard and Horace Murphy had appeared in small roles with Tex, and they took over the sidekick duties. Pollard played in nine Ritter movies, while Murphy was in fifteen, and they were paired as a lackluster comic duo eight times with Tex ("a couple of lame-wits," according to one

Snub Pollard appeared in nine films with Tex, but the former Keystone Kop was too silly even for juvenile audiences in the 1930s.

Snub Pollard (left), Tex, and Horace Murphy, who played in fifteen Ritter films. Pollard and Murphy teamed up as an uninspiring sidekick duo eight times in 1937 and 1938.

Al St. John started in films as a Keystone Kop (his uncle was the famous silent comedian, Fatty Arbuckle). He was a popular sidekick in Westerns ("Fuzzy Q. Jones") for many years, but he was Tex Ritter's pal just once, in Sing, Cowboy Sing (1937).

reviewer). Pollard was a member of the Keystone Kops of slapstick fame during the silent era, and he was a boyhood favorite of Ritter. Tex persuaded Ed Finney to hire Pollard, but the fake moustache Snub painted on for Tex Ritter movies seemed as outdated as the rest of his comedy tricks. Horace Murphy, blustery and pompous, used the same broad style. At least Pollard and Murphy were faithful companions to Tex. Like any singing cowboy star, Tex was clearly superior to his sidekicks with fists, guns, girls and guitars, and they admired him and were as loyal to their hero as any of his juvenile fans.

While Tex was on tour during the 1930s, he met Arkansas Slim Andrews, a musician and comedian who had played tent shows—sometimes as a one-man band—in Arkansas and Louisiana since the 1920s. Andrews gravitated to Hollywood, where Tex helped arrange a contract with Monogram. In 1940 Andrews had a small role with Tex in *Rhythm of the Rio Grande*, then played Ritter's sidekick in six subsequent films. Andrews had his own sidekick, a mule named Josephine.

In 1941 Tex moved to Columbia Pictures, co-starring in a series with Wild Bill Elliott. The first seven of the Columbia films featured Frank Mitchell as "Cannonball." Relying upon slapstick, Frank had enjoyed Broadway appearances as a member of the comedy team of Mitchell and Durant. After the team broke up, Mitchell appeared in a variety of movies, but the seven Ritter-Elliott films comprised his only experience as a cowboy sidekick.

In his last eight starring films, Tex was joined by fellow Texan Guy Wilkerson as "Panhandle Perkins." Tall and lanky, Wilkerson had started out in minstrel shows and vaudeville, but by the time he assumed the role of Panhandle Perkins he had played in such notable movies as *Gone With the Wind* and *Sergeant York*. One of his last films was John Wayne's *True Grit*.

In *Cowboy From Sundown*, bumbling

Roscoe Ates made his sole effort as a Tex Ritter sidekick, and there were other "comedians" who lasted just one film. As if to make up for all of the weak comedy support in Ritter movies, in 1944 Columbia put Max Terhune, Dub "Cannonball" Taylor, and Guinn "Big Boy" Williams in the same film, *Cowboy Canteen*. But it was the only time Tex enjoyed such strong comedy relief, and the other Ritter sidekicks did little to enhance the Tex Ritter mystique.

Roscoe Ates played "Gloomy" in Cowboy From Sundown *(1938). Mercifully, it was his only appearance with Tex, but Ates was "Soapy Jones," Eddie Dean's sidekick, in fifteen films from 1946 through 1948.*

Dub "Cannonball" Taylor made his film debut in 1938 in You Can't Take It With You, *starring James Stewart. The next year he began working as a sidekick with Wild Bill Elliott, and in 1941 he played Cannonball with Elliott and Tex in* King of Dodge City. *Taylor and Tex teamed again in 1944 in* Cowboy Canteen. *Later in his career Taylor became a well-known character actor in movies and television, and his son, Buck Taylor, played Newly on the television series* Gunsmoke.

Tex with sidekick—and one-man band—Arkansas Slim Andrews. Andrews toured with Tex for years after his film career ended.

The Bad Guys

During a decade as a cowboy star, Tex Ritter appeared with most of the character actors who repeatedly played villains during the profusion of B Westerns of the 1930s and 1940s. Arrayed against Tex in one film or another was a roster of familiar screen scoundrels which included Glenn Strange, Warner Richmond, Earl Dwire, Yakima Canutt, Bud Osborne, George Chesebro, Roy Barcroft, I. Standard Jolley, Ed Cassidy, and Charles King. Fans may not have known their names, but there was instant recognition of their surly faces. Each of these men lined up against Tex in several of their hundreds of film appearances. Charlie King appeared in nearly half of the Tex Ritter films, twenty-five, more than any other actor who teamed with Tex.

Sometimes Tex had to face more than one of these formidable tough guys in the same film. In *Trouble in Texas* (1937) Earl Dwire led a gang which included Yakima Canutt, Glenn Strange, and Charles King. *Riders of the Rockies* (1937) again pitted Tex against Dwire, Canutt, and King. King and George Cheseboro led the opposition in *Starlight Over Texas* (1938), and Bud Osborne and Glenn Strange ganged up on Tex in *Cowboy From Sundown* (1940). It was tough enough to face one notable villain, but when two or three or four well-known bad guys ganged up in a single film, young fans knew that their hero was in for a dangerous hour.

Tex wallops Charlie King in Sing, Cowboy Sing *(1937). King appeared in twenty-five Tex Ritter movies, and spent a great deal of time figuring out "new ways for Tex to beat me up."*

Tex gets the drop on villain Glenn Strange in Pals of the Silver Sage *(1940). Like Charlie King, Strange was in countless Westerns—including Ritter's first— before settling in as Sam the Bartender on the TV series* Gunsmoke.

The bad guys in a B Western usually were led by a villain posing as a respectable citizen. During the Great Depression of the 1930s, when hard times generally were blamed on financiers and bankers, the villain leader in a B Western often was a banker. Although he generally donned a gunbelt and boots, he was attired in a three-piece suit and tie, and with a thin moustache he closely resembled a banker of the 1930s. Even if the movie villain was a businessman or a rival rancher or a crooked judge, as long as he wore a three-piece suit and moustache he *looked* like a banker and therefore was easy for audiences to hate. The "banker look" became a convention for B Western villain masterminds. Earl Dwire—tall, thin, and sporting a pencil moustache—employed the banker look in numerous Tex Ritter movies.

Tex was often filmed in closeup during a hard ride on White Flash so that audiences could see that the star was not using a double. This scene is from Oklahoma Raiders *(1941).*

The henchmen did not share their leader's suave appearance. Gang members were burly and unshaven, and they wore black hats and scruffy range clothes. They were belligerent troublemakers who hung around saloons and tried to pick fights, and the hero always was badly outnumbered. By the early 1950s cost-cutting in B Westerns had reduced "gangs" to just three bad guys, but during Tex Ritter's heyday, 1936-1945, small roles could be filled for $10 to $25 per film, and every cowboy hero was menaced by large outlaw gangs. Young cowboys came to Hollywood and gathered daily outside studios which filmed Westerns, hoping to be hired to gallop hell-for-leather across a movie location. The Wild West had ended, but cowboys could still find work on the cinematic frontier.

Despite being badly outnumbered, B Western heroes rarely killed their adversaries. The public regarded blood violence as generally unwholesome for youthful audiences, so B Western gunfights rarely produced fatalities. Tex Ritter shootouts were typical of the genre: a furious exchange of gunfire between good guys and bad guys usually resulted in only one or two wounded men, and blood from these wounds was never seen. When Tex pulled a revolver against a villain, Ritter almost always—with unerring marksmanship—shot the gun out of his opponent's hand.

Of course, B Western audiences expected action, and simply pulling a trigger—without producing blood—offered limited excitement. There was far more sustained action in a horseback chase, or a runaway stagecoach, or a fist-flinging brawl. Faceless stunt men proved to be the real stars of B Westerns.

Tex became a good rider, and his movies were filled with scenes of him galloping full-speed astride White Flash. Such shots were filmed in sufficient closeup for audiences to see that it was Tex, not a double, spurring across the countryside. Tex also was carefully tutored in handling his fists by an expert in screen brawls, Charles King.

"Roy and Gene sang more—I killed more—I must have killed old Charlie King at least twenty times," reminisced Tex. "Usually behind the same rock." If not killed, King at least had once more been beaten senseless, this time in Sundown on the Prairie *(1939).*

Charlie King was a decade older than Tex, born in 1895 in Hillsboro, Texas. Attracted to the movie business, at the age of twenty Charlie caught on as an extra in *Birth of a Nation*. By the 1920s he was starring in short comedies, but when sound arrived his deep growl of a voice and heavyset physique made him a natural villain for the enormous number of Westerns that were being filmed. Charlie sported a black moustache and a threatening scowl, and he learned to handle himself on horseback and in fights. He became one of the most recognizable of the sagebrush heavies, playing in hundreds of oaters opposite virtually every cowboy star of the 1930s and 1940s. Offscreen he was renowned for his rowdy sense of humor, and he was such a freespender that his wife began going to studio business offices to pick up his paycheck.

Charlie appeared in the second Tex Ritter film, as "Tick," and in two dozen more. In other Ritter movies he was called "Bull," "Blackie," "Stark," "Badger," "Trigger," and "Slub," as well as more pedestrian names.

Charlie had a thick build, while Tex was tall and rangy. They looked good as opponents, and Tex demonstrated a knack for screen fisticuffs, which were choreographed by Charlie. The two men enjoyed staging brawls, and Tex rarely used a double. Onscreen Charlie would pick a fight, Tex would quickly rise to the challenge, and fists—and furniture—would begin flying. Finally beaten senseless, Charlie sometimes could not resist a reflexive kick as he lapsed into unconsciousness. Pounding a villain into submission was an exciting and satisfying way to produce justice, and energetic fistfights became a trademark of Tex Ritter movies.

Action films demand interesting and dangerous villains who provide perilous opposition for the hero. Tex Ritter films exhibited an impressive lineup of intimidating heavies. Although the mediocrity of his sidekicks was a drawback to Tex Ritter movies, an unquestionable strong point was the continuing quality of the bad guys.

Top Ten

Early in January 1937, Tex left Hollywood on a personal appearance tour through Texas, Arkansas, Missouri, and Illinois. He was accompanied by comedian Snub Pollard, a white horse, and a sideman. The William Morris Agency set up the tour, and Ed Finney kept in touch with Tex while he was on the road. Finney received five percent of the profits, and when he later made tour arrangements himself, his contract with Tex brought him ten percent. Tex and Finney each would enjoy handsome earnings from these tours. Tex was a natural on the road: He was a tireless traveler, and with his engaging personality and gifts as an entertainer, he quickly learned to cultivate his fans.

Tex handles a buckboard team for Ethelind Terry in his third film, Arizona Days *(1937).*

His fans soon had a new Tex Ritter movie to enjoy. *Arizona Days* was released before the end of the month, and the star cut a much better figure onscreen. Tex was noticeably more comfortable as an actor, while his costume now included a big white hat which he wore with impressive style. "This boy Tex Ritter gets under my skin and I like him," said W. H. Brenner, owner of the Cozy Theater in Winchester, Indiana. "Tex certainly is on the way."

Several of Ritter's friends from New York City journeyed to Hollywood to see if the up and coming Western star could help them break into movies. Chick Hannon and Shorty Miller arrived first, soon followed by Hank Worden, Ray Whitley, Tex Cooper, and Everett Cheetham. When another friend, writer Tex Sherman, came to California, Ritter welcomed him in style. "Tex threw a party for me when I arrived in Hollywood," reported Sherman, "and what a party! Several beautiful gals from the studios were on hand, and many famous cowboys were there," along with Cheetham, Miller, and other old pals. Often one or more of his friends bunked with Tex at his apartment.

Ritter was able to find work for most of his cronies at Grand National, sometimes in his own films. Tall, gangling Hank Worden would appear in eleven Tex Ritter movies. Worden, Miller, and Cooper had small parts in the next Tex Ritter release, *Trouble in Texas*. Glenn Strange, Charles King, and Earl Dwire were part of a strong cast which included two future Hollywood legends.

Yakima Canutt was a former rodeo star who had worked steadily in B Westerns since the 1920s. Yak had starred in his own series of silent Westerns, and while acting in the films of other stars he became Hollywood's finest stunt man. He staged breathtaking action scenes, calculating dangerous movements with unprecedented care and developing an imaginative variety of safety devices. Usually playing a villain, he also doubled for the star, and in many movies in long shots he chased himself on horseback.

Yak appeared frequently in John Wayne films of the 1930s, and the two men notably advanced the art of screen brawling. Appearing with Ritter in *Trouble in Texas* and, later in the year, *Riders of the Rockies*, Yak provided Tex with valuable instruction in handling himself during screen fights. Ritter quickly became adept at fight scenes, thanks to Canutt and Charlie King. One of the strongest features of Tex Ritter movies was the quality of the hero's fights, because Tex was handier with his fists than any other singing cowboy. Gene Autry fight scenes were unconvincing at best; he was visibly unathletic, and it was part of his screen persona to sing his way out of conflicts. Roy Rogers fought frequently in his films, but a slender physique belied his triumphs over burly villains. Tex, on the other hand, was taller than most of his screen opponents, and accepted their fistic challenges with a gleeful readiness and a degree of skill which radiated a visceral appeal to the boys who comprised the majority of his audiences.

Tex, Rita Cansino, and comic sidekick Horace Murphy in Trouble in Texas *(1937). The vivacious young actress soon changed her name, and when she became a superstar,* Trouble in Texas *was re-released with Rita Hayworth in the top billing.*

The leading lady in *Trouble in Texas* soon would become a superstar. She was billed as Rita Cansino, but her real name was Marguerita Carmen Cansino. Her father and mother were professional dancers, and Rita began appearing with the Dancing Cansinos when she was a little girl. A vivacious and pretty brunette, she moved with grace and an unconscious seductiveness, and in 1935 she began making films. Half of her ten movies as Rita Cansino were Westerns, and *Trouble in Texas* was the last feature she filmed before changing her name to Rita Hayworth. Later she changed her hair color to red, and by the 1940s Rita Hayworth was one of Hollywood's biggest stars. Because of her box-office appeal, *Trouble in Texas* was re-released during the 1940s with Rita Hayworth advertised as the star.

"We had a couple of dates," related Tex. "We played tennis a time or two and I took her to a horse race. The horse we betted on lost. After that, I would call her house again and her papa would answer. At first, he would answer, 'Rita isn't in.' Finally he said, 'She won't be in.' He didn't much like his daughter going out with a cowboy-type from Texas. And I guess he thought a cowboy from Texas should be able to pick the winning horse."

Tex dated his beautiful, young co-star, but Rita's father discouraged the match.

Although Rita Cansino was just eighteen when *Trouble in Texas* was lensed, the beautiful young actress played opposite Tex as a leading lady named Carmen, which happened to be her real middle name. She portrayed an undercover government agent disguised as a dancer, and during one of the film's highlights she performed a superb saloon dance. *Variety* usually ignored the actresses who played heroines in B Westerns, but the reviewer of *Trouble in Texas* could not contain himself: "Perhaps the best looker of any of the girls working in hoss pics to date is Grand

National's latest recruit, Rita Cansino. She classes up the company she's in here."

Trouble in Texas revolved around a rodeo setting, and excellent film clips from an actual Wild West show were edited in, including expert trick ropers, Roman riders, and a wild stagecoach chase. Yakima Canutt developed a number of exciting action scenes, and he doubled for Tex during the hair-raising climax. "Tex" (Yak) galloped up to a racing wagon loaded with dynamite, jumped aboard and began fighting two bad guys. After throwing his two opponents over the side, "Tex" climbed out to fight another villain who had ridden up and jumped onto the lead horse. The two combatants fell under the team and, in a scene which preceded Canutt's famous stunt in *Stagecoach* two years later, Yak (still doubling for Tex) passed under the wagon, recovered, and saved the horses before the wagon lurched away and exploded.

"This picture has more action sequences than is common even to these outdoor dramas," enthused the *Motion Picture Herald*. "The action includes an attempted holdup of a stagecoach, two man-to-man struggles, a rodeo that is part acting and part genuine, and a bank robbery that culminates in a wild ride as Ritter and the bandits struggle on a dynamite laden buckboard drawn by runaway horses." Yakima Canutt, Rita Hayworth, nonstop action! *Trouble in Texas* was just the fourth of threescore Tex Ritter films, but it was one of the best he ever made.

Part of the music in *Trouble in Texas* was provided by "Tex Ritter's Tornadoes." Eager to capitalize on his burgeoning fame, Tex organized a little band, the Tornadoes, to accompany him at personal appearances. Tex Ritter's Tornadoes were in his next film, *Hittin' the Trail*, and so were two other musical groups, including Ray Whitley and his Range Ramblers. Makers of singing cowboy movies quickly realized that hillbilly bands provided a major appeal for rural audiences. Musicians were eager for the publicity that could be generated by a movie appearance, so they donned Western duds and accompanied the star and, if they were lucky, performed their best number onscreen. Resourceful directors usually had the musicians change costumes and participate in crowd

scenes. In addition to his own Tornadoes and Ray Whitley's Range Ramblers, Tex Ritter found room in his movies for such groups as The Beverly Hill Billies, The Tennessee Ramblers, The Tailor Maids, The Emerson Mountaineers, The Westerners, The Northwesterners, Art Wilcox and his Arizona Rangers, Carl Shrum and the Rhythm Rangers, Johnny Bond and his Red River Valley Boys, Roy Acuff and his

Latter-Day 49er

Like any capitalist, Tex Ritter invested part of his income in promising ventures. At the old East Texas home place at Murvaul, Tex helped fund a polled Hereford operation with his brother David, the only family member who stayed in Panola County. Tex also tried the mining business in California, hoping to strike it rich in the High Sierras, about 300 miles north of Hollywood.

"I couldn't lose enough money in Hollywood—I had to find some other way to lose it," Tex later laughed. "I was in that for a year. I got more holes in that country than all the gold in Fort Knox. But I loved it because it got me out in the open, instead of attending all the Hollywood parties."

Smokey Mountain Boys, and Jimmy Wakely and his Saddle Pals. The biggest musical coup in a Tex Ritter movie came in 1940, when Bob Wills and his Texas Playboys made their first appearance in *Take Me Back to Oklahoma*.

In addition to finding a spot for his old friend, Ray Whitley, and his band in *Hittin' the Trail*, Tex tried another pal, Hank Worden, as his sidekick. This sidekick experiment lasted for just one film, although Worden continued to appear with Tex in other roles.

Hittin' the Trail was filmed at Kernville, about 100 miles north of Los Angeles. The picturesque little town in the Sequoia National Forest hosted a production unit about three weeks every month. "Hotels, boarding houses and auto camps are having their busiest season in a long while," reported a trade paper, "with town crowded with studio cowboys, generator trucks and other production paraphernalia." Tex soon would return to Kernville for his next film, *Sing, Cowboy Sing*.

For the second Tex Ritter movie in a row, a spectacular stunt climaxed *Hittin' the Trail*. The bad guys stampede a horse herd, but Tex gallops alongside the herd on White Flash. His double leaves White Flash and leaps onto the adjacent horse, then jumps from one running horse to another to drag a villain off his mount on the opposite side of the herd. *Hittin' the Trail* is worth viewing today just to see this stunning scene, which ranks at the top of any list of horseback stunts on film.

In the opening scene of *Hittin' the Trail*, a man on the run tells Tex, "Cast your bread upon the waters. . . ." Tex replies, "That's from the Bible." Throughout his career Tex supported patriotism and religious values. A year after *Hittin' the Trail*, Tex managed to quote from the book of Samuel in *Rollin' Plains*.

The title song of *Hittin' the Trail* was one of six tunes recorded by Tex in his most recent Decca session at the Melrose Studios. On March 17, 1937, Tex again recorded six songs: "Hittin' the Trail," "I'm a Natural Born Cowboy" (also from *Hittin' the Trail*), "Down the Colorado Trail" (from the recent release, *Trouble in Texas*), "Sing, Cowboy Sing" (the title song from a Ritter film scheduled for release in May), "Ride, Ride, Ride" (from a Ritter film scheduled for August), and "Ridin' Down the Trail to Albuquerque." Sheet music advertising

In Where the Buffalo Roam *(1938) Tex sang with Louise Massey and the Westerners, one of the many groups which performed in his films. These various country and western bands were part of the rural audience appeal for singing cowboy Westerns.*

the film connection was published. Each movie gave Tex another record and another song or two in demand when he made personal appearances. Finney even lined up an endorsement, with Frostilla shaving cream, and he actively shopped for more products for Tex.

Tex Ritter was on a roll. "Play my pictures every month and pay your rent," promised Tex in a card sent to theater owners. Grand National produced reams of publicity about the "husky young Adonis from the prairies" and arranged to publish the *Tex Ritter Songbook Number One*. The studio also started the Tex Ritter Fan Club, with chapters in "the first 100 cities in which Ritter has been seen on the

Tex lives up to the title Sing, Cowboy Sing *(1937).*

Tex *Who* ?

The villainous Charlie King sneaks up on Tex in Sing, Cowboy Sing.

Tex pummels Charlie King in a saloon fight in Sing, Cowboy Sing. *King appeared opposite Tex in twenty-five films, and constantly tried to devise "new ways for Tex to beat me up."*

Part of the success formula for Gene Autry movies was the use of his real name for his screen character. As "Gene" and "Gene Autry" in each of his films, he built a strong sense of identity and familiarity with his fans. The Tex Ritter movies partially utilized this same device: The star was called "Tex," but different last names were used.

He was just plain "Tex" in fifteen films. In other movies he was assigned a variety of last names, from Tex Archer to Tex Yancey. Twenty-six different last names were used: the star was Tex Martin in four films; Tex Lawrence and Tex Lansing each were used in two movies; and he was "Texas Dan" in *Song of the Buckaroo* (1938).

When Tex moved to Universal in 1942 to co-star in a series with Johnny Mack Brown, he was assigned a different character for each film: *Montana* Smith (instead of Tex!), Fargo Steele, Bob Brewster, and eight other mundane names. Finally, in 1944, he moved to PRC for his last starring series, and he was called Tex Haines for all eight movies.

screen." At Tex Ritter movies, theater owners distributed fan club buttons, "cheer leader slogans," and the "official Tex Ritter song."

The next Ritter movie was *Sing, Cowboy Sing*, with Al St. John as sidekick and Charlie King as punching bag. Just before their big brawl, King snarls the classic line, "This town ain't big enough for you and me." Unjustly thrown in jail with St. John, Tex tries to cheer up his partner. "Say, do you know what I tell folks down in my home town of Nederland, Texas, when they get to feeling blue?" Having mentioned the family home, Tex then sings "Cowboy Medicine."

The title song of *Sing, Cowboy Sing* was one of six tunes recorded by Tex at Melrose Studios on March 17, 1937. He recorded the title song to his recent release, *Hittin' the Trail*, as well as "Down the Colorado Trail" from *Trouble in Texas*. Tex was alone with his guitar in the studio; producer David Kapp provided no sidemen to add depth to the music. The resulting records did not sell well, and nearly two years would pass before Tex would be given another recording session.

Ritter's next film, *Riders of the Rockies*, featured a trio of villains: Yakima Canutt, Earl

Tex and White Flash sandwiched between outlaw leader Earl Dwire (black hat, of course) and perpetual bad guy Charlie King (right), in Riders of the Rockies.

Dwire, and, of course, Charlie King. During the climactic slugfest between Charlie and Tex, the hero ripped open King's cheek in rather grisly detail for 1937. For the first time Snub Pollard and Horace Murphy teamed up to provide com-

edy relief, and lovely Louise Stanley was the leading lady. Filmed late in April and released early in July 1937, *Riders of the Rockies* was followed a month later by *Mystery of the Hooded Horsemen*.

Mystery of the Hooded Horsemen involved riders with black hoods and capes, decorated with skulls and crossbones. There was a contemporary interest to the storyline, because just the previous year a hooded "Black Legion" caused great turmoil in Michigan. The masked riders of the Tex Ritter movie provided a mys-

Tex welcomes Reginal Baker of the Associated British Film Distributors to the Grand National studio lot. Tex Ritter movies, under different titles, were popular in England.

terious element dear to juvenile audiences, who also enjoyed the familiar presence of Charlie King, Earl Dwire, Horace Murphy, and Hank Worden. Phil Hardy in *The Western* pronounced "the film one of Ritter's best." In New York City *Mystery of the Hooded Horsemen* was scheduled for the Republic Theatre on Broadway. It was the first time a Tex Ritter film had played in a Broadway house, attesting to the growing popularity of the new star.

One of the advertising posters for Mystery of the
Hooded Horsemen *(1937)*.

Mystery of the Hooded Horsemen was the
last of eight films in the initial Range Rider
series, but Grand National immediately com-
missioned Ed Finney to begin another series.
Tex went on a ten-week promotional tour
through the South and East. Shooting began
late in August on the first film in the new
series, *Tex Rides With the Boy Scouts*, which
was ready for release by October 1937. Charlie
King led the bad guys, and Marjorie Reynolds
was one of the prettiest of an impressive succession of lovely leading ladies who graced Tex
Ritter movies.

But the greatest appeal of *Tex Rides With the
Boy Scouts* was the participation of a number of
real Boy Scouts, members of Troop 13 of Los
Angeles. Film also was included of the 1936 Boy
Scout Jamboree, which was held in Washington,
D.C. The Boy Scouts enjoyed a heyday during the
1930s, and a great many audience members
readily identified with their movie counterparts.
"Why have the movies neglected the Boy Scouts
before this?" asked one reviewer. "Has swell
appeal for kids," commented the *Film Daily*,
while shrewdly observing, "Ready made exploita-
tion angle evident in the title."

Tex Rides With the Boy Scouts was set in a
mountain Scout camp. An abandoned mine
shaft nearby was a hideout for train robbers,
but the Boy Scouts helped Tex corral the bad
guys. Although Boy Scout officials at first were
displeased with their youthful members becoming celluloid crime fighters, Ed Finney pointed
out the wholesome example of Scouts standing

Tex Rides With the Boy Scouts *was Ritter's last film
of 1937. Boy Scout Troop 13 of Los Angeles appeared
in the movie.*

up for justice, then he dedicated the film to the
Boy Scouts of America. The organization gave
official approval to the movie and praised the
novice actors for playing "their part like real
showmen." The film premiered on Broadway in
October 1937, and Boy Scouts in every audience eagerly imagined such exciting adventures
enlivening their own summer camp.

Most Gene Autry films were set in the West
of the 1930s and, later, in the West of the
1940s and then the 1950s. During the 1930s,
gangster movies were immensely popular with
audiences, so filmmakers began sending hood-
lums with tommy guns and automobiles out
West, where they were chased down on horseback by sagebrush heroes wielding six-guns.
During World War II Nazi and Japanese spies
carried out their intrigues in the West, until
they were pounded senseless by patriotic cowboys. The frontier had only been closed for a
generation or so, and it was easy for young fans
to imagine such adventures taking place
Somewhere Out West. Battling modern evil-
doers proved to be such a popular plot device

that Roy Rogers and many other cowboy stars engaged in most of their cinematic adventures in the contemporary West.

The majority of Tex Ritter movies were set in the traditional frontier West, but occasionally, as in *Tex Rides With the Boy Scouts*, the plot ventured into the twentieth century. Although response to contemporary Westerns was always good, Tex Ritter and his authentic cowboy music seemed more suited to the nineteenth century.

When Tex filmed *Frontier Town*, it was his eighth movie of 1937. At $2,000 per picture, he earned $16,000 for the year, although movie stars who were paid weekly salaries by their studios generated far more princely sums. Tex supplemented his movie earnings with a busy personal appearance schedule. Enthusiastically received on tour, Tex soon learned that in his first full year of filmmaking he had become one of Hollywood's most popular Western stars.

In 1936 the *Motion Picture Herald*, which annually listed the Top Ten Box Office Stars, began releasing a separate list of Top Ten Western Stars. Only two Tex Ritter films were released in 1936, making the Top Ten Western Stars an impossibility for his first year in Hollywood. But seven Tex Ritter movies hit the screens in 1937, and Tex became the sixth-best moneymaker among cowboy stars. The 1937 Top Ten Western Stars included:

Total Points

1. Gene Autry	946
2. William Boyd (Hopalong Cassidy)	941
3. Buck Jones	783
4. Dick Foran (a talented singer)	733
5. George O'Brien	687
6. TEX RITTER	593
7. Three Mesquiteers	586
8. Charles Starrett	583
9. Ken Maynard	567
10. Bob Steele	554
(13. John Wayne	224)

During his first full year in Hollywood Tex made the Top Ten, and he would be on the list seven times in the next nine years. Tex never reached the Number One status of Gene Autry or Roy Rogers, but he quickly built and maintained strong fan support.

The Demise of Grand National

At the same time that Tex Ritter's career was expanding, his studio suffered severe financial difficulties. Grand National's number one box-office attraction, James Cagney, essentially had gone on strike against Warner Brothers by signing with the new studio in 1936. Although Cagney's first film for Grand National, *Great Guy*, lacked the budget of his Warner Brothers features, it was well-received. But in 1937 Grand National spent $900,000—much more than it could afford—on *Something to Sing About*, and the Cagney musical bombed. Then Warner Brothers lured Cagney back with an eye-popping contract, and Grand National lost its biggest star. The financial losses from *Something to Sing About* (referred to around Grand National offices as *Something to Cry About*) staggered the little studio, which tried to stay afloat on the modest profits generated by Tex Ritter movies and similar films with small budgets and solid returns. But funding became so scarce at Grand National that long intervals passed between production work on Ritter films.

Ed Finney sensed that Grand National was sinking. Ritter was under contract to Finney, rather than to Grand National, and Ed began legal maneuvers to free himself and Tex from the troubled studio. Late in February, Tex, along with Snub Pollard and some musicians, left for a tour of Midwestern theaters. In the meantime, Finney sent feelers to Columbia, Universal, Monogram, and other studios to produce a new series of Tex Ritter movies. Finney simultaneously tried to line up more endorsements for Tex, including a deal with a milk company and with a dime store chain for Tex Ritter holsters. While Tex was on tour, Finney moved into his apartment.

While Grand National was suffering collapse, Tex was on tour, as he would be for much of the rest of his life.

In March 1938 Grand National filed a petition for bankruptcy. Grand National lawyers insisted that the studio "is solvent and termed the bankruptcy action an expedient for reorganization, expressing confidence in continuation of production and distribution activity." But during the bankruptcy hearing, the financier who was expected to bankroll the studio "was conspicuously absent."

At Finney's direction, Tex wrote Edward Alperson, stating that it had been five months since he had filmed a feature, and requesting a release from his Grand National contract. Ed Finney then brought suit to gain his own release, contending that Grand National was in contract violation by failing to film and release Tex Ritter movies on schedule. Indeed, when *Frontier Town* was released, on March 4, 1938, more than four months had elapsed since the release of *Tex Rides With the Boy Scouts*, and another four months would pass before the next Ritter movie, *Rollin' Plains*, was sent to the theaters.

While Ed Finney avoided repeated phone calls from Edward Alperson, the Grand National president tried to lure Tex back to California for personal discussions. Finney stayed in contact with Tex by letter, telegram, and long distance phone calls. The producer reminded Tex of their commitments to various theaters, while urging him to "stick to an outlined diet which will protect you against colds and enable you to better withstand the rigors of the tour." Apparently, Tex failed to stick to his "outlined diet," because he caught a heavy cold. Then the troupe was caught in a Kansas blizzard. There was some consolation when the tour reached Dodge City and Tex was named "Honorary Marshal" of the famous old frontier town.

While Finney tried to arrange a new contract with another studio, Tex urged him to negotiate a large salary increase, perhaps $3,500 per picture for a new series. In addition to his series work, Tex wanted a guarantee that the new studio would loan him to a major studio for a featured role in a big budget motion picture. Finney was convinced that the best route to major stardom was a substantial increase in production budgets with which "we'll be able to give the pictures a finish" that would make Ritter movies "sought after by the more important houses." Finney emphasized to Tex his determination "to make our singing westerns the very best pictures on the market."

During March and April of 1938, while Tex toured theaters in Kansas and Oklahoma, other executives joined Ed Finney in defecting from Grand National. Desperately trying to hold his failing studio together, Ed Alperson fought a holding action in court and tried to find the money to produce films. Finney had produced only two of the eight contracted movies in the

second Tex Ritter series: *Tex Rides With the Boy Scouts* and *Frontier Town*. Alperson insisted that the other six films be completed, while Finney, citing breach of contract, wanted to go immediately to another studio without making any more pictures for Grand National.

Frontier Town, in circulation during this turbulent period, was the second Tex Ritter movie with a rodeo setting. The rodeo announcer was played by Earl Dwire, the chief bad guy was played by Charlie King, and the sidekicks were Horace Murphy and Snub Pollard. One unimpressed critic disparaged Murphy and Pollard, and pointed out that Tex "rides steers, bulldogs, bucks, broncs, and then halters himself to a guitar for a song until the rodeo sponsors give him the prize to get rid of him."

Perhaps the lackluster qualities of *Frontier Town* made it difficult for Finney to cut a deal with another studio. Each studio he contacted steadfastly declined to pay Tex more than $2,000 per film, which was what he earned at Grand National. Finally, Finney negotiated a contract with Monogram calling for four films at $2,000 each for Tex, then $2,500 for the next eight, along with a budget increase to $12,000 to $15,000 per movie. Tex balked at the deal, but Finney telegraphed that this was a "great opportunity to go to town," and he urged Tex to return a signed contract by "air mail special delivery."

Tex grudgingly complied, then also agreed to make two more films for Grand National. Alperson was willing to release Finney and Tex from their Grand National obligation if he received *Rollin' Plains* and *Utah Trail*, which meant cancellation of the final four films of the series. Finney was anxious to begin working with a new studio: "We must start shooting as

"Tex" for Sale

As soon as Tex Ritter's star began to rise, Ed Finney actively sought endorsements. One of the first products to use the new star's name was Frostilla shaving cream. There was a deal with a milk company to put Tex Ritter labels on ice cream cartons. A set of Tex Ritter playing cards featured an image of Tex in the center of the face, and a clothes brush set was labeled "Tex."

Many products, of course, were cowboy items aimed at juveniles. There were little hats and small knives and bandannas with "Tex" on them. A set of little chaps proclaimed, "Tex Ritter Range Rider." A badge announced that the wearer was a member of the "Tex Ritter Colorado Junior Rangers," and there was an assortment of other badges. A set of Tex Ritter and Dorothy Fay paper dolls was aimed at little girls, but more than one boy secretly changed the cutout clothes on his sister's Tex doll.

Tex, a two-gun man in the movies, also was an avid pipe smoker, and he raises his hands in the face of two pipes brandished by actor Jean Hersholt. Hersholt served as president of the Screen Actors' Guild and the Academy of Motion Pictures Arts and Sciences, and the Academy named its humanitarian award after him.

soon as you get back so that you'll be right in the swim again."

Before Tex could return to Hollywood for filming, he was expected to attend Monogram's annual convention for distributors at the Netherland-Plaza Hotel in Cincinnati on May 9 and 10. Tex was scheduled to end his tour in Kentucky at the end of April, then he intended to spend a week there for rest and recreation. "Gather that since you intend to meet Zelma and spend some time with her," wrote Finney, "that you will want to be alone, so I will plan to see you in Cincinnati about the 7th of May at the Netherland-Plaza."

Tex received a standing ovation when he was introduced at the convention. So did child star Jackie Cooper, who was scheduled to make four films for Monogram; Boris Karloff also was signed for four movies. Tex then drove cross-country to California, where he made several more scheduled personal appearances before filming his last two movies for Grand National.

Ed Finney intended to complete these two features as rapidly as possible. Al Herman would direct both films, and Horace Murphy, Snub Pollard, Charlie King, Karl Hackett, Ed Cassidy, and Lynton Brant acted in both movies. To save time and money, the last reel of *Sing, Cowboy Sing*, released just a year earlier, was recycled as the last reel of *Rollin' Plains*.

Tex enjoying the fan mail that his Top Ten status attracted.

The storyline for the final Grand National film, *Utah Trail*—cattle rustlers who use an elusive "ghost train"—was supplied by Tex. A railroad siding was found at Bakersfield for a day of shooting, and four days were spent at Chatham Ranch. During the film Tex sang tenderly to White Flash, "There's no cow like a pony, A joggin' prairie crony. . . ."

After filming concluded, Tex had to make a court appearance in June to finalize his contract cancellation at Grand National. On July 8, 1938, *Rollin' Plains* was released. It was the first Tex Ritter film in four months, and only the second in the past eight months. But within four days, on July 12, *Utah Trail* was shipped to theaters.

Grand National attempted to reorganize under new leadership while continuing to produce cheaper and cheaper films. Desperately the studio promoted Dorothy Page as the "Singing Cowgirl," but the idea of a female heroine was too alien for the time, and her series of musical Westerns lasted for only three films. By 1940, Grand National was defunct.

Tex Ritter had made twelve films for Grand National. These features were produced with small budgets on tight shooting schedules, but so were hundreds of other B Westerns. The Ritter films at Grand National, emphasizing rugged brawls and authentic cowboy tunes, quickly vaulted Tex to the front rank of B Western stars. Tex and Ed Finney both hoped that the move to a new studio would bring an even higher level of stardom.

Monogram

Monogram Pictures was founded by W. Ray Johnston, a precocious young executive who lined up a number of independent producers and began releasing features in 1931. The next year Monogram released an impressive thirty-two films. The studio's Westerns starred Tim McCoy or Bob Steele or Rex Bell, and in 1933 John Wayne came to Monogram for the next two years. Most of his sixteen Monogram features were written and directed by Robert N. Bradbury, the father of Wayne's boyhood friend, Bob Steele. In 1935 Johnston agreed to a merger engineered by Herbert J. Yates of Consolidated Film Laboratories. The new studio, Republic Pictures, was headed by Yates and became the giant of Poverty Row. By 1937 Johnston restlessly left Republic and revived Monogram, releasing a score of features by the end of the year.

Johnston ambitiously planned even more films for 1938. Monogram would release a wide variety of movies, but like any independent the studio counted upon inexpensive "bread and butter" Westerns to provide dependable profits. Tom Keene and Jack Randall were Monogram's principal Western stars in 1937, and Johnston was eager to bring Tex Ritter and his Top Ten audiences to his studio. At the Monogram convention in Cincinnati in May 1939, Tex was given a standing ovation by studio executives and distributors who hoped he would greatly improve the company's Western offerings. Johnston announced that there would be forty-two Monogram features during the coming year, including sixteen Westerns.

Tom Keene was dropped as a Western star, and although Jack Randall was signed for another series of eight Monogram Westerns, he never captured the public imagination. Randall was the brother of Three Mesquiteers star Bob Livingston. In 1942 he joined the Air Force, rising to the rank of captain by the time of his 1945 discharge. Randall immediately returned to moviemaking, but in July 1945 he was fatally injured in a fall from a horse while filming a serial about Mounties.

The other eight Monogram Westerns of 1938 would star Tex Ritter. Eagerly anticipating the Ritter movies, Monogram exhibitors and salesmen wrote to Tex, asking him to send autographed photos or to make theater appearances, and offering best wishes and encouragement.

Ed Finney kept the nucleus of his Boots and Saddles production unit intact: Al Herman, who had directed the last two Ritter Westerns for Grand National, would direct the first nine and most of the rest of the Ritter features for Monogram; Charlie King came along, too, and so did Snub Pollard and Horace Murphy and several background actors familiar to Tex Ritter fans. With Boots and Saddles remaining in charge of Tex Ritter movies, audiences could still expect their hero to use his fists and guns and guitar energetically. Tex Ritter fans could continue to enjoy familiar villains, rip-snorting action, and authentic music in a setting of the traditional frontier West.

But if the strengths of the first twelve Tex Ritter films were continued by Monogram, so were the weaknesses. The plots of Ritter movies always had been simple, with trite dialogue, and in between action or musical sequences the films moved slowly. Ritter film budgets at Monogram only increased slightly, not enough to noticeably improve his movies. During this same period Republic Studios appreciably

Starlight Over Texas *(1938), the first Tex Ritter movie for Monogram, featured an eye-catching fiesta scene.*

Tex pulls Charles King away from sidekick Snub Pollard in Where the Buffalo Roam.

Tex in Starlight Over Texas, *with sidekicks Horace Murphy and Snub Pollard (moustache), leading lady Carmen LaRoux, and a youngster who generated appeal with juvenile audiences.*

increased the budgets on Gene Autry and Roy Rogers features, eventually filming in technicolor, and the increase in production values was obvious to audiences. Ritter movies, however, were never improved to a higher level. And Ritter continued to work with lackluster sidekicks, while Autry and Rogers movies were enlivened by Smiley Burnette and Gabby Hayes. Smiley and Gabby generated such appeal that in 1943 they finished in the Top *Five* of Western Stars, ahead of Tex and almost all of the other sagebrush heroes.

The first three Tex Ritter Monogram features were produced as quickly as possible. *Starlight Over Texas*, with Horace Murphy and Snub Pollard as sidekicks and Charles King and George Chesebro the most notable villains, was released on September 7, 1938.

The next month *Where the Buffalo Roam* was ready for theaters. Murphy and Pollard again played "Ananias" and "Pee Wee," while Tex once more traded punches with Charlie King. Frank Sanucci, musical director on most of the Grand National films, became the regular musical director for the Monogram movies. There were seven musical numbers in *Where the Buffalo Roam*, and Tex and Sanucci frequently would collaborate on songs, as they had in the past. Despite the emphasis on music, other production values suffered. Especially glaring were the inserts of grainy stock footage of buffalo herds.

Song of the Buckaroo would prove memorable for Tex. It was one of the best of his twenty Monogram features, despite the presence of Horace Murphy and Snub Pollard. In the film Tex ran for mayor of a town beleaguered by crooks. The villains, led by Charlie King and George Chesebro, tried to rig the election, but Tex whipped King and defeated the rest of the bad guys. The leading lady was beautiful Jinx Falkenberg, and a smaller female part was played by the equally beautiful Dorothy Fay.

Her full name was Dorothy Fay Southworth. She was from Prescott, Arizona, and she had received theatrical training in London, at USC, and at the Pasadena Playhouse. In 1938 in her first film, the twenty-three-year-old actress was

Tex and Jinx Falkenberg in Song of the Buckaroo *(1938).*

Tex points the way to Dave O'Brien and Dorothy Fay in Song of the Buckaroo. *She accepted a bit part in this film with the promise of a leading role in a future Tex Ritter movie.*

the leading lady for Buck Jones in *Stranger from Arizona*, with Hank Worden, Horace Murphy, and other Ritter regulars. The Buck Jones movie was filmed by Coronet Pictures, another Poverty Row studio, and Hank Worden persuaded Dorothy Fay to let him introduce her to Tex on the set of his latest Monogram feature. She quickly filmed three more Westerns, including another Buck Jones movie.

While Ed Finney was making preparations to film *Song of the Buckaroo*, he was approached by Dorothy Fay's agent. At that point she had worked in four films, three as leading lady.

Finney was impressed by her credentials and her picture portfolio, but he already had cast Jinx Falkenberg as leading lady. Finney offered a smaller part (a pioneer woman killed early in the film), and the agent agreed when Ed promised the lead in the next Ritter movie.

After Dorothy Fay filmed *Song of the Buckaroo*, she appeared in two more movies, then reported for *Sundown on the Prairie*. Hank Worden was in the cast, and Charlie King led the bad guys. Horace Murphy as "Ananias" had to handle the sidekick duties alone, because Snub Pollard was dropped.

As soon as filming ended, Tex went on tour. In addition to his usual performances at theaters and auditoriums, Tex also was booked for some of his singing lectures on cowboy music. On January 4, 1939, he recorded four songs, and many experts contend that his unbilled accompanists were the Sons of the Pioneers. The recordings were four country songs, including two from recent Monogram movies: the title tune from *Sundown on the Prairie*, and "Viva Tequila" from *Starlight Over Texas*. These records did little business, and none of Ritter's other Decca recordings had enjoyed much success. Tex had been under contract to Decca since 1935, but after four years and thirty sides the company dropped his option. With cowboy songs making little impact on the market, Tex was unable to land another recording contract.

Sundown on the Prairie *(1939). From left: Horace Murphy, Tex, Dorothy Fay, and Hank Worden. An old friend from New York, Worden appeared in eleven Ritter films, and he introduced Tex to Dorothy Fay.*

A month after his final Decca session, the first Tex Ritter film of 1939, *Sundown on the Prairie*, was released. By that time the next Ritter movie had been lensed. *Sundown on the Prairie* featured Charlie King, Horace Murphy, Tex Ritter's Tornadoes—and lovely Dorothy Fay. The movie's world premiere was held at the Studio Theatre in Prescott, the hometown of Dorothy Fay Southworth. In his first sixteen films, Tex had fifteen different leading ladies. In 1937 pretty Louise Stanley, who was married to cowboy star Jack Randall, played the feminine lead in back-to-back Ritter films, *Sing, Cowboy Sing* and *Riders of the Rockies*. She was the only actress to play Ritter's leading lady twice until Dorothy Fay—and the next year Dorothy Fay would return for a third film with Tex. These three assignments would prove to be rehearsals for a permanent role as Tex Ritter's leading lady.

Tex and Mary Brodel and a herd of elk (on rear-screen projection) in Down the Wyoming Trail *(1939). Tex is about to sing "In Elk Valley."*

There was another pretty leading lady, dark-haired Mary Brodel, in the next Ritter film, *Down the Wyoming Trail*. Monogram nearly doubled the usual budget for a Ritter film. Cast and crew traveled to snowy mountain locations, and in front of an elk herd on a rear projection screen Tex sang "In Elk Valley" to his leading lady. Charlie King, leader of a gang of rustlers, drove elk into the midst of grazing cattle in order to scatter the herds. Tex foiled this scheme, and Charlie King, having suffered one frustration too many at the hands of Ritter, committed suicide in the snow.

Horace Murphy was dropped after *Down the Wyoming Trail*, and in the next movie, *The Man From Texas*, Tex had no sidekick. He also had no fights with Charlie King, who appeared only in a minor role. The principal bad guy was Roy Barcroft, eventually acknowledged as the king of Western villains after menacing roles in more than 150 films. The "Shooting Kid," a two-gun criminal played by bass-voiced Charles Wood, had been taught to shoot by Tex. Although hired to kill Tex, the Shooting Kid redeemed himself by defending Tex at the cost of his life. There were several fatal shootings, but the gunplay was slow and rather dull. What passed for dialogue was a series of stilted clichés. The story was simple and predictable, and there were only two songs. With none of the trademark Tex Ritter brawls, and with little other action, a limp plot, and a minimum of music, *The Man From Texas* was one of the poorest movies Tex ever made. It was his seventh film for Monogram, but the new studio was doing little to advance his career.

Tex shows sidekick Nelson McDowell a stolen army rifle in Roll, Wagons, Roll *(1939).*

Riders of the Frontier was next, with Tex disguised as an outlaw to trap Roy Barcroft, in the role of a crooked foreman. Again the story line was simplistic, even for a B Western, and the film displayed a cheap look. So did *Roll, Wagons, Roll*, which was largely pasted together from stock footage from earlier films, including silent Westerns. *Roll, Wagons, Roll* and Ritter's next movie, *Westbound Stage*, both featured Muriel Evans in back-to-back leading lady

Tex and leading lady Muriel Evans—also a favorite leading lady of Buck Jones—in Roll, Wagons, Roll.

appearances. But neither Roy Barcroft nor Charlie King was around to add their sinister qualities to the villainy, and again there were only two songs in each feature.

Roll, Wagons, Roll was the last Ritter Western of 1939, while *Westbound Stage* was released on the second day of 1940. The erratic release of Grand National features had damaged Tex Ritter's standings in the Top Ten Western Stars, dropping him to ninth place. But the Monogram films of 1939 boosted Tex back to seventh place, and he remained at seventh in 1940.

Tex and White Flash in Westbound Stage *(1939).*

The bad guys in *Rhythm of the Rio Grande*, released on March 2, 1940, were bolstered by the presence of lantern-jawed Warner Richmond and big Glenn Strange. Tex also found a small part for Slim Andrews. Andrews was a native of Arkansas, and when Tex played the state on a personal appearance tour he caught the act of Arkansas Slim. A gifted musician, the tall, lean Andrews performed as a one-man band during his comedy and music act. Tex invited Andrews to come to Hollywood, and later Arkansas Slim traveled to California to see if Tex could help him break into the movies. Tex arranged the bit in *Rhythm of the Rio Grande*, then worked him into his next nine films, usually as sidekick. The two men became close friends, and Arkansas Slim toured with Tex for the next decade.

A musical interlude with the cavalry in Westbound Stage.

Along with Andrews, Glenn Strange appeared in the next two Ritter movies, *Pals of the Silver Sage* and *Cowboy From Sundown*. The later film also featured another classic Western bad guy, Bud Osborne, although one unimpressed critic described *Cowboy From Sundown* as "a cactus opera that's got plenty of thorns." A new Tex Ritter song, "I've Done the Best I Could," was sung in *Cowboy From Sundown*. Tex admired the work of Hudie "Leadbelly" Ledbetter, a black folk musician from Louisiana and Texas. During the early 1930s John A. Lomax brought Leadbelly to New York, where he arranged recording sessions and where Tex met Hudie and was reunited with his old University of Texas mentor. Impressed by the folk singer, Tex later told Leadbelly, according to Johnny Bond, that he used part of the melody line from Hudie's great hit "Goodnight Irene" while composing "I've Done the Best I Could." The heritage of an earlier America continued to be the driving force behind Tex Ritter's music.

His next film was *The Golden Trail*, with Slim Andrews as sidekick, Warner Richmond as a bad guy, and Eddie Dean as "Injun." A fine singer, Eddie Dean had left radio work in Chicago to try Hollywood. Beginning in 1938, Dean landed a succession of small parts in Western movies. *The Golden Trail* was his first appearance with Tex Ritter, and eventually he would star in his own singing cowboy series.

In the Top Ten

Tex Ritter arrived in Hollywood in 1936 and immediately began filming Westerns. He starred in oaters through 1945. From 1936 through 1954 the *Motion Picture Herald* annually compiled a "Top Ten Money-Making Western Stars" list, based on a poll asking exhibitors to "name in order the ten players in Westerns who drew the greatest attendance to your theaters." Gene Autry was number one from 1936 through 1942, when he joined the Air Force, and Roy Rogers led the list from 1943 through 1954. Dale Evans sometimes made the list, and so did Smiley Burnette and Gabby Hayes and a few other sidekicks. Tex was ranked number six in 1937, and he made the list a total of seven times in nine years.

Year	No. of Tex R. Movies	Top Ten List
1936	2	
1937	7	#6
1938	6	#9
1939	6	#7
1940	9	#7
1941	4	#10
1942	9	
1943	6	
1944	6	#10
1945	5	#9

Tex and a Monogram film crew prepare for a mobile shot on the set of Westbound Stage.

Tex ready for action in Rhythm of the Rio Grande *(1940).*

A few weeks after *The Golden Trail* was released, *Rainbow Over the Range* hit the screens. Slim Andrews played "Slim Chance," Warner Richmond led the villains, and Dorothy Fay essayed her third turn as Tex Ritter's leading lady. By this time Tex and Dorothy were dating, and it required only a little nepotism to secure a small role for her young nephew, Tommy Southworth.

The next feature, *Arizona Frontier*, cast legendary athlete Jim Thorpe as an Apache chief. Thorpe, a Sauk and Fox from Oklahoma, starred in football and track in college. He was the dominant player in early pro football, while simultaneously playing six seasons of major league baseball. Following a superb performance in the 1912 Olympics, his medals were presented by King Gustav of Sweden. "Sir," the King remarked with admiration and accuracy, "you are the greatest athlete in the world." But when his athletic career ended, Thorpe began drinking heavily, and he fell on hard times. Hoping to capitalize on his name, Thorpe found a few roles in Hollywood, and at fifty-two he appeared in *Arizona Frontier*. Tex enjoyed the company of the genial, good-natured Thorpe.

After working with Thorpe, Tex then welcomed Bob Wills and His Texas Playboys to a feature appropriately titled *Take Me Back to Oklahoma*. At the height of his career as the "King of Western Swing," Wills had been trying for over a year to break into the movies through the Bruce Gear Agency of Hollywood. There was a Poverty Row offer for a cheap Western series, but the agency advised Wills not to make those "stinkeroos." Offers from other studios included only a few of Bob's musicians. But he had built a large swing band, and he wanted to bring all of the Texas Playboys to the silver screen. Tex told Bob's biographer, Charles R. Townsend, that when Ritter called Wills, the King of Western Swing told his fellow musician: "Tex, for you I will split my band."

Along with his fiddle, Bob brought his brother, Johnnie Lee Wills, on guitar, Leon McAuliffe on steel guitar, Eldon Shamblin on guitar, Wayne Johnson on clarinet, and Son Lansford on bass. Bob was togged out in duds

Tex and Pablo the Bandit in Rhythm of the Rio Grande.

Visitors to the set of Rhythm of the Rio Grande.

Cantina scene in Rhythm of the Rio Grande.

suitable to a singing cowboy, and the Texas Playboys were costumed in matching Western outfits: tan pants, dark shirts, white bandanna ties, and light-colored Stetsons.

Take Me Back to Oklahoma premiered on November 1, 1940, at the Rialto Theatre in Tulsa, home base for Bob and the Texas Playboys. Bob, Tex, and Lieutenant Governor James Berry led a parade through the streets of Tulsa, and ads loyally indicated that the film starred Bob Wills and His Texas Playboys, "with Tex Ritter." Bob

Tex, Sugar Dawn, and Clarissa Curtis in Pals of the Silver Sage *(1940).*

and his band initially appeared in the movie atop a stagecoach, singing and playing the first of six numbers, including such Wills standards as "Take Me Back to Tulsa" and "Lone Star Rag." During a church social scene, Bob and his band performed four numbers in a row. Although playing himself, Bob delivered his dialogue awkwardly, but B Western audiences were accustomed to wooden actors. Most Bob Wills fans had never seen him. They listened to his music over the radio and on records, but now they could see Bob Wills and His Texas Playboys in performance on movie screens. From 1942 through 1944, Wills and his band appeared in eleven Westerns for Columbia Pictures, backing up Russell Hayden and later Charles Starrett. But Tex Ritter and Monogram had introduced Bob Wills and His Texas Playboys to motion pictures.

Following this coup, Monogram introduced more music into Tex Ritter movies. Earlier Ritter films for Monogram had included only two or perhaps three songs, but *Rollin' Home to Texas*, the first movie after *Take Me Back to Oklahoma*, featured eight musical numbers. Eddie Dean had a prominent role as a singing sheriff in *Rollin' Home to Texas*, which was the final Ritter film in 1940. The next movie, *Ridin' the Cherokee Trail*, included seven musical numbers.

Another country music legend made his movie debut in the next Tex Ritter film, *The Pioneers*. Red Foley, like Tex and Bob Wills, was a future member of the Country Music Hall of Fame. Already a veteran radio star, in 1941 he signed a lifetime recording contract with Decca Records, and four years later he became the first major artist to record in Nashville. Early in 1941 Foley, like Bob Wills, played himself opposite Tex as *The Pioneers* was lensed. Arkansas Slim Andrews again was the sidekick, and scowling George Chesebro led the bad guys. *The Pioneers* was based on the novel of the same title by James Fenimore Cooper. In the spirit of Cooper's *Leather Stocking Tales*, Tex and Arkansas Slim wore fringed buckskin jackets, and Andrews also donned a coonskin cap.

The Pioneers, released on May 10, 1941, completed Ritter's current contrac-

Lone Star Heritage

Tex Ritter's work repeatedly reflected the entertainer's deep interest in his Texas heritage. He participated in the story conferences of his movies, and the Texas influence is indicated by the titles: *Trouble in Texas, Starlight Over Texas, The Man From Texas, Rollin' Home to Texas, Under Texas Stars, The Lone Star Vigilantes, Deep in the Heart of Texas*, and *The Lone Star Trail*.

Tex helped write the songs for his movies, including: "Starlight Over Texas," "Ridin' Down to Texas," "Goin' Back to Texas," "Texas Dan," "Headin' Home to Texas," "Out on the Lone Star Trail," and "I've Got to See Texas Just One More Time." When he was growing up on a Texas cotton farm, he learned "Boll Weevil," a folk song that would become a Tex Ritter standard. Also during his boyhood, a nearby railroad went through the communities of Tenaha, Timpson, Bobo and Blair, and Tex later would score a hit with the novelty ballad based on the conductor's call, "Tenaha, Timpson, Bobo and Blair."

Tex was a prolific songwriter, and many of the songs he wrote and/or recorded displayed his Lone Star roots: "My Brown Eyed Texas Rose," "San Antonio Rose," "Texas Rangers," "Fort Worth Jail," "Dallas Darlin'," "The Eyes of Texas," "Love You as Big as Texas," "The San Antone Story," "Old Tex Kringle," "Remember the Alamo," "Sam Bass," "Streets of Laredo," "Red River Valley," "A Message From the Alamo," and "Texas."

Tex and another sidekick, Slim Andrews, in Cowboy From Sundown.

tual obligation to Monogram, as well as his five-year contract with Ed Finney. He starred in thirty-two Westerns produced by Finney, the last twenty for Monogram. Finney had brought Tex to Hollywood, but after a promising start, Tex's film career had stagnated. The first successful singing cowboy, Gene Autry, was the perennial leader of the Top Ten Western Stars. Roy Rogers, who did not star in a musical Western until 1938, two years after Tex Ritter's screen debut, rapidly gained momentum and became the second most popular singing cowboy. Tex was the third most popular singing cowboy, but in 1941 he finished only tenth among the Top Ten Western Stars, while Roy Rogers finished third. Autry and Rogers benefited from large budgets and the expertise of Republic Studios, while Ed Finney had been unable to boost Tex past the low budgets and unimaginative approach of Poverty Row's Grand National and Monogram studios. Slipping in screen populari-ty, still collecting only a modest salary for each film, and with no recording contract, Tex decided to break away from Ed Finney. A major reason for the rejuvenation of Ritter's career was because Tex was about to take a wife.

Tex and White Flash and a horse herd at a river crossing in Rainbow Over the Range *(1940).*

Right: Tex tips his hat to Dorothy Fay in Rainbow Over the Range.

Tex is Ridin' the Cherokee Trail—*in a buckboard and away from his pursuers as fast as possible.*

In Arizona Frontier *(1940) Chief Grey Cloud, pointing for Tex and Slim Andrews, was played by famed athlete Jim Thorpe. Tex constantly pressured casting directors to fill Indian roles with authentic Native Americans.*

Tex and the Tennessee Ramblers entertain convicts in Ridin' the Cherokee Trail *(1941).*

Tex and Bob Wills hold their hats and shake hands, along with Monogram studio executives, over the deal to film Take Me Back to Oklahoma *(1940). Bob Wills and His Texas Playboys were the most notable of the country and western groups which appeared in Tex Ritter movies. Ed Finney, the producer who brought Tex to Hollywoood, has his hand across the star's shoulder.*

Tex and Wanda McKay in The Pioneers *(1941). It was Ritter's final Monogram movie, and the last of thirty-two films he made for producer Ed Finney.*

For The Pioneers, *Tex donned a buckskin jacket, and sidekick Slim Andrews wore a coonskin cap.*

Lifetime Leading Lady

"With people you can't get bored," said Tex Ritter, revealing his gregarious nature to interviewer Kathy Sawyer. Even as a teenager in Carthage, he had taken dates to school parties and other social occasions. A popular man about campus in high school and at the University of Texas, Ritter then led a carefree bachelor's existence for eight years in New York City. He was in his thirties by the time he became a Hollywood movie star, and he enjoyed the company of starlets and of young women he encountered on his road tours.

Tex explained to a Hollywood reporter that he was "scared to get married" because of the young boys who formed the core of his audience. "The kids looked on me as a happy-go-lucky singing cowboy, fancy free and inclined to wander and live as I pleased," he cheerfully rationalized. "I was afraid that if I got married they would think I was a sissy."

Avoiding such a label, Tex Ritter happily continued to date while ducking permanent commitments. But bachelors are inevitable targets of matchmakers, even by their own friends. Hank Worden, apparently with the complicity of Horace Murphy, introduced Tex to a lovely blonde actress, Dorothy Fay Southworth, on a movie set in 1938—while he was in a makeup chair. She soon appeared in a Ritter film, then played his leading lady in three subsequent movies.

Tex wasted little time in arranging a date with his beautiful co-star. An inveterate sports fan, Tex had tickets to a football game at Hollywood's Gilmore Stadium between Loyola and Hardin-Simmons, a Baptist college from Ritter's home state. After picking up Dorothy, Tex had to drive back to his apartment because

Dorothy Fay's skills as a horsewoman helped her win roles in Western films.

he had forgotten the tickets. Their seats were in the end zone facing the sun, and Tex muttered something about needing to improve his tan for a new movie that was about to begin filming. He did not offer to buy soft drinks or hot dogs or a game program. Dorothy perhaps stiffened up, and there was little conversation, an unusual condition for the customarily talkative Ritter.

After the game Tex drove Dorothy home, then left to keep a dinner date with a young woman who wanted to confer with him about starting a dude ranch. During the evening they were robbed at gunpoint.

"I thought about fighting him," a smiling Tex later told his son Tom. "But he didn't look like Charlie King, and the bullets in his gun didn't look like blanks."

When Dorothy learned that Tex had scheduled a date immediately after the football game, she said that being robbed served him right. Despite their shaky start, however, Tex and Dorothy continued to date. One day Western star Bill Elliott asked, "Dorothy, what was Tex's car doing in front of your apartment the other night?" "Bill," she fired back, "what were you doing driving by my apartment the other night?"

Dorothy Fay Southworth was beautiful, personable, and confident. Born in 1915, she was the daughter of Dr. and Mrs. Harry Thomas Southworth of Prescott, Arizona. A number of Western movies were filmed around Prescott, and Dr. Southworth often treated actors, stunt men, and crew members for injuries and illnesses. When Tom Mix fell ill while on location, he stayed with the Southworths for three weeks. Exposed to the world of Western filmmaking, Dorothy learned to ride and became an excellent horsewoman.

Dr. Southworth, a prominent physician who had served as president of the Arizona State Medical Society, died while his daughter still was in high school. Dorothy's brother, Dr. Harry T. Southworth, Jr., was interning in a Chicago hospital, so the widowed Harriett Fay Southworth took her daughter to Los Angeles. Dorothy finished secondary school at Hollywood High. She also took drama lessons, and appeared in a play with Alan Ladd of North Hollywood High. Both young actors were offered contracts by Universal Pictures. Alan Ladd signed with Universal, but Dorothy decided to pursue further training. Dorothy and her mother went to England, where the aspiring actress studied at the Royal Academy of Dramatic Arts and at the Central School of Speech at the University of London. Returning to Los Angeles with her mother, Dorothy enrolled at the University of Southern California. She joined Pi Beta Phi social sorority and Phi Beta speech and music honor fraternity, and she also trained at the Pasadena Playhouse.

In her first movie, Stranger From Arizona *(1938), Dorothy Fay co-starred opposite cowboy great Buck Jones. Jones had just stunned Hank Worden, who would introduce Dorothy Fay to Tex Ritter.*

When Dorothy acquired an agent who learned of her riding skills, in 1938 she was signed to co-star in a Buck Jones Western. Using her first two names as a stage name, Dorothy Fay made thirteen feature films and two chapter serials from 1938 through the early months of 1941. Dorothy Fay co-starred with Buck Jones three times, appeared in four Tex Ritter movies, and played opposite Bill Elliott, Bob Baker, and other Western stars. Her most memorable non-

Bob Baker and Dorothy Fay co-starred in Prairie Justice *(1938).*

Western appearance was a small role in the sophisticated comedy *The Philadelphia Story*, starring Katharine Hepburn, Cary Grant and James Stewart, who won an Academy Award for Best Actor.

Dorothy Fay first acted in a Tex Ritter movie in 1938. There were two more Ritter films in 1939, and another in 1940. By this time Tex had given Dorothy a ring. She gave it back a couple of times, dubious of his heavy travel schedule, but Tex now was thinking of marriage and a home. Since coming to Hollywood, Tex had lived in apartments. Usually he had shared his apartment with Hank Worden, and sometimes Everett Cheetham or some other pal. But Tex decided he wanted to buy a house with acreage, and when he found a promising property he asked Dorothy to inspect it with him before he bought it.

"I had a place for stables and in the back of the stables there was an 80 acre field where I raised squashes," described Tex. "In front of my house, a little to the right, there was

Films of Dorothy Fay

Stranger From Arizona (Buck Jones—1938)
Frontier Scout (George Houston—1938)
Law of the Texan (Buck Jones—1938)
Prairie Justice (Bob Baker—1938)
Song of the Buckaroo (Tex Ritter—1938)
The Long Shot (Gordon Jones—1939)
Trigger Pals (Art Jarrett—1939)
Sundown on the Prairie (Tex Ritter—1939)
Rollin' Westward (Tex Ritter—1939)
Rainbow Over the Range (Tex Ritter—1940)
The Green Archer (15-Chapter Serial, Victor Jory—1940)
Glamour for Sale (Anita Louise—1940)
The Philadelphia Story (Katharine Hepburn, Cary Grant, James Stewart—1940)
North From the Lone Star (Bill Elliott—1940)
White Eagle (15-Chapter Serial, Buck Jones—1941)

Dorothy Fay co-starred with Buck Jones in two movies and a fifteen-chapter serial. In 1942, a year after they filmed the serial, Buck died a hero's death in Boston's Coconut Grove nightclub fire.

a 50 acre walnut orchard. And then about two or three blocks from my house was a stream; it was a perfect place to exercise a horse, which I used to ride every morning."

The house was one-story, and the little spread was located at 13610 Erwin Street in Van Nuys, a community north of Hollywood. A menagerie of horses, dogs (including Tex's pet Dittyboo) and chickens also made the East Texas country boy feel at home. A number of actors and stunt men found a haven at Tex Ritter's Lazy TNT Ranch, until he brought a bride to his new home.

Dorothy Fay announced at a Hollywood tea that she would marry Tex Ritter in Prescott on Saturday, June 14, 1941. In May, Dorothy and her mother returned to Prescott, where they stayed with Dr. Harry Southworth, Jr., and with other friends. Following another announcement tea, Dorothy "was the recipient of many prenuptial courtesies," according to the *Arizona Republic* of Phoenix. In addition to numerous

Tex and Dorothy Fay were in four films together.

Not confined to Westerns, in 1940 the beautiful Dorothy Fay appeared in a contemporary drama, Glamour For Sale, *and the classic comedy,* The Philadelphia Story.

bridal showers and luncheons and dinners, a mountain picnic was held near Prescott at Camp Dr. Harry Thomas Southworth, named after Dorothy's father during the 1930s. The picnic was a copper shower, with all gifts made of Arizona copper.

The formal wedding ceremony was conducted at 8:30 in the evening at the First Congregational Church of Prescott. The church's minister was assisted by Rev. Bruce Power, Tex's brother-in-law (Power was married to Lucille Ritter) and pastor of St. Luke's Methodist Church of Houston. Attired in a magnificent bridal gown with a long train, Dorothy was given in marriage by her brother. The bride and groom each had six attendants, and there were two flower girls, along with "several hundred guests."

Among the guests were Western actors Buck Jones, Tim McCoy, Bob Baker, Guinn "Big Boy" Williams and Raymond Hatton, as well as actresses Luana Walters and Betty Miles. Singing cowboy Dick Foran performed "I Love You Truly" and "Because" during the ceremony. Tex wrote "In Your Lovely Veil of White" for

Dorothy the night before the wedding (the song later was recorded by Bing Crosby and became a hit single). After the wedding there was a reception at the Hassayampa Country Club, followed by music and dancing. Mr. and Mrs. Ritter were driven to a honeymoon suite in Phoenix. Then they traveled to the California coast for a few days before settling in at the Lazy TNT and resuming film work.

Dorothy completed a serial for Columbia, *White Eagle*, with Buck Jones. She fulfilled her Columbia contract with *Summer Sun Valley*, a short film about vacationing in Sun Valley, Idaho. Then Dorothy Fay retired from the screen. She had been a busy movie actress, appearing in fifteen films in less then three years. Now that she was married, however, she intended to be a full-time wife and a deeply involved participant in social and community activities.

"The miracles Dorothy has wrought around

Tex and Dorothy were married at Prescott, Arizona, on June 14, 1941.

Dorothy Fay and her Special Services troupe brought a lovely touch of home to Pacific bases.

Dorothy Fay firing a machine gun from the hip, a technique that would be emulated by actors in war movies.

my Van Nuys ranch are something to behold," Tex proudly told a Hollywood reporter. "Just little touches here and there, but now the place feels like a real home."

Harriett Fay Southworth spent a great deal of time at the Lazy TNT, although she periodically visited her son's home in Prescott. Tex had long absences on extended tours, and Dorothy sometimes went on the road with her husband. Although she did not sing, she would appear onstage and take part in the patter. At home she performed considerable charity work, served as a hospital volunteer, and was an active member of the Beverly Hills Flower Guild, Assistance League, and National Charity League.

Dorothy became an officer of Pi Iota chapter of Phi Beta, and during the year of her presidency, 1943-44, she was awarded the National Gavel for the most outstanding alumnae chapter in the United States. She obtained the California State Adult Education credential in order to teach in Southern California and Los Angeles City schools. For two years she taught

speech in night classes at USC, and she spent four years as director of training at Caroline Leonetti Women's Center in Los Angeles.

Dorothy frequently opened her home for social events, and when Tex was off the road there was a virtual open house at the Lazy TNT. Tex still liked to play poker, often with a group that included Roy Rogers. "What I used to do, when I wasn't touring, was get together with a bunch of the western guys," Tex said. "I spent a lot of time with people not in the business. I had met people in New York and Hollywood, and that's all they could talk about—show business. So, many of my friends in Hollywood were not in the industry."

Tex had taken Masonic orders, joining Metropolitan Lodge 646 of Los Angeles, and he and Dorothy frequently visited children at the Shrine Hospital. During the war years of the 1940s, Tex and Dorothy performed at military bases for the USO. She joined the Fourth Regiment of the Women's Ambulance and Defense Corps of America, taking classes in first aid, motor mechanics, emergency obstetrics, and the handling of ambulances and patients for evacuation. She also received credentials in aerial navigation and meteorology at Los Angeles City College. Dorothy eagerly accepted assignments with the Special Services of the U.S. Armed Forces, and she went on a six-month tour of overseas bases, managing the first Hollywood Victory Committee Troop in the Central Pacific. Decked out in fatigues, Dorothy and her fellow troupers tirelessly and courageously brought a touch of home to servicemen and reminded them of what they were defending.

This tour of Pacific bases, typical of her generous spirit of involvement, marked Dorothy's final sustained entertainment effort. She modeled at charitable fashion shows, and her occasional tours with Tex would briefly place her in front of an audience. But for the rest of her life Dorothy Ritter expended herself as a devoted wife and citizen—and mother.

Columbia Co-Star

After leaving Monogram Pictures and long-time producer Ed Finney, Tex Ritter soon found a new celluloid home with a major studio, Columbia Pictures. The studio was founded as a Poverty Row outfit in 1920 by Harry and Jack Cohn and Joe Brandt. Originally called CBC—for Cohn-Brandt-Cohn, but nicknamed "Corn Beef and Cabbage"—the studio was renamed Columbia in 1924. By 1931 hard-nosed Harry Cohn had established himself as studio head. His best director was young Frank Capra, who turned out a classic comedy in 1934. *It Happened One Night* starred Clark Gable and Claudette Colbert. The sparkling film won the Academy Award for Best Picture, and Gable, Colbert and Capra also were awarded Oscars. *It Happened One Night* was the first motion picture to win Academy Awards in all four major categories and earned Columbia widespread recognition. The studio's reputation was enhanced during the next few years by such Capra gems as *Mr. Deeds Goes to Town* (1936), *You Can't Take It With You* (1938), and *Mr. Smith Goes To Washington* (1939). By the 1940s Columbia was producing an average of fifty features per year, to meet Cohn's goal of completing a film each week. "I want one good picture a year," said Cohn, who filmed a great many B features and serials to underwrite a few prestige movies.

Columbia therefore produced more B films, including Westerns, than any other major studio. Columbia's Western stars were Wild Bill Elliott and Charles Starrett, neither of whom sang onscreen. Republic dominated B Westerns with singing cowboys Gene Autry and Roy Rogers, and Columbia executives intended to compete in the musical Western field by employing Tex Ritter. Tex signed with Columbia as a contract player. At Grand National and Monogram Tex had been paid on a per picture basis, but as a Columbia contract player his weekly salary almost doubled his annual income from motion pictures.

But there was a major drawback to working with Columbia: The studio decided to co-star Tex in a series with Wild Bill Elliott. A third featured role, a sidekick called "Cannonball," was played at first by Dub Taylor. Such trio Westerns had been popularized by The Three Mesquiteers, a 1936 Republic oater based on characters from the novels of William Colt MacDonald, who transposed the Three Musketeers of Alexander Dumas to the Wild West. The Mesquiteers were Stony Brook, impulsive and romantic, Tucson Smith, strong and steady, and Lullaby Joslin, a comic sidekick who was reliable in a fight and therefore more than a hick comedian. The Three Mesquiteers was a hit with B Western audiences, and series after series of Three Mesquiteers films—totaling fifty-one features—was made by Republic during the 1930s and 1940s. The best Mesquiteer combination was Bob Livingston as Stony, Ray Corrigan as Tucson, and ventriloquist Max Terhune as Lullaby. Through the years, however, there were many combinations of actors—John Wayne played Stony alongside Corrigan and Terhune during a memorable 1938-39 Mesquiteers series. The trio concept, emphasizing men of action working as a team, had a special appeal during World War II, and other studios imitated the Mesquiteers with such groups as the Rough Riders (Buck Jones, Tim McCoy and Raymond Hatton), the Trail Blazers (Ken Maynard, Hoot Gibson and Bob Steele), and the Range Busters (Ray Corrigan, Max Terhune and Dennis Moore).

Tex Ritter was accustomed to starring in his own series, and once he became a trio co-star he would find it difficult to regain individual stardom. After signing Tex, Columbia determined to combine the singing cowboy concept with the trio. Elliott no more wanted to be relegated to co-star status than did Ritter, but Wild Bill and the amiable Tex remained friendly, even though onscreen Tex became the less important of the two heroes. Elliott, who was reserved by nature, played a strong, silent peace officer, while Ritter's hotheaded character often clashed with the sensible Wild Bill. The formula called for Tex and Wild Bill to conflict with each other throughout most of each film, before combining at last to thwart the villains.

Elliott was two years older then Tex. Born Gordon Nance in Missouri, his boyhood idol was William S. Hart, and as a teenager he became a rodeo performer. He gravitated to Hollywood, changed his name to Gordon Elliott, and worked at the Pasadena Playhouse. Tall, lean, and ruggedly handsome, Elliott began appearing in silent films in 1925. He acted in more than sixty movies before first playing in a Western in 1936. Two years later he starred in the popular Columbia serial, *The Great Adventures of Wild Bill Hickok*. Hickok wore his revolvers butts forward, and reversed six-guns became the trademark of Wild Bill Elliott. Elliott went on to star in twenty-four Westerns for Columbia, often portraying Wild Bill Hickok. Elliott played Hickok in six of his eight movies with Tex Ritter.

Columbia always tried to make the first film of a new series the best. *King of Dodge City* featured rousing action, four musical numbers, George Chesebro and Edmund Cobb as bad guys, and a wild shootout at the end. Columbia budgets were far larger than those at Monogram or Grand National, and the production values improved noticeably over previous Ritter movies. Well-received by audiences, *King of Dodge City* was released on August 14, 1941, just three months after Ritter's last film for Monogram.

Two months later the second film of the series, *Roaring Frontiers*, hit the theaters. Elliott once again played Wild Bill Hickok, while Ritter was "Tex Rawlings." Dub Taylor departed after

King of Dodge City *(1941) was the first of eight films teaming Tex with Wild Bill Elliott.*

King of Dodge City *was Ritter's first film for Columbia and brought him another sidekick, Dub "Cannonball" Taylor.*

the first movie, replaced as "Cannonball" by Frank Mitchell, a former member of the vaudeville comedy team of Mitchell and Durant. George Chesebro was back, and so was suavely handsome Tris Coffin, who usually portrayed gangsters when not playing Western bad guys. Tex again took the lead in four musical interludes.

On the first day of 1942 *The Lone Star Vigilantes* was released. There were just two songs, and the film was rather routine. The following month *Bullets for Bandits* came out, with four songs but little else of note. By this time, of course, Pearl Harbor was a month in the past and the United States was at war. At the age of

White Flash

One of the most important elements of B Westerns was the hero's horse. The immensely popular Tom Mix rode "Tony, The Wonder Horse," to such fame that the horse received fan mail; one letter arrived at the Mix ranch addressed simply, "Just Tony, Somewhere in the U.S.A." William S. Hart appeared with Fritz, a smart horse which delighted fans with an assortment of tricks. Buck Jones was identified with Silver, Hopalong Cassidy with Topper, and Ken Maynard, a superb rider, with Tarzan. Among the singing cowboys, Gene Autry would ride Champion and Roy Rogers galloped astride a magnificent Palomino, Trigger, through all eighty-eight of his movies and each of his 101 television shows.

For *Song of the Gringo*, Grand National provided Tex Ritter with White Flash, and he would ride a big, white horse in all of his subsequent films. From the first, White Flash was listed in the credits of Tex Ritter movies, and Tex quickly became identified onscreen with a striking white mount. But "White Flash" actually was a succession of white horses—whatever animal was available to rent when a Tex Ritter movie was being filmed.

In 1941 Tex bought a young, white stallion from Jerome Eddy of Chino Valley, Arizona. Eddy was a family friend of the Southworths, including the future Mrs. Tex Ritter. Tex hired noted trainer Glenn Randall (who trained Trigger and, later, Rex Allen's Koko) to train the new White Flash. Tex rode his own horse in his later movies, and the striking, well-trained animal was a hit on personal appearance tours. When White Flash was twenty-seven, in 1966, Tex reluctantly had to put his beloved steed to sleep.

Poster for Roaring Frontiers *(1941), the second Columbia movie teaming Tex and Wild Bill Elliott.*

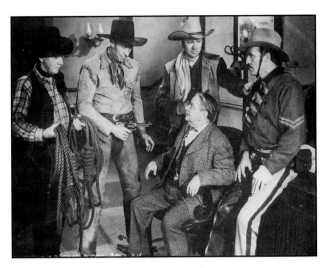

Tex with Wild Bill Elliott in The Lone Star Vigilantes. *Although Ritter and Elliott were friends, neither man liked sharing top billing with another actor.*

thirty-seven, Tex was not subject to the draft. The Selective Service Act, in effect since September 1940, drew upon a manpower pool of healthy men between the ages of twenty-one and thirty-five. In July 1942, thirty-four-year-old Gene Autry dismayed Republic Pictures by volunteering for the Air Force. At first he was used for recruiting and entertaining troops, but he earned pilot's wings, and Tech Sergeant Autry served the Air Ferry Command as a co-pilot until 1946. Roy Rogers, twenty-nine and a husband and father when the war started, was boasted by Republic as "King of the Cowboys" and replaced Sergeant Autry as first among the Top Ten Western Stars. Like Autry, many other actors served in the armed forces, but entertainers were crucial to maintaining public morale during the war. Tex Ritter and Roy Rogers and a host of other performers would entertain at military bases throughout World War II. At these same bases Tex Ritter Westerns were shown to off-duty soldiers and sailors, and many urban young men were exposed for the first time to Ritter's persona and style of music. (In addition to entertaining the troops, Tex joined the California Militia, helping to organize and provide mounts for a horse patrol for emergencies in the rugged San Fernando Valley.)

In the next movie of the Elliott-Ritter series, *North of the Rockies*, Elliott became "Sgt. Wild Bill Cameron" of the Canadian Mounties, while Ritter was "Tex Martin." Ian MacDonald was a bad guy, while young Lloyd Bridges

played a constable. A decade later MacDonald was the head villain and Bridges a deputy marshal in the memorable *High Noon*.

Not so memorable were the next two Elliott-Ritter films, *The Devil's Trail* and *Prairie Gunsmoke*. There were only two songs in each

Tex delivering one of three songs in North of the Rockies *(1942).*

In Prairie Gunsmoke *(1942) Tex and sidekick Frank Mitchell subdue Tris Coffin, who appeared in several Ritter films.*

movie. Tris Coffin was in both pictures, and Glenn Strange appeared in *Prairie Gunsmoke*.

The last film of the series was *Vengeance of the West*, released on September 3, 1942. Elliott played "Joaquin Murietta," and Ritter was "Ranger Captain Tex Lake." Frank Mitchell finished the series as "Cannonball," and the leading lady was lovely Adele Mara.

Although the series was concluded, contract players Ritter and Elliott each owed Columbia one more movie. Elliott filmed *The*

Valley of Vanishing Men, released late in 1942. For 1942 Elliott rose to seventh among the Top Ten Western Stars, his highest finish to date. Co-starring with Tex Ritter apparently boosted Elliott's career, but he had no intention of continuing to share Columbia's screen. For 1943 Elliott left Columbia for Republic, the best in the business at making B Westerns. Republic starred Elliott, most notably as "Red Ryder," and by 1946 he was second in the Top Ten, just behind Roy Rogers.

Unlike Elliott, Ritter's year as a co-star dropped him out of the ranks of the Top Ten Western Stars. His Columbia films were set in the historical West, where he was most comfortable. But Columbia's musical content was uninspired, Ritter's fans missed the rousing fisticuffs with Charlie King, and playing second fiddle to Elliott definitely was a step away from stardom. With Elliott gone, Tex declined to pick up the option on his contract for another year, and he quickly signed with Universal. Although he owed Columbia one more film, the studio agreed to postpone this obligation until a future date. When this feature finally was filmed, in 1944, it proved to be a unique Western. In the meantime, Tex Ritter hoped to revive his once-promising movie career at a new studio.

Capitol Recording Star

Tex Ritter's status as a singing cowboy was declining by 1942, but in that year he made a move that would favorably influence his career for more than three decades. On June 1, 1942, Tex signed a recording contract with Capitol Records. Tex had not recorded since 1939, when he was dropped by Decca. Capitol was organized in Los Angeles in 1941, and Tex was the new company's first Western artist. For both parties it was a profitable union that would last the remainder of his life.

In 1942 Tex became the first country artist signed by newly organized Capitol Records. He turned out a succession of hits, and recorded for Capitol until his death more than three decades later.

Although Tex had not cut a record in more than two years, he had regularly provided visually recorded musical performances in his movies. Between films Tex constantly worked the road, singing Western songs before a wide variety of audiences. Selling merchandise was an important source of income for live performers, and Tex Ritter songbooks were the most popular items during that era of his career. His musical portfolio bulged with songs and ballads which could be used in movies or songbooks or live performances—or on records.

Ritter's lack of success with Decca in the 1930s was in great part attributed to a general lack of interest in Western music, including songs from popular Western movies. But during the 1930s many farm people from the Midwest and South moved to California searching for work. This migration accelerated during the 1940s as the West Coast economy expanded for war production. The shift of rural families to the West Coast soon created a demand for nightclubs and ballrooms and other venues for country/western music. Singing cowboy star Tex Ritter, who performed with unexcelled frequency before live audiences, finally was in a favorable position to capitalize on his recording potential.

Composer-performer Johnny Mercer, one of three men who founded Capitol Records, had heard Tex sing "The Old Chisholm Trail" on the radio in the 1930s. "He was as distinctive as Bob Nolan of the Sons of the Pioneers," said Mercer, who had never forgotten Ritter's sound, "and when we started Capitol, I signed him before I even met him."

Tex would become the new company's first star. But when he signed in 1942, the record

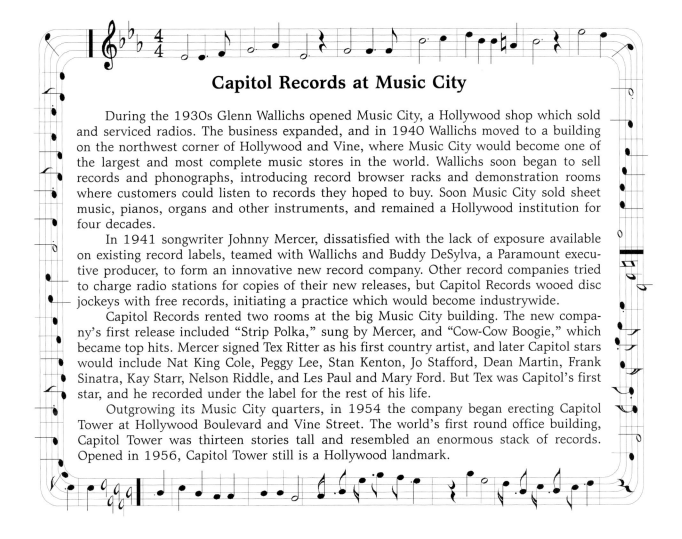

Capitol Records at Music City

During the 1930s Glenn Wallichs opened Music City, a Hollywood shop which sold and serviced radios. The business expanded, and in 1940 Wallichs moved to a building on the northwest corner of Hollywood and Vine, where Music City would become one of the largest and most complete music stores in the world. Wallichs soon began to sell records and phonographs, introducing record browser racks and demonstration rooms where customers could listen to records they hoped to buy. Soon Music City sold sheet music, pianos, organs and other instruments, and remained a Hollywood institution for four decades.

In 1941 songwriter Johnny Mercer, dissatisfied with the lack of exposure available on existing record labels, teamed with Wallichs and Buddy DeSylva, a Paramount executive producer, to form an innovative new record company. Other record companies tried to charge radio stations for copies of their new releases, but Capitol Records wooed disc jockeys with free records, initiating a practice which would become industrywide.

Capitol Records rented two rooms at the big Music City building. The new company's first release included "Strip Polka," sung by Mercer, and "Cow-Cow Boogie," which became top hits. Mercer signed Tex Ritter as his first country artist, and later Capitol stars would include Nat King Cole, Peggy Lee, Stan Kenton, Jo Stafford, Dean Martin, Frank Sinatra, Kay Starr, Nelson Riddle, and Les Paul and Mary Ford. But Tex was Capitol's first star, and he recorded under the label for the rest of his life.

Outgrowing its Music City quarters, in 1954 the company began erecting Capitol Tower at Hollywood Boulevard and Vine Street. The world's first round office building, Capitol Tower was thirteen stories tall and resembled an enormous stack of records. Opened in 1956, Capitol Tower still is a Hollywood landmark.

industry faced a double crisis. The United States had recently entered World War II, and wartime rationing included shellac, needed to press records. The government placed controls on how much shellac could be used by a record company. An even greater threat to the recording industry was a proposed strike by the American Federation of Musicians, scheduled to begin on August 1, 1942. Financial demands of the AFM were generated by the musicians' resistance to the growing trend of radio stations to play records rather than employ live musicians for programming. Long-term opposition to this trend would prove futile, but the imminent likelihood of a strike by musicians made it imperative for recording companies to schedule sessions and stockpile records before August 1.

Johnny Mercer set up a recording session for Tex Ritter for June 11, 1942. Although the company later would erect Capitol Tower, at this beginning stage Capitol simply rented two rooms at Sunset and Vine. Early Capitol recording sessions were held at the C. P. MacGregor Studios. Johnny Mercer served as producer and A & R man (Artist and Repertoire) for most of Capitol's early recording sessions, and he was in the control room when Tex and a group of musicians assembled on June 11.

Johnny Marvin, named musical contractor, had lined up a number of talented musicians: his brother, Frank Marvin, on steel guitar; Paul Sells, accordion, piano and organ; Charlie and Margie Linville, violins; Johnny Bond, guitar and vocal; Eddie Kirk, guitar and vocal; Harold Hensley, violin; Buddy Cole, organ; Cliff Stone, bass violin; Wesley Tuttle, guitar and vocal; and Merle Travis, guitar and vocal. Most of these fine artists frequently worked in Tex Ritter recording

Tex proudly holding up his latest Capitol hit, on a 78 RPM record. There were more than half a million juke-boxes in America during the 1940s.

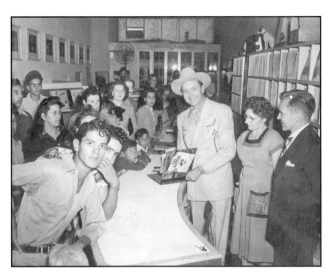

Tex signing record covers at May's Record Shop in Albuquerque.

sessions, and Travis, Tuttle and Stone would themselves become Capitol recording stars.

Johnny Mercer and Tex selected four songs for their first session: "Jingle, Jangle, Jingle," "Someone," "Goodbye, My Little Cherokee," and "I've Done the Best I Could." The first song recorded was "Jingle, Jangle, Jingle," soon to be used in a Paramount movie and written by future Broadway play producer Frank Loesser. The lively tune featured jingling spurs and a chorus, and Ritter's first recording for Capitol proved to be his first hit. Indeed, "Jingle, Jangle, Jingle" also would be successfully recorded by Gene Autry and Bing Crosby.

Another song from his first session, "I've Done the Best I Could," was written by Ritter. "I wrote it," explained Tex, "and I stole it." In 1935 John A. Lomax had brought folk singer Hudie "Leadbelly" Ledbetter to New York and immediately looked up his former student, who was then a veteran Broadway and radio singer-actor. Tex promptly introduced Hudie to Dave Kapp, who arranged a Decca recording session for Ledbetter. Ledbetter sang "Goodnight Irene"—later a great hit—several times to Tex. "I loved the melody, so I just took it,"

laughed Tex, shortly before his death. "After this many years I can confess to my crimes."

But Tex returned favor for favor. Ten years after their first meeting, Leadbelly came to Hollywood. Tex brought the gifted black musician to his home. Dorothy Ritter was on a tour of Pacific military bases, but Merle Travis came to the ranch house. After the three musicians played and sang, Tex called Lee Gillette of Capitol Records and invited him to the ranch to audition Leadbelly and his twelve-string guitar. Gillette arranged for Leadbelly to make an album for Capitol, and it was gratifying to Tex that "I got him two record contracts." Indeed, as the years passed Tex would be instrumental in helping numerous artists begin their recording careers.

Less than two months after Capitol's first session with Tex Ritter, the American Federation of Musicians went on strike, and the recording industry virtually halted for more than a year. During this period Tex Ritter switched from Columbia Pictures to Universal, where he co-starred in an unsatisfactory film series with Johnny Mack Brown. Finally, on November 23, 1943, Johnny Mercer arranged another recording session with Tex.

The four songs selected included "I'm Wastin' My Tears on You," "Have I Stayed Away Too Long," and the patriotic "There's A Gold Star In Her Window." For the fourth number, Tex told Johnny Mercer he was undecided between two songs. Mercer preferred the melody of "There's A New Moon Over My Shoulder," and the song went on the flip side of

At May's Record Shop in Albuquerque, Tex was on tour promoting Tex Ritter, *a set of four 78 RPM records with eight songs recorded in 1945:* "San Antonio Rose"/ "Blood on the Saddle"; "Try Me One More Time"/ "The Old Chisholm Trail"; "Boll Weevil"/ "Bad Brahma Bull"; "Round Up in Glory"/ "Rye Whiskey."

Tex at the Adams Record Shop in Temple, Texas.

"I'm Wastin' My Tears Over You." "I'm Wastin' My Tears Over You" went to the top of the country chart and remained Number One for six weeks, while crossing to the pop chart Top Fifteen. "There's A New Moon Over My Shoulder" climbed to the Top Three, while also crossing over to the pop chart Top Twenty-Five.

The shortage of shellac postponed another Ritter session for ten months. On September 20, 1944, Tex and Johnny Mercer recorded

four songs, including "Jealous Heart" and "I'm Gonna Leave You Like I Found You." Tex picked "Jealous Heart" from about ten selections of sheet music, and the song rose to Number Three, while spending twenty-three weeks on the country chart. The flip side, "I'm Gonna Leave You Like I Found You," had a good beat and also was a hit. The number was written by Tex and Frank Hartford, who teamed to write several songs for Ritter movies. Tex later confessed to lifting this melody from the old "Ta Ra Ra Boom De Ay" he had heard while watching "Flora Dora Girls" in Hoboken during the 1930s. "I hope I don't get sued," he laughed.

Tex signing record sets for young fans in Abilene, Texas.

On September 27, only a week after his first 1944 recording session, Tex and Johnny Mercer and their musicians were back in the studio. Among the four songs, "You Will Have To Pay (For Your Yesterday)" eventually spent three weeks at Number One. Tex helped write "You Will Have To Pay," along with Bonnie Dodd, an Arkansas girl who played steel guitar for Ritter, and another young woman from Arkansas, Sarah Jane Cooper. "Long Time Gone" reached the Top Five.

In 1945, with the war coming to a close, Tex had eight recording sessions within three months: April 30 and May 1, with the Paul Sells Orchestra; May 7, with Merle Travis and his Orchestra: May 9, 15 and 18, with Wesley Tuttle and his Orchestra; and on July 27 and 28. Among the songs recorded with the Paul Sells Orchestra were "Blood On the Saddle," a comedy tune written by Everett Cheetham, "Boll

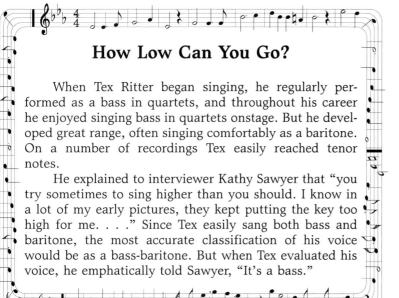

How Low Can You Go?

When Tex Ritter began singing, he regularly performed as a bass in quartets, and throughout his career he enjoyed singing bass in quartets onstage. But he developed great range, often singing comfortably as a baritone. On a number of recordings Tex easily reached tenor notes.

He explained to interviewer Kathy Sawyer that "you try sometimes to sing higher than you should. I know in a lot of my early pictures, they kept putting the key too high for me. . . ." Since Tex easily sang both bass and baritone, the most accurate classification of his voice would be as a bass-baritone. But when Tex evaluated his voice, he emphatically told Sawyer, "It's a bass."

In 1945 Tex was voted one of the Top Ten Western Stars for the seventh time, and he also became the first recording artist to dominate the top three slots on the country charts.

Tex on tour in New Mexico with his new record set.

Weevil," and "You Two Timed Me One Time Too Often," a song by Jenny Lou Carson which spent eleven weeks at Number One.

With Merle Travis and his Orchestra, Tex recorded "Bad Bramha Bull," a ballad about a bull rider that was constantly requested when Ritter played rodeos. Tex and Travis also recorded "The Old Chisholm Trail" and "Rye Whiskey," which reached the Top Ten. The three sessions with Wesley Tuttle and his Orchestra produced "Green Grow the Lilacs"

and "Froggie Went a Courtin'," a folk song which Tex always sang when there were numerous children in an audience, and which later became a staple of his children's albums. On July 27 Tex recorded "Christmas Carols by the Old Corral," which made the Top Three. Capitol was the first company to send free records to radio stations, and Tex was benefiting from this farsighted strategy.

In 1945 Tex Ritter filmed his final movie as a singing cowboy. But in January of that same year, Tex established an enviable standard for country recording artists. The January 20, 1945, issue of *Billboard* magazine announced that three Tex Ritter records ranked One, Two and Three on the country chart: "I'm Wastin' My Tears on You," "There's a New Moon Over My Shoulder," and "Jealous Heart." Tex was the first country singer to monopolize the Top Three, and he became a Capitol artist for as long as he would live—a total of thirty-two years.

Tex recorded for Capitol the rest of his life, a total of thirty-two years.

The Universal Years

Universal Studio wanted Tex Ritter to co-star in a movie series with long-time Western hero Johnny Mack Brown. Tex did not want to play second banana again, but filming on the series was ready to begin and there would be no interruption in his screen appearances (Ritter's final Columbia movie was released on September 3, 1942, while his first Universal picture followed three weeks later, on September 25). Tex was promised his own starring series after the seven films with Brown, along with acting roles in A features for Universal. Hoping that these developments might boost his career, Tex signed with Universal and promptly went to work opposite another co-star.

A year older than Tex, Johnny Mack Brown was a native of Alabama who had been an All-American running back at the University of Alabama. Brown scored the winning touchdown in two consecutive Rose Bowls. While in California for the 1927 Rose Bowl, Brown filmed a screen test, and later that year he began appearing in silent movies such as *Our Dancing Daughter* with Joan Crawford. He made the first of more than 130 Westerns in 1930, *Montana Moon*, again with Joan Crawford. Later in 1930 his second Western, *Billy the Kid*, made him a sagebrush star. Brown rode a Palomino named Rebel, and by 1942 he was a fixture among the Top Ten Western Stars. The budgets for his Westerns at Universal were higher than for any previous Tex Ritter films.

Universal had been founded in 1912, and within three years moved to a new studio called Universal City. Studio head Carl Laemmle opened the lot to paying tourists eager to see how movies were made, and today Universal

Deep in the Heart of Texas *(1942) was Ritter's first film for Universal. A new studio brought another co-star, Johnny Mack Brown.*

City is still a favorite for visitors to Hollywood. Universal released such varied hits as *All Quiet on the Western Front*, the Dracula and Frankenstein movies of Bela Lugosi and Boris Karloff, and the comedy features of Bud Abbott and Lou Costello. Universal B Westerns enjoyed good production values and shooting schedules that sometimes extended to ten days.

Universal had just signed Jennifer Holt to a contract, and she would play the leading lady in all seven of the Brown-Ritter films. Born in Hollywood in 1920, she was the daughter of noted actor Jack Holt and the younger sister of future cowboy star Tim Holt. She made her film debut in a 1942 Hopalong Cassidy film, then promptly joined Universal. Jennifer was pretty and a fine horsewoman, and she sang skillfully throughout the series.

The sidekick in the Brown-Ritter films was Fuzzy Knight. A talented musician from West

Virginia, John Forrest Knight played tent shows and vaudeville as a comic musician, and reached Broadway by the late 1920s. He came to Hollywood in 1932, and from 1935 through 1953 he was the sidekick in scores of B Westerns. Fuzzy sang a song or at least provided musical accompaniment in all the Brown-Ritter movies.

The Jimmy Wakely Trio appeared in each film of the series. Shortly after Wakely formed his trio in 1937, Tex met Jimmy, Johnny Bond, and Scotty Harrell while he was touring in Oklahoma. They introduced themselves to him when he reached Oklahoma City, and he generously agreed to appear on their early morning radio show. After Wakely made his film debut in a 1939 Roy Rogers feature, he and his trio were signed by Gene Autry as regulars on his *Melody Ranch* radio program. There were appearances in Autry movies, and by 1944 Wakely would begin starring in his own series.

During the Brown-Ritter films, Wakely, Bond and Harrel were used in crowd scenes. Bond recalled one scene in which they appeared four times. The scene began with a song by the Jimmy Wakely Trio. Then the musicians changed hats and coats and were filmed in the crowd. After watching themselves perform, they again changed hats and coats and joined the gang of bad guys galloping down the street. Following another costume change, they mounted up again and joined a posse led by Tex and Brown in pursuit of the bad guys. In a single scene they performed a number, joined their own audience, rode with the outlaw gang, and chased themselves as posse members.

Home Again...

After Tex began touring regularly during the 1930s, whenever his travels took him to Texas he tried to visit his family in Nederland. Sometimes Tex attended one of his movies with family members, and occasionally he sang in the First Methodist Church of Nederland. Late in 1941 Tex and his bride drove to Nederland during their first Christmas season as a married couple. Throughout the remainder of his life Tex dropped in to visit his family in Nederland near Beaumont, and it was there that he chose to be buried.

His brother David remained in Panola County, along with other relatives, and Tex visited any time he was in the vicinity. In 1952 Tex was on hand for the thirtieth anniversary of his Carthage High School class, and nearly two decades later he made an appearance on the town square on behalf of Republican political candidates. During his adulthood Tex was a nomad, but he touched his roots at every opportunity.

With Fuzzy Knight, Jennifer Holt, and the Jimmy Wakely Trio providing music, Tex usually sang just one song in each film. But thanks to his many fistic duels with Charlie King, he handled action scenes as well as the former All-American. As in the series with Wild Bill Elliott, the two heroes usually clashed for most of the film before combining to defeat the villains. The conflict between Brown and Ritter usually erupted in a fistfight, with Tex—as the lesser of the two stars—the inevitable loser.

The inspiration for these brawls between the stars was *The Spoilers*, a classic Rex Beach story of the Alaska gold rush that has been filmed five times (1913, 1923, 1930, 1942, and 1955). The 1942 version starred John Wayne and Randolph Scott and was lensed by Universal on the same lot where the Brown-Ritter series was about to be filmed. The climax of *The Spoilers* is a fistfight between the two main characters, and the best of the five versions is the rousing slugfest between Wayne and Scott. With the Wayne-Scott fisticuffs such a spectacular success for Universal, it was natural for a similar faceoff to be written into the Brown-Ritter movies.

The first film of the series was *Deep in the Heart of Texas*. Universal had bought rights to the popular song and used it for the title. Although it seemed a tailor-made number for Tex, it was performed by Fuzzy Knight onscreen. Tex sang the traditional cowboy lament, "Streets of Laredo." The movie found Brown returning home to Texas after the Civil War to foil a gang of landgrabbers—led by his father. The villainous father was played by William Farnum, who

Tex and Fuzzy Knight hogtie the bad guys in Deep in the Heart of Texas. *Reunited with Tex at Columbia, Fuzzy Knight had been Ritter's sidekick in his first film in 1936.*

Tex and Jennifer Holt watch Johnny Mack Brown contend with Mady Correll in The Old Chisholm Trail. *The daughter of actor Jack Holt and the younger sister of cowboy star Tim Holt, Jennifer was the leading lady in nine Tex Ritter films (thirty-eight Westerns overall).*

With Johnny Mack Brown riding alongside, Tex drives a wagon across the set of The Old Chisholm Trail *(1943).*

had starred in the original screen version of *The Spoilers* three decades earlier.

The second film of the series, *Little Joe the Wrangler*, featured Glenn Strange as leader of a gang stealing gold shipments. Johnny Mack Brown, framed for a murder, teamed up with a discredited sheriff—played by Tex—to corral the gang. The plot, like most of the Brown-Ritter storylines, was complex for a B Western.

The last release of 1942 was *The Old*

Chisholm Trail. There was a female villain, whose chief henchman was the unsurpassed bad guy, Roy Barcroft. The heavies were charging cattlemen to use a key water hole on the Chisholm Trail, but Brown and Tex managed to reopen the hole and the trail. Tex sang the title song, another traditional cowboy ballad. Four of the seven Brown-Ritter films were titled after a familiar tune.

In *Raiders of San Joaquin*, another complicated plot pitted Johnny Mack Brown and Tex against a crooked land-grabber. Like many other oaters of the period, *Raiders of San Joaquin* was set in the contemporary West, but it was one of the few Ritter films that did not take place in frontier times.

It was back to the Old West in *Tenting Tonight on the Old Camp Ground*. The two heroes helped Jennifer Holt win a stagecoach mail contract, thwarting the villains who opposed her. Ritter's old friend, Hank Worden, had a small part, and so did veteran bad guy Bud Osborne.

Roy Barcroft added menace to *Cheyenne Roundup*. A familiar plot twist for B Westerns placed Johnny Mack Brown in dual roles as twin brothers, one good and one bad. The

Johnny Mack Brown and Tex in Cheyenne Roundup *(1943). An All-American halfback at the University of Alabama, Brown twice led his team to the Rose Bowl. In California he was given a screen test which led to a long career in movies, including more than 130 Westerns.*

Tex riding undercover with the bad guys in Cheyenne Roundup. *The mask might disguise Tex, but it would be hard for a witness to miss White Flash.*

claim-jumping twin is brought to justice by his look-alike brother, who is aided by Tex.

The last film in the series, *The Lone Star Trail,* was perhaps the best, "a rip-snorting Western," according to *Film Daily.* Brown was the victim of a frame-up. After serving a two-year prison sentence, he was aided by Tex—as "U.S. Marshal Fargo Steele"—in clearing his name. As in the other films of the series, Jennifer Holt was pretty and lively, Fuzzy Knight contributed effective humor and music, and the Jimmy Wakely Trio added to the music and crowd scenes. One of the principal bad guys was young, moustachioed Robert Mitchum, playing in his eleventh movie. The future superstar participated in one of the best saloon brawls ever filmed for a B Western.

The Lone Star Trail was released on August 6, 1943. On that same date Universal released *Frontier Badmen*, an A Western starring Robert Paige and Diana Barrymore. The cast also featured Noah Beery, Jr., Anne Gwynne, Andy Devine, Leo Carillo, Lon Chaney, Jr.—and Tex Ritter. Tex had been promised roles in bigger budget scenes, but despite some exciting cattle stampede scenes, *Frontier Badmen* was not much of a Western. Tex expected more of these roles, but even though his contract was renewed, no more parts in A features materialized.

Universal did not renew Johnny Mack

Tex (far right, next to Andy Devine) played a small part in Frontier Badmen *(1943). He hoped to expand his acting career at Universal with character roles in quality features. But* Frontier Badmen *was a mediocre Western, and Tex was offered no other character parts.*

Brown's option. The studio intended to reduce its production of B features, and it was rumored that Brown was dropped because he commanded a larger salary than Ritter. Another rumor suggested that Brown quit Universal rather than continue as a co-star. In any event, Brown signed with Monogram, again starred in his own series, and maintained a strong position among the Top Ten Western Stars through 1950.

Tex immediately went to work on another series for Universal, assuming the headliner role that originally may have been written for the departed Johnny Mack Brown. Elevated to the second banana role was Dennis Moore, who had played supporting parts in B Westerns and crime films. Fuzzy Knight continued as sidekick, and Glenn Strange added a familiar face. The leading lady was Janet Shaw. Although Jimmy Wakely had left Universal to pursue his acting career, Johnny Bond, a member of the old Jimmy Wakely Trio, formed the Red River Valley Boys, a four-man band which signed for the series.

Tex and Dennis Moore in Arizona Trail *(1943).*

The first film of the series, *Arizona Trail*, was released on September 24, 1943. Tex and Dennis Moore played contentious stepbrothers who patch up their differences long enough to foil landgrabbers. *Arizona Trail* was fast-paced and exciting, and Tex seemed back on track as a Western star. Dennis Moore, Jennifer Holt, and Fuzzy Knight would be featured in the second film of the series, *Frontier Law*. It was a film Tex never made.

The night before the production meeting for *Frontier Law*, Tex climbed to his hayloft to feed his five horses. He had cautioned Dorothy never to pull a bale of hay backward. But Tex, puffing on a pipe, forked a bale with a hay hook and pulled it, moving backward toward the double doors of the loft, intending to drop the bale into the corral. As Tex tugged forcefully on the bale, the hook slipped off the wire and he staggered backward.

Suddenly, he felt himself tumbling out of the loft. He hurled the hay hook aside before thudding to the ground. Tex took the weight of the fall on his left hip and thigh, and bit his

pipestem in half. Stunned, he managed to call Dr. George Berg on the barn telephone, then tried to get to the house, where Dorothy was preparing dinner. His leg would not hold him up, but he crawled about seventy feet toward the house.

Dorothy thought Tex had been delayed at the barn with a phone call. Finally, she walked outside and saw him lying among the chickens. She called out to him to come to dinner, then heard his cries for help. When she rushed to his side he told her he had called Dr. Berg. Covering him with a saddle blanket, she again called the doctor, then waited by her husband's side. Dr. Berg arrived with an X-ray truck, and pictures taken at the site revealed no broken bones.

Torn ligaments and muscles put Tex on crutches, but he immediately began therapy. At the production conference for *Frontier Law*, the assembled cast was told that Tex had been injured the previous evening. Veteran Western actor Russell Hayden was hastily brought in from Columbia to star in the second movie of the series. Within a few days a battered Tex Ritter came to the set of *Frontier Law* on crutches. He was welcomed by the cast and crew, but it must have been painful to watch another actor play the starring role Tex had so long coveted.

Within two weeks of his accident Tex traveled to Dallas for an important personal appearance. Although Tex could not yet walk onstage, he was placed atop a stool with his guitar, and

Tex and Russell Hayden played brothers in Marshal of Gunsmoke *(1944). From left: Hayden, Jennifer Holt, Fuzzy Knight, Tex.*

when the curtain was drawn he launched his performance.

By the time the third film of the series, *Marshal of Gunsmoke*, was ready for production, Tex had recovered sufficiently to take the lead role. But Russell Hayden returned to co-star. Fuzzy Knight was still the sidekick, and Jennifer Holt, who had played opposite Hayden in *Frontier Law*, again was the leading lady. The gang of villains featured George Chesebro, William Desmond, and Bob Osborne. Tex played a U.S. marshal who, aided by his brother (Hayden), restored order to a town by cleaning up crooked elections. Jennifer Holt sang two songs, the Red River Valley Boys performed "Saddle Serenade," and Tex warbled the traditional "Git Along Little Dogies."

Tex, playing the title role as the Marshal of Gunsmoke, *stands beside the door at right while a trial is conducted in the bank.*

Tex Ritter's next film appearance finished his remaining contractual obligation to Columbia. Still owing Columbia one movie when he left for Universal in 1942, Tex agreed to co-star in *Cowboy Canteen*. One of Warner Brothers' biggest hits of 1944 was *Hollywood Canteen*. The film was set in the famous wartime *Hollywood Canteen* where soldiers and sailors were served refreshments and entertained by movie stars, with Bette Davis as chief hostess and guest appearances by everyone from Joan Crawford to the Andrews Sisters. Columbia immediately put together a Western version of the popular movie, featuring the studio's great cowboy star, Charles Starrett. A standout football player at Dartmouth, the handsome, athlet-

ic Starrett starred in 131 Westerns for Columbia from 1935 through 1952; in almost half of his films he played the masked "Durango Kid."

In *Cowboy Canteen* Starrett portrayed a rancher-turned-soldier. Starrett and Tex played opposite pretty Jane Frazee, who later would be the leading lady in half a dozen Roy Rogers movies. Max Terhune and Bob Taylor were the sidekicks, backed up by the colorful Guinn "Big Boy" Williams. Like *Hollywood Canteen*, the emphasis in *Cowboy Canteen* was on patriotism and entertainment, with nearly a dozen musical numbers provided by Tex, Roy Acuff and his Smoky Mountain Boys, Jimmy Wakely and his Saddle Pals, the Tailor Maids, and, among other groups, the Mills Brothers. Commenting upon the strength of Western movies, Phil Hardy, author of the encyclopedic *The Western*, observed about *Cowboy Canteen*: "Imagine a film called *Detective Canteen*."

A grizzled Tex in Oklahoma Raiders *(1944), his final film for Universal. The "Bandit Known as EL VENGADOR" turned out to be leading lady Jennifer Holt.*

Oklahoma Raiders was the next Ritter movie for Universal, with Jennifer Holt as "El Vengador," a masked vigilante assumed to be a man. Russell Hayden had returned to Columbia, but Dennis Moore was elevated to co-star. Tex played an army officer who, along with Fuzzy Knight, encountered assorted villainy while trying to buy horses for the cavalry. Tex and Jennifer Holt were effective together, and there were five musical numbers. *Oklahoma Raiders* was crisp and entertaining, but it would prove to be the last good starring film for Tex Ritter.

Marshal of Gunsmoke and *Oklahoma Raiders* were filmed in late 1943 for release early the next year. Tex went on tour, expecting to make the remaining movies of the series in the early months of 1944. But Universal had decided to phase out its B units: The studio would film no more B Westerns after 1944. Along with many other B contract players, Universal did not renew Tex Ritter's option for 1944. Rod Cameron and Kirby Grant starred in Universal's last few B Westerns.

The Universal films of Tex Ritter were well-plotted and enjoyed good production values and casts. Despite his co-star status, Tex was played to advantage with exciting fight scenes and traditional Western songs. Although he again missed the Top Ten, he managed the number twelve ranking among Western stars. Just when he regained a starring series, Tex suffered an untimely accident, then was caught in the beginning of the decline of B Westerns. His years at Universal had been frustrating, and he hoped that a starring series at another studio might jump start a movie career that was headed in the wrong direction.

Riding Into the Sunset at PRC

Producers Releasing Corporation (PRC) was a Poverty Row studio organized in 1940. PRC filmed Westerns, mysteries, comedies, and musicals aimed at bobbysoxers. George Houston starred in a Lone Rider Western series for PRC. Another PRC Western star was Buster Crabbe, who once had played Tarzan, and PRC sometimes put him in low-budget jungle movies. In his Westerns the athletic Crabbe usually slugged it out with Charlie King. Producer Ed Finney also worked at PRC during the 1940s.

PRC produced a Texas Rangers series starring James Newill as a lawyer, backed up by co-star Dave O'Brien and sidekick Guy Wilkerson. Newill was an opera-trained singer who had worked on vaudeville and radio shows. From 1937 to 1940, Newill starred as "Renfrew of the Royal Mounted" for Grand National and Monogram. But the wavy-haired singer did not cut much of a figure as a Western hero, and after fourteen Texas Rangers films Newill left the movies to concentrate on his musical career.

With Tex Ritter suddenly available, PRC executives decided that the veteran singing cowboy was ideal to head the Texas Rangers series. Tex signed for eight pictures. The Texas Rangers was a trio series: Tex, with his legal training, played lawyer "Tex Haines"; Dave O'Brien, who had worked with Tex in earlier films, was Texas Ranger "Dave Wyatt"; and gangly Guy Wilkerson was a rather unfunny "Panhandle Perkins." Tex was reunited with his friend and long-time celluloid foe Charlie King, who was a bad guy in seven of the eight films. King had grown a large paunch, and he sometimes wore a ragged hat and helped Guy Wilkerson with the comedy. Although still one of the villains, King's fights now were exercises

In 1944 Tex began a series as one of The Texas Rangers for PRC. Dave O'Brien (left) played "Dave Wyatt" in the eight films, Tex was "Tex Haines," and Guy Wilkerson was their sidekick, "Panhandle Perkins."

in slapstick, and the films were not helped by the loss of his menace.

The co-stars dressed the same in each film of the series. Tex wore black pants and a big black hat, with a light cowboy shirt. Dave O'Brien was togged out in a black outfit with a white hat and a long white neckerchief. Dave wore one six-gun, and Tex still sported two revolvers in a magnificently tooled rig. The same costumes helped identify the Texas Rangers from other cowboy heroes of the period. But use of the same skimpy town set in film after film merely demonstrated economy, and the entire series had a cheap look. Each movie ran the following Foreword after the opening credits: "Dedicated to the law officers of the Old West, who led the fight for law and order in the pioneer days of this country in 1880."

The first film of the series, *Gangsters of the Frontier*, was released on September 21, 1944. There were three musical numbers in *Gangsters of the Frontier*. The climax was unusually deadly for a B Western. Two villains, each squared off against one of the heroes, carefully entered a room. Mistaking each other for Tex and Dave, the outlaws suddenly whirled and shot each other to death.

"This is a free country," emphasized Tex in one speech, "where nobody can set themselves up as absolute ruler and force other people to do their bidding."

Such sentiments were eagerly received by wartime audiences, and Tex increasingly looked for opportunities to express patriotic or religious convictions. The script also saluted women who had enlisted in the armed forces, or who had participated in unprecedented numbers in the wartime economy, by having Texas ladies offer to join the Rangers.

"As our country grows," observed Tex, "more and more you'll find men and women working and fighting side by side."

The second film of the series was *Dead or Alive*. Tex co-wrote both of the songs he briefly performed. When asked by a judge early in the movie if he had his law books with him, Tex put his hands on his holstered six-guns: "Yep—both of 'em." Dave posed as an escaped outlaw to infiltrate the gang of villains. Bud Osborne helped Charlie King with the villainy, and Charlie squared off against Tex in a fistfight. The climax was an extended action scene with brawls, chases, and shootouts.

The Whispering Skull was the last Texas Rangers film released in 1944. But again there were only two songs, Charlie King was absent, and there was little to recommend the movie. At least Tex was the star. The three starring films for PRC, plus two co-starring roles at Universal and *Cowboy Canteen* for Columbia, were enough to bring Tex back to the Top Ten after a two-year absence. With only a modest film output for 1944, Tex Ritter reclaimed the number ten slot.

Marked For Murder, the first release of 1945, opened with Tex in his law office playing his guitar and singing "Tears of Regret." Dave O'Brien rode up to enlist Ritter's help in subduing a range conflict between cattlemen and sheep ranchers. Guy Wilkerson had been

Tex helps Denny Burke step out of a stagecoach in The Whispering Skull *(1944).*

During a tour between PRC filming, Tex met Governor Jimmie Davis of Louisiana. In addition to his political skills, Governor Davis was a talented country performer and songwriter who would be elected to the CMA Hall of Fame in 1971. Tex noted the success of Davis in both country music and politics, and one day he would run for high office himself.

assigned by O'Brien to work undercover as a tinker around the suspected villains. He performed his first comedy routine with rotund bad guy Charlie King, and later tried another piece of business with the Milo Twins, supposedly confusing the look-alike brother duo. The guitar-playing twins then performed a song, and

Tex and Dave O'Brien seize an Enemy of the Law *(1945). During his last eight films, Tex was co-starred with Dave O'Brien as The Texas Rangers, in a series shot by PRC.*

Tex with Dave O'Brien and Lorraine Miller in Three in the Saddle *(1945).*

Tex belted out the folk number, "Froggie Went a Courtin'." After Tex and Dave and Guy cleared up the trouble, Ritter sang "Long Time Gone," which he had co-written.

Tex also co-wrote both of his songs, "Teach Me to Forget" and "You Will Have to Pay," for his next film, *Enemy of the Law*. Leading lady Kay Hughes called him the "singing lawyer." The Texas Rangers rounded up Tex to help recover $250,000 stolen from the federal government. "Uncle Sam, eh," commented Tex, with the pro-government sentiment of wartime America, "count me in."

Guy Wilkerson, posing as a convict, was put in the same cell as prison inmate Charlie King, who knew the whereabouts of the stolen money. Once again Guy and Charlie tried to act as a good guy-bad guy comedy team. Released from prison together, Guy joined Charlie's gang, which included old-time Western star Kermit Maynard. Although the younger Dave O'Brien handled most of the fisticuffs in the series, *Enemy of the Law* featured three fights pitting the outnumbered co-stars against the gang.

Three in the Saddle referred to Tex, Dave, and Guy Wilkerson. Lorraine Miller was the leading lady, and she played the same role in the next film, *Frontier Fugitives*. There were only two songs in each of these movies, as in most of the films of this series. A musical score tried to whip up excitement during chase scenes and fights, but these movies would have been better off with more cowboy songs from Tex.

In Three in the Saddle *Tex and Dave O'Brien face a band of bad guys led by the sheriff, played by veteran Western villain Bud Osborne, and, between Osborne and O'Brien, Ritter's old nemesis, Charlie King.*

The final movie of the Texas Ranger series was *Flaming Bullets*. Dave O'Brien played a dual role—his usual character, "Ranger Dave Wyatt," and look-alike bad guy "Steve Carson." Bud Osborne and Kermit Maynard were in the cast, along with Charlie King, who, as "Porky Smith," tried to help Guy Wilkerson with the lame antics of "Panhandle Perkins." Songs were limited to "Be Honest With Me" and "I Hang My Head and Cry," two numbers popularized by Gene Autry. Released on October 15, 1945, *Flaming Bullets* was Tex Ritter's sixtieth film, and his last as a singing cowboy. "A lot of people have told me that I shouldn't have made those [PRC] pictures,"

Tex told Jon Tuska, a leading authority on Western movies. "I suppose they were right."

But the PRC films kept Tex on the big screen for one more year. Even though he made just five low-budget films in 1945, Tex moved up to number nine on the list of Top Ten Western Stars. He was forty now, and with the B Western beginning a steady decline, Tex was not extended any more worthwhile movie offers. But Tex had made his mark on the public consciousness.

For sixty movies throughout an entire decade, Tex Ritter had championed the frontier West. Resisting the trend to set musical Westerns in the contemporary West, Tex consistently performed in the heroic pioneer period. For ten years Tex blazed away at bad guys with a six-gun in each hand. He handled fistfights more convincingly then any other singing cowboy. He galloped across the screen on White Flash, with cameras recording closeups to prove that it was not a double but Tex riding hell for leather. And more than any other sagebrush star, he preserved the music of the Old West, singing old-time cowboy ballads with obvious relish in his rich, deep voice. It still is fun to watch the Texan in the big hat handle a brace of revolvers and ride a striking white horse and brawl with Charlie King. But the greatest plea-sure of viewing a Ritter movie is to enjoy his performance of traditional Western music.

Tex Ritter arrived in Hollywood just as the singing cowboy became popular, and only Gene Autry and Roy Rogers, who starred in about ninety films each, made more musical Westerns than Tex. If Tex had worked for a major studio early in his career, his success might have equaled that of Gene or Roy. Instead, Tex starred for years with Grand National and Monogram and PRC, Poverty Row outfits that could not provide him with proper budgets or scripts or promotion. And when he filmed for major studios, Columbia and Universal, Tex was saddled with co-stars—Wild Bill Elliott and Johnny Mack Brown—who were given the dominant roles. Although Tex starred in poorly mounted films, even though he was mired as the secondary co-star in more than a quarter of his movies, he still earned repeated recognition as one of Hollywood's most appealing Western actors. If his movie career was not what it might have been, it nevertheless developed a legion of Tex Ritter fans who would loyally support him for three more decades. The little boy riding a stick horse around his yard at Murvaul had become a two-gun hero astride a magnificent white stallion.

Hollywood's Most Traveled Performer

Tex Ritter's movie career and World War II ended at about the same time. The greatest war in history brought enormous change throughout the world, including the world of country music. Before the war, country music consisted primarily of folk ballads and mountain tunes, along with cowboy songs. Although popular in the South, hillbilly music enjoyed little commercial success across the nation. But by the mid-1930s Bob Wills and His Texas Playboys were leading the popularization of western swing, a big band country sound. During these same years Gene Autry, Tex Ritter, and lesser stars vastly increased the popularity of cowboy songs through their singing cowboy movies. Indeed, through his scores of films, countless personal appearances, and successful Capitol recordings, Tex Ritter was instrumental in putting the "western" in country and western.

During the war years, Tex continued to make movies and personal appearance tours. Wartime rationing of gasoline and tires restricted travel, but Tex cultivated the friendship of service station owners and continued to drive his entourage in a battered 1940 station wagon to theaters and gymnasiums and outdoor arenas. He did not have to range as far as before on his tours, because during the war the West Coast became a hotbed of country music. Southerners moved to the West Coast, along with everywhere else that war plants were built, and they brought their musical tastes with them. At the same time, a majority of military training bases were established in the South, which exposed young men from all over the nation to Southern country music. By the war's end country music had expanded out of the South.

From 1938 through 1940, Monogram sent their "Cowboy Troubadour From Texas" on promotional tours.

Tex, Slim Andrews, and Dorothy Fay promoting their 1940 film Rainbow Over the Range.

In 1946 eight million records were sold, and more than thirteen percent were country recordings (only popular music, with fifty percent, and classical, with nearly nineteen percent, had a larger share of the business). Before the war most country records were played on jukeboxes, but after the war only ten percent of country records went into America's half a million jukeboxes. Country fans who heard catchy songs on jukeboxes or over the radio now bought their own records to play on their own phonographs. By war's end there was at least one radio in almost every American home, and an increasing number of automobiles also were equipped with radios. During the war years, Americans listened more avidly than ever to their radios, for war news as well as for entertainment. Hundreds of new stations were licensed in the postwar years, as radio enjoyed the peak of its popularity.

These years also brought the peak of Tex Ritter's popularity as a recording artist. Early in 1945 Tex Ritter songs ranked Number One, Two, and Three on the country chart, and later in the year "You Two-Timed Me Once Too Often" stayed at Number One for eleven weeks. Capitol staged eight recording sessions, from the end of April through the end of July, for Tex in 1945. Lee Gillette became the A & R man for Ritter recording sessions, and with some interruptions he would work with Tex in this capacity for two decades.

In 1946 "You Will Have to Pay," recorded more than a year earlier, was the Number One country hit for three weeks. On July 31, 1946, Tex and Lee Gillette cut four sides, including "Have I Told You Lately That I Love You," written by Scott Wiseman. Wiseman was part of the country comedy-singing team of Lulu Belle and Scotty. During the 1940s, they made musical films for Republic Studios, and they performed "Have I Told You Lately" in one of those movies.

"I always thought that this was one of the great country songs of all time," said Tex. When he learned that "Have I Told You Lately" had not been recorded, Tex immediately tried to locate Wiseman. He was playing the Corn Palace in Mitchell, South Dakota, where Tex reached him by phone. A deal was struck, but Gene Autry also obtained recording rights. Although the Autry version was released about a week before Ritter's, "Have I Told You Lately" reached the Top Three for Tex. The flip side, "When You Leave Don't Slam the Door," also made the Top Three.

"When You Leave Don't Slam the Door" was written by Joe Allison. Tex met the young disc jockey in San Antonio, where Allison was working for KMAC. Allison toured with Tex for a couple of years as a performer and emcee. Returning to broadcasting, Allison eventually earned induction into the D. J. Hall of Fame. He authored a number of hit songs, most notably "He'll Have To Go" for Jim Reeves. One of country music's most multi-talented personalities, Allison would be reunited with Tex on numerous future occasions.

Allison was with the band on a trip through Arkansas a year or two after the end of the war. The roads were wretched, and when Tex took the wheel he growled an oath each time the station wagon slammed into a chughole. Tex was often teased by band members about his tendency to sleep while driving, and with a straight face.

Kiss and Tell

Tex always used humor throughout his live performances, and a favorite comic monologue dealt with learning to kiss his leading ladies for Western films.

"I never forgot the first girl I kissed in the movies," grinned Tex. "I was a boy fresh out of East Texas and I didn't know much about kissing. I had kissed my mother and my aunt and my cousins, but kissing a girl in the movies was another story.

"The director told me how to do it. When I saw it later on the screen, it looked like I was eating a head of lettuce. There's a special way you kiss a girl in the movies, and the director showed me how. You put your lips together. She tries to push your teeth down your gullet, and you try to push her plates into her nasal passage. Then you pull apart. There's a little suction, but you can make it.

"You've got to hold a girl just right, too. I would come around with my left hand and place my fingers one inch above the sacroiliac, with my fingers closed. Then I would come around with my right hand and we'd go into my clinch."

Singin' in the Rain

Tex Ritter was an indefatigable trouper. He endlessly drove the highways and backroads of America to bring his music to audiences, and once he was in front of an audience, he delivered a show, come hell—or high water.

"I remember seeing him when he was playing at a fair in Oklahoma," recalled Harry Mills of the Mills Brothers, who had appeared with Tex in the 1944 film, *Cowboy Canteen.* "It was raining, just pouring. The people were sitting in the grandstands under a cover, but Tex Ritter was in the open, singing to them. The natural thing to do is to get in the dry, out of the wet. But Tex didn't. He just stayed out there, entertaining those folks."

Tex and his Musical Tornadoes, performing between showings of the 1940 Western, Virginia City, *starring Errol Flynn and Randolph Scott.*

Allison asked his boss how he liked Arkansas. "If they gave the nation an enema," grumbled Tex, "right here is where they would insert the plunger."

The Tex Ritter record hits of the mid-1940s greatly stimulated his personal appearance opportunities. Tex had worked the road since coming to Hollywood in 1936. After his film career ended in 1945, there was more time for personal appearances. Sometimes he was on tour for sixteen weeks at a time, and once he played ninety cities in ninety days. Tex Ritter

became known as "Hollywood's most traveled performer."

His first backup group was called "Tex Ritter's Tornadoes," then "Tex Ritter's Texas Tornadoes." By the mid-1940s he named his band "Tex Ritter and His Texans." Spud Goodale was lead guitarist from 1944 to 1951, and sometimes only Tex and Spud climbed into the 1940 station wagon to drive to an appearance. Band personnel were constantly in flux, but a 1947 photo of the Texans included Tex, Spud, Joe Allison, Pete Martinez, and Bob Morgan. White Flash often was hauled along in a trailer, and a chimpanzee called Cheetah was part of an expanded "Tex Ritter Festival and Circus," which toured more than one hundred towns and cities.

The long stretches away from home helped to frustrate the family plans of Tex and Dorothy, and after five years of marriage the couple began to consider adoption. But Dorothy worked a tour of the Pacific Northwest with Tex, and their time together produced happy results. Tex and Dorothy became parents on January 8, 1947, when Thomas Southworth Ritter was born. Tommy soon was diagnosed with cerebral palsy, and Dorothy became active in the United Cerebral Palsy Association, eventually becoming the first woman selected as national vice-president. On September 17, 1948, Jonathan Southworth Ritter was born into the family. The Lazy TNT Ranch house became a lively home place, but Tex had to spend much of his time on the road earning a living.

In 1948 Tex organized a larger road show, "Tex Ritter and His Hollywood Revue." A photo taken in August 1948 in Pennsylvania shows Tex, White Flash, eight male performers, and one female musician. The Western Revue traveled in two station wagons and a horse trailer. Another vehicle soon was added, when Tex expanded the Western Revue to more than twenty performers: Spud Goodale still was lead guitarist; Slim Andrews was comedian-fiddler; Tommy Durden played steel guitar and was a featured soloist; Boots Gilbert was another fea-

For more than a decade White Flash was an immensely popular part of the Tex Ritter show. Onstage he would perform tricks, then take a bow.

Comedian Slim Andrews with fiddle, lead guitarist Spud Goodale, bass fiddler Boots Gilbert, Tex, and steel guitarist Tommy Durden, who later wrote "Heartbreak Hotel."

The Show MUST Go On

On May 5, 1947, Tex was in Richmond, Virginia. His usual hectic schedule called for a 2:30 matinee appearance in Tappahannock, about forty-five miles to the northeast. Tex decided to fly in a small plane, but on takeoff at 2:00 the little craft could not gain altitude and crashed. Tex was bruised on the arms and legs, while the pilot, Richmond radio announcer Ira Hull, suffered head injuries and glass fragments in an eye. "It's a miracle we weren't both killed," said Tex.

Undaunted by his brush with death, Tex climbed into a car and was driven to Tappahannock. The performance was delayed about thirty minutes, but Tex gamely limped onstage, and in the best showbiz tradition, the show went on!

Ritters vs. Cerebral Palsy

When Tommy Ritter was diagnosed with cerebral palsy, Dorothy went to war against the disease. She became the first secretary of the California Cerebral Palsy Association, a member of the Board of Governors of the Los Angeles County United Cerebral Palsy Association, Pacific regional vice-president and first female national vice-president of the United Cerebral Palsy Association, was appointed to the California Governor's Committee to Employ the Physically Handicapped, and for this work she was cited by President Eisenhower for "exceptional contributions." Dorothy was a driving force behind the organization and construction of the Charles LeRoy Lowman School for Physically Handicapped Children, and she was den mother for the Lowman School Pack 177 for Handicapped Cub Scouts.

Tex took Tommy with him to ballgames and personal appearances. Encouraged by the support of his parents, Tommy excelled at his studies. In later years Tex enjoyed talking with Tommy and his fellow law students (during this same period the well-rounded father conversed with John Ritter and his friends about theater and acting). Tom Ritter eventually produced television programs and documentaries dealing with a variety of subjects, including people with disabilities. He lectured widely on disability issues before local, state and national organizations, corporations, universities, and governmental agencies. Every year Tom interviews people with cerebral palsy for the United Cerebral Palsy Telethon. His career and attitude proclaim the victory won by the Ritters over cerebral palsy.

tured soloist and bass-fiddler; Rusty McDonald and Paul Buskirk were guitarists; the Skyline Boys were a quartet; and other musicians were in and out of the large group.

Tex emphasized the Western Revue because another musicians' strike again would shackle the recording industry for most of 1948. With the American Federation of Musicians scheduling a strike for January 1948, recording companies busily piled up records late in 1947. Tex and Lee Gillette cut seventeen sides in four sessions during the final week of 1947. The resulting records, along with re-releases, were rationed out during the strike year. The strike went on until December 1948, but during the year "Rock and Rye" reached the Top Five and "Pecos Bill" made the Top Fifteen. Both of these numbers were recorded during the December

30 session, and "Pecos Bill" was from the Walt Disney film, *Melody Time*. A re-release from 1945, the Tex Ritter standard "Rye Whiskey," rose to the Top Ten.

Another Top Ten hit, "Deck of Cards," was recorded during 1948, despite the musicians' strike. Before Tex left on a spring tour, he suggested to Lee Gillette that an offbeat religious recitation, "Deck of Cards," could be recorded without music. Tex left for the South, and while he was in Montgomery, Alabama, he received a phone call from Gillette to record the material. Gillette emphasized that the recording had to be less than three minutes, the limit preferred by disc jockeys. The resulting recitation, recorded in a Montgomery radio station, was brisk and sharp. "Deck of Cards" is the tale of a World War II soldier during the North African campaign who

Tex and guitarist Spud Goodale performing at a New Orleans children's hospital in 1949.

Tex and his band traveled in a station wagon, with a trailer for White Flash.

Bass fiddler Boots Gilbert with Tex and White Flash at a 1948 appearance.

Tex interrupted a Bingo and Coke party, but these Western-dressed fans are delighted to be with their hero.

was accused by his sergeant of playing cards in chapel. The soldier explains that the deck of cards served as his Bible and prayer book: "When I see the trey I think of the Father, the Son, and the Holy Ghost," for example, and "When I see the ten I think of the Ten Commandments God handed down to Moses. . . ." Tex shipped the recording from Montgomery by airplane, and in California the talented Buddy Cole added organ music in the background. "Deck of Cards" reached the Top Ten and became a favorite request on his tour appearances for the rest of his career.

Tex made another recitation recording, on June 25, 1948, at the Capitol studio in Hollywood. He dramatically recited "The Pledge of Allegiance" and "Lincoln's Gettysburg Address." Although the record did not become a best-seller, one side received a great deal of play for years. Many radio stations played the National Anthem or the Pledge of Allegiance at signoff, and upon receiving a free copy of this record, Tex Ritter's reading of the Pledge was aired every night. Although recitations were resorted to because of the musicians' strike, Tex was a natural at this form. In deep, authoritative tones he recited patriotic or religious material with sincerity, and recitations would become a growing part of his performance and recording career.

On tour, Tex and his band often were scheduled for several shows daily. At a theater there might be a live performance, then a western movie, followed by another live show. Tex carried a comedian, Slim Andrews, for several years and Hank Morton for another lengthy period. Tex interacted with his comedian, and provided a lot of laughs by himself. The band backed Tex in his

Steel guitarist Bonnie Dodd, lead guitarist Spud Goodale, Tex, unidentified, and bass fiddler Bob Morgan. Bonnie helped Tex write his hit, "You Will Have to Pay."

Slim Andrews and Spud Goodale holding Tex Ritter songbooks, which band members sold between shows.

most popular standards and in numbers appropriate to the occasion, and Tex often gave solo spots to band members who had written a song. At one point in the show Tex would dismiss his band and sit on a stool to become intimate with his audience. He made humorous comments, sang and played on his guitar, then delivered a mock-drunken version of "Rye Whiskey": "If the ocean was whiskey and I was a duck, I'd dive to the bottom and never come—hiccup!" Eddy Arnold's biographer, Don Cusic, related that after observing Tex on tour, Arnold began to dis-

miss his band and perform songs with only his guitar, and in time this acoustic set "would become the favorite part of his live performance."

In addition to influencing a notable star such as Arnold, Tex always was willing to help young performers. Not long after the war, for example, Tex encountered young Hank Thompson in Waco, Texas. Tex arranged for Hank to sign a contract with Capitol, and Thompson's first session in 1947 produced a dual hit record, "Humpty Dumpty Heart," which reached Number Two, and "Yesterday's Mail." Hank had hit songs during a five-decade span, and he was elected to the CMA Hall of Fame in 1989. Through the years Tex is generally acknowledged also to have aided the careers of Jim Reeves, Jan Howard, Charlie Walker, and Barbara Mandrell, among other young performers.

After the recording ban ended in December 1948, Tex recorded only twice in 1949, and four of the six sides were for children: "Jesus Loves Me," "I'll Be a Sunbeam," "Yankee Doodle," and "She'll Be Comin' Round the Mountain." In 1950 there were seven recording sessions, which included several more children's numbers. His only record to make the Top Ten in 1950 was "Daddy's Last Letter (A Letter From Korea)," a timely recitation recorded on September 26—a few months after the outbreak of combat in Korea. This September 26 recording session was produced by Ken Nelson. Nelson

In 1948 Tex took his Western Revue to Baltimore's Hippodrome, one of America's last vaudeville theaters.

was an experienced radio executive when he was hired by Capitol Records in 1946. Nelson would produce Ritter's sessions from 1950 until 1954, when he was appointed head of Capitol's Country Music Department. Lee Gillette then resumed producing the Ritter sessions, although Nelson would return from time to time. In 1951 Tex had only three sessions, recording ten sides, none of which were hits. There were four sessions in the first five months of 1952, but half of the sides were not even issued. Public tastes were changing rapidly: Eddy Arnold and Hank

Williams and other artists dominated country music, while the soaring popularity of television hastened the demise of B Westerns in the early 1950s. By 1952 Tex had not starred in a movie in seven years, and for the past few years his recording career had made little impression on the charts. With no recent hit records or movies, his tour bookings were not as choice or lucrative. Hollywood's Most Traveled Performer continued to work the road as his principal means of support, but he badly needed a hit.

After signing an autograph, Tex is amply rewarded by a little fan.

For years Hank Morton toured with Tex as comedian and bass fiddler.

Three members of the Western Revue at this Toronto appearance were female performers, including steel guitarist Bonnie Dodd (center) and Dorothy Fay (left).

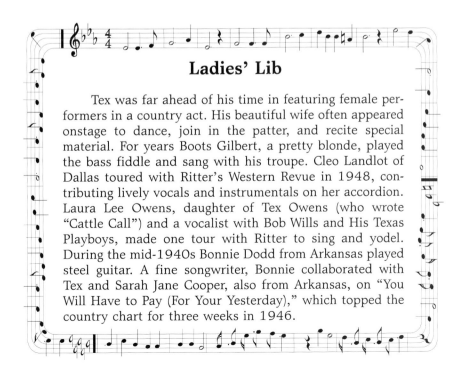

Ladies' Lib

Tex was far ahead of his time in featuring female performers in a country act. His beautiful wife often appeared onstage to dance, join in the patter, and recite special material. For years Boots Gilbert, a pretty blonde, played the bass fiddle and sang with his troupe. Cleo Landlot of Dallas toured with Ritter's Western Revue in 1948, contributing lively vocals and instrumentals on her accordion. Laura Lee Owens, daughter of Tex Owens (who wrote "Cattle Call") and a vocalist with Bob Wills and His Texas Playboys, made one tour with Ritter to sing and yodel. During the mid-1940s Bonnie Dodd from Arkansas played steel guitar. A fine songwriter, Bonnie collaborated with Tex and Sarah Jane Cooper, also from Arkansas, on "You Will Have to Pay (For Your Yesterday)," which topped the country chart for three weeks in 1946.

High Noon

Tex Ritter made *Flaming Bullets*, his last film as a singing cowboy, in 1945. He stayed busy with personal appearances and Capitol recording sessions, but after 1948 his records enjoyed only modest success. In 1950 Tex, with the Cass County Boys, performed "The Old Chisholm Trail" in *Holiday Rhythm*, a romantic comedy starring blonde Mary Beth Hughes. This minor film had no impact on his career, and by the early 1950s his lack of a recent hit had begun to affect the quality of his tour bookings. It was fitting that a Western movie would provide the musical hit he needed to rejuvenate his career.

High Noon, a major Western starring Gary Cooper, was filmed in 1951. The project was produced by Stanley Foreman, directed by Fred Zinnemann, and written by Carl Foreman, three talented moviemakers who had worked together on other noted films. A strong supporting cast included lovely Grace Kelly, Oscar-winner Thomas Mitchell (for his role in *Stagecoach*), Lloyd Bridges, Katy Jurado, Lee Van Cleef, and Robert Wilke. *High Noon* was filmed in black and white, achieving the realistic effect of a newsreel. The suspenseful story, climaxing in an inventive shootout, covered an hour and a half on a Sunday, and the final cut ran a taut eighty-five minutes.

But at a sneak preview, *High Noon* fell surprisingly flat with the audience. Kramer tightened the film and inserted a number of shots of ticking clocks, which greatly heightened the suspense. Kramer also instructed musical director Dimitri Tiomkin to compose a ballad which would run throughout the film. Despite Tiomkin's protests that he was not a songwriter, the gifted musician soon produced a melody

Gary Cooper and Grace Kelly in High Noon. *Although he did not appear onscreen, Tex made a major contribution to the success of the award-winning movie.*

with a driving beat. Ned Washington provided lyrics, and Elmo Williams, involved in the editing of *High Noon* and formerly a Capitol employee, suggested Tex Ritter as singer of the ballad, "Do Not Forsake Me, Oh My Darlin'."

Tiomkin called Tex on a Sunday and asked him to come to his home to study the ballad. Tex rounded up Merle Travis and another musician or two, then went to Tiomkin's house. Tex noticed a number of record albums around Tiomkin's piano: there were three or four by Burl Ives, two or three by Merle Travis—and one by Tex Ritter. The movie was explained to Tex, who also studied a number of photo stills from *High Noon*.

"It wasn't supposed to be Gary Cooper's voice necessarily; it could have been his thoughts," explained Tex. "But it was used instead of [instrumental] music to create the mood."

The musicians worked on the ballad and music, then Tex recorded "Do Not Forsake Me" for the soundtrack. *High Noon* was expected to become a popular release, and Tiomkin suggested that Tex record "Do Not Forsake Me" for Capitol. Capitol was reluctant, however, because cowboy songs and movie themes were not selling well as records. Tiomkin showed the song to Mitch Miller, who recorded it with Frankie Laine on Columbia Records. This news galvanized Capitol into action, and a recording session was hastily arranged for May 14, 1952.

Capitol released "Do Not Forsake Me" on June 21, 1952. Frankie Laine's version was released by Columbia a week later. *High Noon* would not hit the movie theaters for four more months, but a promotional campaign by Columbia quickly thrust the number onto the charts. In the meantime, Capitol producer Ken Nelson realized that the Tex Ritter recording lacked power without the steady tom-tom drumbeat. Nelson brought Lee Gillette into the studio to overdub the drumbeat onto the master, and the Ritter version without drums was recalled.

Tex sang "Do Not Forsake Me" in his deep, strong drawl. A violin and accordion added plaintive notes in the background, and the tom-tom effect drove the ballad relentlessly. Both the Ritter and Frankie Laine versions sold well, paving the way for the movie. When *High Noon* was released in the fall, Ritter's song—which was the only music on the soundtrack—contributed notably to a film which quickly became a Western classic. The popularity of *High Noon* then triggered explosive record sales. Frankie Laine's version eventually sold more than one million records and topped the pop charts. Tex Ritter's "Do Not Forsake Me" sold approximately 800,000 copies and reached *Billboard's* Top Ten "Honor Roll of Hits" for September

Tex and White Flash in front of the Granada Theatre in London. Tex retired White Flash soon after this tour.

1952. Ritter's version was Number One on Capitol's Western Best-Sellers List for three consecutive weeks, and stayed among the Top Ten of that list for eight months. For many of us who were captivated by *High Noon*, the only version of the title song that ever rang true was by Tex Ritter.

Tex went on his first European tour late in the summer of 1952, starring in a Wild West show. He performed "Do Not Forsake Me" for the first time in public to a London audience. His films had been shown throughout England during the 1930s and 1940s, and were the first Westerns to be televised over the BBC. Tex Ritter fans turned out in droves, and the two-week tour of England and France was extended by popular demand to seven weeks. In Paris, Tex and Dorothy had their first opportunity to see *High Noon*. Until the movie started they did not know if the music had been dubbed in French, but during the opening scene Tex was gratified to hear his own voice singing, with French subtitles.

The New York Film Critics voted *High Noon* the best picture of 1952 and designated Fred Zinnemann as best director, while the Screenwriters' Guild named Carl Foreman's script the year's best. Academy Award nominations went to *High Noon* for best picture, best actor, best direction, best screenplay, best film editing, best song, and best score.

When "Do Not Forsake Me" was first nominated for an Oscar, early in 1953, Dimitri Tiomkin called Tex, who had returned from his European tour. Initially, Tex was reluctant to commit to perform at the Academy Awards,

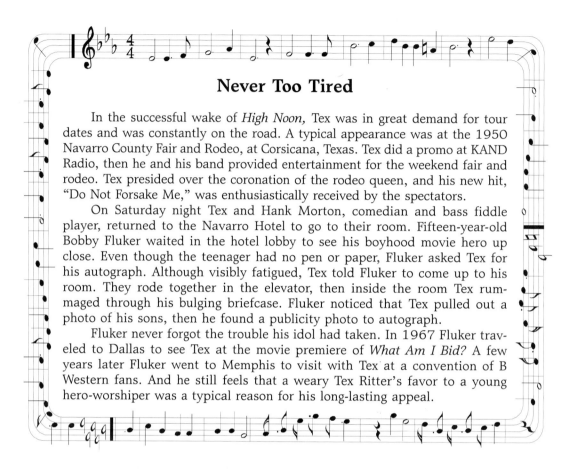

Never Too Tired

In the successful wake of *High Noon,* Tex was in great demand for tour dates and was constantly on the road. A typical appearance was at the 1950 Navarro County Fair and Rodeo, at Corsicana, Texas. Tex did a promo at KAND Radio, then he and his band provided entertainment for the weekend fair and rodeo. Tex presided over the coronation of the rodeo queen, and his new hit, "Do Not Forsake Me," was enthusiastically received by the spectators.

On Saturday night Tex and Hank Morton, comedian and bass fiddle player, returned to the Navarro Hotel to go to their room. Fifteen-year-old Bobby Fluker waited in the hotel lobby to see his boyhood movie hero up close. Even though the teenager had no pen or paper, Fluker asked Tex for his autograph. Although visibly fatigued, Tex told Fluker to come up to his room. They rode together in the elevator, then inside the room Tex rummaged through his bulging briefcase. Fluker noticed that Tex pulled out a photo of his sons, then he found a publicity photo to autograph.

Fluker never forgot the trouble his idol had taken. In 1967 Fluker traveled to Dallas to see Tex at the movie premiere of *What Am I Bid?* A few years later Fluker went to Memphis to visit with Tex at a convention of B Western fans. And he still feels that a weary Tex Ritter's favor to a young hero-worshiper was a typical reason for his long-lasting appeal.

Tex surrounded by properly attired young fans in England, where his films had been screened for more than a decade. Dorothy stands in the back.

thinking that there might be a conflict with a tour date. By now a number of artists had recorded "Do Not Forsake Me," but Tiomkin persuaded Tex that it was imperative that the performance should be delivered by the man who had originally sung the ballad so memorably on film.

With television only in its fifth year of commercial programming, NBC-RCA bid $100,000 for TV and radio rights to the awards ceremony. The twenty-fifth annual presentation of Oscars was scheduled for March 19, 1953. Bob Hope emceed Hollywood activities at the RKO Pantages Theatre, while a companion show was hosted by Conrad Nagel at the International Theatre in New York. The cameras switched back and forth from coast to coast, depending on whether the presenter or winner was in Hollywood or New York. The viewers of 1953 were unaccustomed to seeing such a large and glamorous assemblage of celebrities, and the Oscar show attracted the largest audience in the brief history of network TV.

On the evening of March 19, Tex Ritter sang "Do Not Forsake Me" before the first nationwide audience ever to watch the Academy Awards. His appearance on this notable evening was one of the personal highlights of his career, exceeded only by making his first film, *Song of the Gringo*. *High Noon* was awarded several Oscars, although Cecil B. DeMille's spectacular circus movie, *The Greatest Show on Earth*, won the best picture award. But Gary Cooper, who had received the best actor award in 1941 for *Sergeant York*, earned his second Oscar for his

Amen!

Tom Ritter recalled an evening during his boyhood when the family was invited to dinner by Jimmy and Inez Wakely. Tex was asked to say grace, and everyone bowed their heads. After the prayer ended, John Ritter's head remained bowed. Tex, under no illusions about his youngest son's meditation habits, quietly sidled over to the boy—and found him absorbed in the comic book in his lap.

ing technique predictably spawned imitation. Soon Frankie Laine, Rosemary Clooney, Gordon McCrea, Nat King Cole, Johnny Cash, and other popular singers performed title songs for motion pictures. Tex, naturally, was signed to sing ballads for other Westerns, with the hope that he could duplicate the magic of *High Noon*. In 1953 Tex sang for *The Marshal's Daughter*, a poor film which included old-timers such as Hoot Gibson and Johnny Mack Brown. Tex was one of the narrators for an excellent 1954 documentary, *The Cowboy*, which was produced and directed by Elmo Williams. The next year Tex sang the background music for *Wichita*, starring Joel

Tex with sons, Tommy and John.

grim portrayal of Marshal Will Kane. Oscars also were presented to Elmo Williams and Harry Gerstad for film editing, to Dimitri Tiomkin and Ned Washington for best song, and to Tiomkin for best scoring of a dramatic or comedy picture. Tiomkin's score, of course, consisted entirely of Tex Ritter's ballad, artfully utilized throughout the story like a Greek chorus.

The success of Tiomkin's innovative scor-

The cast of Apache Ambush *(1955) clustered around director Fred Sears. A bearded Tex stands next to star Bill Williams, whose New York accent proved unconvincing in a Western. Standing in back of everyone is old-timer Kermit Maynard, who had played in earlier Tex Ritter films.*

McCrea as Wyatt Earp. Also in 1955 Tex played a non-singing role in the low-budget, slow-moving *Apache Ambush*. Tex narrated *The First Badman*, a seven-minute Western cartoon that hit the screens in 1955. Tex sang and acted in a television episode of Dick Powell's *Zane Grey Theatre*, and he sang "Remember the Alamo" in a featurette released by Warner Brothers in 1956, *Down Liberty Road*. In 1957 Tex sang background music for *Trooper Hook*, starring Joel McCrea and Barbara Stanwyck.

Tex performed from the back of a truck at a 1953 rodeo in Pampa, Texas. After the 1952 release of High Noon, *"Do Not Forsake Me" became his most requested song.*

None of these projects captured the public imagination like *High Noon*, nor produced a hit song remotely comparable to "Do Not Forsake Me." But the old singing cowboy had helped make *High Noon* one of the most memorable Westerns in film history, while the title song became a permanent hit for him. Tex sang "Do Not Forsake Me" at countless personal appearances, and he realized the lasting impact of the ballad during a tour of England in May 1973. During thirty-one one-nighters, three in Scotland and the rest in England, the most requested song was "Do Not Forsake Me"— "which I sang for the first time in public in London twenty-one years before," he said.

Tex on Television

The success of "Do Not Forsake Me" from *High Noon* helped Tex land a TV series. He had entertained on Broadway, radio, movies, records, and the road, and during the 1950s, as television became America's dominant entertainment medium, Tex Ritter gravitated to TV.

Tex and his road show occasionally had been booked into the Fresno Barn by William B. Wagnon, Jr., a promoter who operated a number of California ballrooms. Bill Wagnon moved into the Los Angeles area early in 1952, leasing the Town Hall building in Compton, an L. A. suburb. A number of country barn dances had been staged in Compton's Town Hall, and Wagnon began to line up country and western acts for a *Town Hall Party* on Saturday nights. Wagnon's *Town Hall Party* would include such California-based artists as Merle Travis, Eddie Dean, and Wesley Tuttle, along with whatever *Grand Ole Opry* acts that might be on tour in California.

Town Hall Party attracted good crowds, and Wagnon persuaded radio station KFI to run an hour of his live entertainment. *Town Hall Party* aired each Saturday night at 8:00. A Los Angeles version of the *Grand Ole Opry* or Chicago's *National Barn Dance*, *Town Hall Party* appealed to the interest in country and western music that had been growing steadily for years on the West Coast. KFI was an NBC affiliate, and the popular new show soon was carried over the network in certain areas. Wagnon then sold Town Hall Party to a new Los Angeles television station, KTTV, Channel 11. *Town Hall Party* was televised from 10:00 until midnight. Fascinated by the novelty of a local barn dance on live television, C & W fans flocked to *Town Hall Party*. The telecast was extended an hour, to 1:00 A.M., and because the Saturday night shows were consistently sold out,

a non-televised version of the *Party* was staged on Friday nights.

Hoping to attract more lucrative sponsors for their promising show, program executives at KTTV and KFI asked Wagnon to find a big-name star to headline *Town Hall Party*. Tex Ritter had just made his memorable appearance on the first nationally televised Academy Awards ceremony, his distinctive voice was heard enhancing the popular film *High Noon* in theaters across America, and "Do Not Forsake Me" was a hit record. Tex already had worked with Wagnon, as well as with most of the *Town Hall* performers. Approached by Wagnon, Tex was delighted to accept a regular—and well-paid—television assignment.

Cast of Town Hall Party. *Tex, standing at left, hosted the show for eight years, 1953-61. Standing in the back row at far right and wearing a white hat and tie is Johnny Bond, Tex's close friend and music publishing partner.*

So Long, White Flash

Tex rode his splendid mount, White Flash, during the last
four years of his music career, and he often took his horse on tour.
For more than a decade Tex hauled White Flash to rodeos and fairs and
parades, riding astride a beautifully decorated saddle. Tex also led White
Flash onstage, where the horse would perform tricks, then execute a bow to
the audience. The team of Tex Ritter and White Flash became as well known
throughout rural America as Tom Mix and Tony had to an earlier generation of
cowboy fans.

In 1953 Tex retired White Flash to the Lazy TNT. But two years later he sold
the little ranch, and White Flash was pastured in Bouquet Canyon near Kernville,
where Tex had filmed movies, nearly a hundred miles north of Los Angeles.

Rex Allen, who had become the last of the singing cowboys in 1950, ran mares
on a ranch in Bouquet. He had noticed an old white horse in a pasture. One day
Allen recognized Tex Ritter, "talking soft and low, while the horse stood with his
head over the cowboy's shoulders." Allen observed "a comradeship that you see
only when a horse and a man come to mean a lot to each other over the years."

Allen was impressed. "The fact that he'd travel a hundred miles or so
over busy weekend freeways just to talk to that old horse tells me what
kind of man Tex Ritter really was."

Sadly, by the time White Flash was twenty-five he had gone
blind, and in 1961 Tex had him put to sleep.

In 1953 Tex began eight years as headliner and host of *Town Hall Party*. It was a happy cast, and Tex Ritter's presence stimulated the growing popularity of the show. Armed Forces Television exhibited *Town Hall Party* overseas, and KCOP, Channel 13, televised a two-hour *Town Hall Party* beginning each weekday afternoon at 4:00. In conjunction with *Town Hall Party*, Tex hosted a C & W music show over KFI (two decades earlier Tex worked as emcee and featured performer on the *WHN Barn Dance*, and of course he had a strong radio background during the 1930s in New York). *Town Hall*

Party was able to book many attractive guest stars, most notably Gene Autry. The two great singing cowboys, Gene and Tex, appeared together on May 8, 1954, and Gene later returned for a second guest appearance on *Town Hall Party*.

In 1954, with television having stabilized his career, Tex and Dorothy decided to move their home to Toluca Lake in the San Fernando Valley. The neighborhood around their Van Nuys ranch had grown considerably. When an elementary school was built near the Lazy TNT, Tex had to ride White Flash through the school-

So long, White Flash

not on the road. And when he was on an extended tour, Dorothy liked to engage in redecorating projects. She was a gifted hostess, entertaining her friends with grace and style, and sometimes throwing a surprise party when Tex returned from the road. There were tall eucalyptus trees in the yard, dressing rooms and a guest house near the swimming pool, and a handsome den for Tex, decorated with guns and saddles and other Western artifacts. On Saturday afternoons during the fall, Tommy Ritter remembered surrendering the television set to his father, as Tex settled down to watch football games in the comfort of his new home.

Tex and Johnny Bond, partners in Vidor Publications. Bond was a singer, guitarist, and songwriter who appeared in Tex Ritter movies and in Town Hall Party. *After Tex died, Bond wrote a biography of his friend.*

yard to the nearby riverbed for exercise. After a subdivision was developed, "I couldn't work my horse in the arena out by the barn because the neighbors would come and hang over the fence." Another subdivision took the place of a walnut orchard in front of the Lazy TNT. "Shortly after that they cemented the river bed for flood control," recalled Tex, "so it was no good for riding there anymore."

The Lazy TNT, which had been the Ritter home for nearly a decade and a half, was sold. The family moved into a handsome, two-story colonial style house with tall columns in front and a swimming pool in back. The big Toluca Lake house would be home for more than a decade, but Tex never lost his affection for the Lazy TNT. Johnny Bond related that occasionally, when Tex was riding home with him after a performance of *Town Hall Party*, Ritter would ask Bond to drive by the old Van Nuys ranch, where he liked to sit in silence for a few minutes before proceeding on to Toluca Lake. But like the Lazy TNT, the colonial house at Toluca Lake became a gathering place when Tex was

Johnny Bond, who had worked in Tex Ritter movies in the early 1940s, was hired as a scriptwriter and performer on *Town Hall Party* in December 1953, and he would stay with the show until it ended early in 1961. Born in Oklahoma in 1915, Bond was fascinated by country music. He became a fine guitarist, and in Oklahoma City formed a trio with Jimmy Wakely and Scotty Harrell. Moving to Hollywood in 1940, the trio began to appear in Westerns with such stars as Tex Ritter and Gene Autry. Bond worked on personal appearance tours with Autry, and on Gene's *Melody Ranch* show on CBS Radio. A prolific songwriter, he began recording with Decca in 1941, and formed his own band, the Red River Valley Boys.

In 1949 he organized his own music publishing company, Red River Songs, Inc.

A few years earlier Tex ostensibly had formed his own publishing firm, Tex Ritter Music Company, Inc. The Tex Ritter Music Company was affiliated with Capitol Records and Tex was not involved in "his" company's operations. After a few years the company ceased to function. But aspiring composers constantly gave Tex unpublished songs, which he jammed into the bulging briefcase he lugged everywhere, and he was in constant contact with talented performers and songwriters on *Town Hall Party.*

Johnny Bond realized that he and Tex were in "an ideal spot in which a music publisher might possibly build a valuable catalog of copyrights." Johnny and Tex, of course, could use their company for their own material. Tex and Wagnon quickly saw the potential, and the three men decided to become partners in a publishing venture designed to assemble a catalog of songs and find talented artists to record the music. Searching for a company label, Bond said that the partners pooled the first names of their wives: both Tex and Johnny were married to a Dorothy, while Wagnon's wife was Veva ("Viva" according to the sound). A shortened combination of Viva and Dorothy translated to "Vidor," and

The Western Ramblers

Despite a regular schedule of television and radio programs, Tex still worked the road at every opportunity. During the mid-1950s he formed a new band, renaming the group the "Western Ramblers." The Western Ramblers included Doug Coats, Jerry Dykes and Johnny Smith on guitars, Maurice Anderson on steel guitar, Lonny Campbell on drums, and Jess Hudson on electric piano and steel guitar. One night in 1957, while traveling on the Bessemer Highway in Alabama, Tex and the Western Ramblers stopped at an all-night diner near Birmingham. Seventeen-year-old Henry Strzlecki watched the tall Texan lead his men inside and he was inspired to write a song. Strzlecki penned "Long Tall Texan," which would sell millions of records.

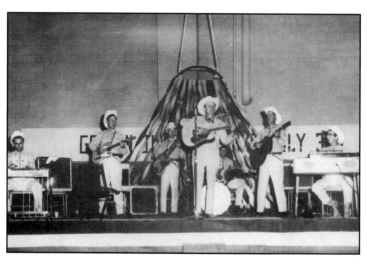

Tex and the Western Ramblers playing in the high school gym at little Buhl, Idaho, in 1956.

the new firm was called Vidor Publications, Inc. An office was set up in an upstairs suite at 5927 Sunset Boulevard in Hollywood, and when he was not on the road, Tex would amble to his Vidor desk late each morning.

The first song in Vidor's catalog, "Remember the Alamo," had been given to Tex by Jane Bower when he was on tour in San Antonio. Johnny Bond recorded "Remember the Alamo" for Columbia Records, and through the years a number of other artists covered the heroic ballad on various labels. Tex recorded it during a 1955 Capitol session, and the next year he sang it in the Warner Brother featurette, *Down Liberty Road.* Providing a nice supplementary income for Tex and Bond and

Wagnon, Vidor catalogued numerous songs that were written and recorded by *Town Hall Party* artists. When *Town Hall Party* finally ended its run in 1961, Wagnon sold his one-third interest in Vidor to his two partners, who eventually moved their headquarters to Nashville.

Throughout the run of *Town Hall Party*, Tex worked several recording sessions each year for Capitol, produced either by Ken Nelson or Lee Gillette. After the success of "Do Not Forsake Me" from *High Noon*, he continued to record movie theme songs, including title ballads he sang for Western soundtracks: "The Marshal's

Daughter" (recorded in 1953), "Wichita" (1955), and "Trooper Hook" (1957). Other films that did not include Tex on their soundtracks yielded songs that he recorded: "The San Antone Story" (recorded in 1953, from the 1953 Western *San Antone*, starring Rod Cameron); "A Whale of a Tale" (recorded in 1954, after being sung by Kirk Douglas in *20,000 Leagues Under the Sea*); "The Last Frontier" (1955, from a Western of the same title starring Victor Mature, Guy Madison, and Robert Preston); and "The Searchers" (1956, from the classic John Wayne Western, *The Searchers*). On April 16, 1956, when Tex recorded "The Searchers," he also cut "The Wayward Wind," which sold well and which became the opening song for his road show. Tex also continued to record children's songs and religious music, as well as such Christmas tunes as "Old Tex Kringle."

During this period long-playing albums were introduced, and Tex went on to record dozens of LPs. He began with a pair of extended play 45 RPM records. Popular for a short time before the twelve-inch 33 RPM LPs became common, the extended 45s had two songs on each side of the record. Entitled *Tex Ritter Sings*, his first extended play 45 featured "High Noon" (the movie title was more recognizable than "Do Not Forsake Me"), along with "I'm Wasting My Tears on You," "Green Grow the Lilacs," and "Jealous Heart." The second extended play 45, *Deck of Cards*, naturally included "Deck of Cards," while also offering "High Noon," "Green Grow the Lilacs," and "Conversation With a Gun."

His first LP, *Songs of the Western Screen*, was released in 1958 and contained eleven movie songs, including "High Noon," "The Searchers," "Wichita," "The Marshal's Daughter," "Trooper Hook," and "Remember the Alamo." The next year Capitol released *Psalms*, which had been recorded on June 25 and July 1, 1958, in the new Capitol Tower. Kathryn Julye arranged the musical background and played the harp, while Tex delivered a magnificent reading of fifteen of the biblical songs and prayers known as the Psalms. The album enjoyed notable success, encouraging Tex and Capitol to continue making religious recordings.

At this time Marty Robbins scored a sensational hit with the Western ballad "El Paso," a tragic tale of fatal shootouts triggered by a saloon girl. Robbins then recorded an LP, *Gunfighter Ballads and Trail Songs*, released in 1959 and featuring "El Paso," traditional cowboy songs, and ballads from Western movies. Inspired by the success of the type of material he had collected and sung since the 1920s, Tex Ritter began putting together an album of folk songs and cowboy ballads. There were five recording sessions in 1959, produced by Lee Gillette, and with accompaniment by Paul Sells on accordion, Skeets McDonald on bass, guitarists Merle Travis, Johnny Bond, Roy Lanham and Joe Maphis, and the Jack Halloran Quartet. The album was entitled *Blood on the Saddle*, an accurate indication of the tragic and sometimes grisly nature of the album's twelve songs. The album's title number, a 1945 hit for Tex that was written by his old friend, Everett Cheetham, was about an injured rodeo cowboy lying in "*a great, big puddle*" of his own blood. Other songs included: "Little Joe the Wrangler," a ballad about a young horse wrangler trampled to death in a cattle stampede; two traditional songs about dying cowboys, "Streets of Laredo" and "Bury Me Not on the Lone Prairie"; and "Billy the Kid" and "Sam Bass," a pair of recitations about legendary outlaws who were shot to death. This dark mood was relieved somewhat by two Tex Ritter folk standards, "Rye Whiskey" and "Boll Weevil." But Ritter's deep love for traditional Western music dovetailed with the public's interest in the Old West. Prime-time television was filled with weekly Western series, while quality Western films graced American movie screens, and *Blood on the Saddle* generated strong appeal, selling profitably for years.

The popularity of Western television series led to numerous TV appearances for Tex Ritter. He played a guest role on *Zane Grey Theatre* with Dick Powell, on *The Rebel* with Nick Adams, on *Shotgun Slade* with Scott Brady, and on *The Adventures of Rin Tin Tin* with the famous dog. Tex often guest-starred on Red Foley's *Ozark Jubilee*, which aired on NBC-TV from 1954 through 1960, and he was one of the co-stars for an *Ozark Jubilee* summer replacement show, *Five Star Jubilee* (the other stars, who rotated on a weekly basis, were Rex Allen, Jimmy Wakely, Carl Smith, and Snooky Lanson). In 1959 Screen Gems contracted with Bill Wagnon to film a thirty-minute version of

A Springfield, Missouri, movie theater was the home of Five Star Jubilee. *The five stars, who alternated weekly as host, were (from left): Tex, Jimmy Wakely, Snooky Lanson, Carl Smith, and Rex Allen.*

Tex appeared on Art Linkletter's popular TV show. Along with many other country stars, Tex wore "Nudies," Western suits designed by "Nudie the Tailor."

the three-hour *Town Hall Party* for syndication. The syndicated show was called *Ranch Party*. Tex headlined *Ranch Party*, which included the cast of *Town Hall Party* and guest stars. Thirty-nine episodes were filmed in Hollywood at the Art Linkletter Theater on Vine Street. (In the early years of television, a series consisted of thirty-nine weekly episodes; the best thirteen episodes were re-run during the summer to round out the fifty-two weeks of a year.) *Ranch Party* was distributed nationwide, but no further episodes were filmed.

After eight seasons *Town Hall Party* finally ran its course, shutting down early in 1961. But Tex appeared on Art Linkletter's popular show, and in the future he would make frequent guest appearances on various programs. In 1960, when Marty Robbins was unavailable to perform the theme music he had sung for the Gary Cooper Western *The Hanging Tree*, Tex sang the ballad on the *Ford Startime Academy Award Theater.*

Tex had maintained a busy personal appearance schedule during his *Town Hall Party* years. Dorothy Ritter answered an appeal from a South African organization of parents of victims of cerebral palsy and put together a benefit show to raise money in South Africa to build a hospital. She lined up Tex, of course, along with Merle Travis, Zsa Zsa Gabor, Pat O'Brien, and a few other performers. Encountering the Pope on the trip, Tex joked to Merle Travis, "This is a fine place for a southern Methodist." Indeed, Tex was able to practice his boyhood religion regularly during the early 1960s. *Town Hall Party* often kept him home on weekends, and he sang in the choir of the First Methodist Church of North Hollywood.

A few months after *Town Hall Party* ended, Tex accepted the lead in *The Stovepipe Hat*—his first play since *Mother Lode* on Broadway back in 1934. *The Stovepipe Hat* was billed as "A New Star Spangled Musical" about Lincoln's famous hat and his wife and John Wilkes Booth. Tex was "a sort of singing-host-narrator," who delivered a prologue to each scene with a narration or song. The play opened at the Music Box Theater in Hollywood on September 20,

Tex found a solid outlet for his recordings with LP albums.

Tex with Dariel Tardiff, one of the forty cast members of the short-lived musicial The Stovepipe Hat.

1961. But *The Stovepipe Hat* did not work with audiences and closed three days later.

The Stovepipe Hat, like many other entertainment events of 1961 and the next four years, attempted to capitalize on the Civil War Centennial, 1961-1965. In this vein, early in 1961 Tex and Lee Gillette put together *The Lincoln Hymns*, an album of religious music favored by the Civil War president. Backed by Ralph Carmichael's Chorus and Orchestra, Tex sang "Let Me Freely Yield," "Grace Has Set Me Free," and ten other traditional hymns. The sixteen-voice chorus produced a large and impressive sound, but, as Tex ruefully admitted, "*The Lincoln Hymns* sold less than any album I ever made."

However, one of the most popular of all Tex Ritter recordings came out of this album's sessions. The album was recorded on February 1-3, 1961. During the February 3 session Tex also recorded "I Dreamed of a Hillbilly Heaven." The song was written by Eddie Dean and Hal Sothern, and Dean made the country chart with it in 1955. Four or five other artists recorded it, but Dean tried for years to persuade Tex to cover

it on a major label. Dean and Sothern agreed that Tex could revise the lyrics, and Ritter's changes were so considerable that they offered him one-third of the royalties on his version of "Hillbilly Heaven."

"Well," Tex laughed, "I took it."

And he deserved it. Tex updated the lyrics, mentioning a wide variety of artists that he found in "the Big Tally Book," and closing with himself. Feeling that the strong backup of Ralph Carmichael's Chorus and Orchestra would greatly aid the song, Tex convinced Lee Gillette to cut "Hillbilly Heaven" during the album sessions. Then a Capitol executive came up with the promotional device of altering the lyrics to include a disc jockey's name on the acetate promotional copies sent to stations. Tex returned to the studio to insert the name of one disc jockey after another, pop DJs as well as country DJs. The strategy vaulted "Hillbilly Heaven" onto both pop and country charts, as disc jockeys played the clever song with their names on it over and over. "Hillbilly Heaven" reached the Top Five on the country chart, and crossed over to the Top Twenty on the pop chart. And, for

Dodger Fan

A lifelong sports enthusiast, Tex was delighted when major league baseball came to California. In 1958 the Brooklyn Dodgers moved to Los Angeles, while the New York Giants transferred to San Francisco. Tex made sure that Vidor Publications purchased box seats for Dodger games. The Dodgers were one of the most famous teams in baseball. Los Angeles baseball fans were treated to Duke Snider, Gil Hodges, Don Drysdale, Carl Furillo, Sandy Koufax and company in action against other National League teams.

Tex happily manned the Vidor box at the Los Angeles Coliseum, a vast football stadium with a tall screen in the short left field (a proper ballpark, Dodger Stadium, was under construction in Chavez Ravine). Tex soon became friendly with many of the Dodgers, a number of whom were country music fans. In 1959 the Dodgers won the World Series against the Chicago White Sox, and Tex, who was provided tickets by Gene Autry, hugely enjoyed games three, four and five in L. A.

During the 1961 season Tex and Dorothy threw a memorable party for the Dodgers. Tex emptied his freezer of wild game he had collected on hunting trips, Gil Hodges tended bar, and Don Drysdale and other players sang while Tex and Johnny Bond played guitar. That same year Gene Autry became owner of an expansion team, the California Angels, and Tex had a chance to see American League clubs. When the Dodgers swept the 1963 World Series from the New York Yankees, Tex was furnished with tickets by Wally Moon, a Dodger outfielder who had played at Texas A&M.

the rest of his career, "I Dreamed of a Hillbilly Heaven" became one of the most requested songs when Tex made personal appearances. (After Patsy Cline, Cowboy Copas and Hawkshaw Hawkins were killed in a plane crash in March 1963, Tex led a tribute in Kansas City by singing a special version of "Hillbilly Heaven," featuring the names of the dead stars.)

Capitol soon followed the success of this hit record with the album *Hillbilly Heaven*. In addition to "I Dreamed of a Hillbilly Heaven," many of his other hits were included: "High Noon," "Jingle, Jangle, Jingle," "Jealous Heart," "Deck of Cards," "Green Grow the Lilacs," "There's a New Moon Over My Shoulder," and "The Pledge of Allegiance." Recorded in July 1961, *Hillbilly Heaven* sold well, like most Tex Ritter albums. The fan base Tex had built with his sixty movies, hit records, and countless personal appearances

was reflected by the consistent success of his LP albums.

His next album afforded Tex a unique experience. *Stan Kenton! Tex Ritter!* was recorded on March 26, 29 and 30, 1962, with Stan Kenton's Orchestra. The album offered "High Noon," "Red River Valley," "Wagon Wheels," "Cool Water," "Home on the Range," and other Western songs. Like Tex, Stan Kenton was an original Capitol recording artist, and his orchestra enjoyed a popular following. Tex, as always, reflected his deep feeling for Western music with a strong performance in his flavorful accent. At the end of a long recording session, Kenton's musicians, visibly impressed, rose from their chairs and gave Tex a standing ovation.

Later in the year Lee Gillette, who owned a yacht, decided to mix business with pleasure by sailing to Mexico to record a Tex Ritter album, *Border Affair*. Tex worked recording sessions in Mexico City. Gillette produced these sessions,

Tex made regular television appearances on variety and country shows. In 1970 Tex and Roy Acuff were guests on ABC's popular Johnny Cash Show. (Photo by Les Leverett.)

Despite all of his accompaniments the songs on this album were undistinguished. For years most Tex Ritter recordings had been produced with the backup sounds of a full orchestra and a singing group or chorus. Although "Hillbilly Heaven" and a few other numbers certainly had benefited from this big accompaniment, Tex began to feel that a large backup was not the best sound for the cowboy ballads and folk songs that were nearest his heart. Yet the orchestral and choral backup was a major part of the "Nashville Sound" that had begun to dominate country music in the late 1950s. During the late 1940s Eddy Arnold, who eventually would spend more time at Number One than any other country artist, began to cross over to the pop charts with many of his country hits. Tex Ritter also enjoyed a certain amount of crossover success in this period, but most country hits that made the pop charts had been re-recorded by pop artists. The really big money in the music industry was made from the vast pop audiences, and Eddy Arnold and other country artists tried to move toward mainstream music. Arnold's sound was smooth, and he became more of a crooner. During this period the Grand Ole Opry helped Nashville became a center of country music, with recording studios and song publishers and talented musicians clustered there. Country music began to lose its twang as the sounds of the steel guitar and fiddle disappeared, replaced by orchestral strings and backup groups like the Jordanaires and the Anita Kerr Singers.

This new Nashville Sound pleased the younger generation of country fans while attracting mainstream audiences. Although Buck Owens and his pop-country "Bakersfield Sound" maintained a country presence in California, country music now was dominated by Nashville. After three decades in Hollywood, Tex Ritter felt strong pressures to move to Nashville.

while Ralph Carmichael conducted an orchestra of Mexican musicians. Thirteen songs—including such material as "High Noon," "Tennessee Waltz," and "San Antonio Rose"—were never completed or released. But eleven others, sung by Tex in Spanish with the accompaniment of mariachi and marimba bands, were made into the album *Border Affair*. *Border Affair* featured "Guadalajara," "Cielito Lindo," "La Cucaracha," and other traditional Mexican numbers.

On November 27, 1963, just five days after President John F. Kennedy was assassinated and one day after his nationally televised funeral, Tex went to the Capitol Tower to record "Dark Day in Dallas." Written in the wrenching aftermath of the assassination by a member of the Boll Weevils, "Dark Day in Dallas" was a musical lament over the tragic event. Capitol decided not to issue "Dark Day," but a few months later Tex began recording *The Friendly Voice of Tex Ritter*. Tex was backed up on this album by the King Sisters, Johnny Bond and young Glen Campbell on guitar, and Ralph Carmichael and his Orchestra.

Living Legend

Rock 'n roll exploded in popularity during the 1950s, dominating the music scene and threatening, among other genres, country music. The Country Music Disc Jockey Association, organized in 1954, went defunct in 1958. Just four months later, the Country Music Association was formed from the membership and monetary remains of the CMDJA. Country artists, DJs, and record company executives organized in an attempt to defend their shrinking industry, with an immediate goal of securing more radio exposure for country music. The CMA would prove instrumental in reversing the course of country music, and Tex Ritter was in the vanguard of the new organization. In August 1958, shortly after the CMA was founded, Vidor Publications submitted a $30 check for dues, and Tex soon became a board member.

In 1960 personable Jo Walker was hired as executive director of the CMA, a post she would hold for more than three decades. Although Nashville record labels were merely branch offices in the 1950s, Ken Nelson of Capitol and RCA's Steve Sholes committed their companies to the struggle. Jo Walker led a campaign to convince radio stations of the market potential for country music, and Tex would play a major role in this effort.

At the April 1963 meeting of the CMA board of directors held in Los Angeles, Tex was elected to succeed Gene Autry as president. Within a month live promotional programs showcasing the CMA were presented to radio executives in New York, Chicago, Detroit, Toronto, and Los Angeles. Tex hosted these live performances, which were written and produced by Joe Allison, then recorded by RCA and packaged by Capitol. The CMA sent copies of the album to each person who had attended one of the shows. Such efforts, along with the growing popularity of country music, stimulated the number of full-time country stations from only eighty-one in 1961 to more than six hundred just eight years later.

Tex immersed himself in the activities of the CMA, and was reelected to the presidency in 1964. After the CMA established a Country Music Hall of Fame, it was imperative to fund and construct a building to house the organization and its museum. President Ritter was instrumental in launching money-raising endeavors and planning this impressive structure. First elected to the CMA Hall of Fame in 1961 were Jimmie Rodgers, Hank Williams, and industry executive Fred Rose. In 1962 Roy Acuff was added to this select group. No one was voted in the next year, but a fifth Hall of Fame member was to be inducted on the evening of November 6, 1964.

The occasion was the premier of the bio-

Country Music Association board meeting in January 1962. Tex stands at right.

Roy Acuff, Gene Autry, and Tex at the 38th anniversary of the Grand Ole Opry on November 1, 1963. Tex was replacing Gene as president of the CMA. (Photo by Les Leverett.)

graphical film about Hank Williams, *Your Cheatin' Heart*, held at Nashville's Loew's Theater. Johnny Bond related that Tex was set up to believe that the new Hall of Fame member was Ernest Tubb (who would be voted in the next year). As CMA president, Tex planned to escort Tubb onto the stage after the announcement was made. Before *Your Cheatin' Heart* was shown, Tex helped with various ceremonies. Then Frances Preston, chairman of the CMA board of directors, took the stage to praise and announce the winner:

> This year's choice is one of the most worthy that will ever be made in the annals of our field of endeavor. His story can never be completely told because it would take more hours than we can count to praise his artistry, his contributions, and his devotion to his chosen work.
>
> He has inspired and shaped the lives of many young entertainers, not only with a kind word, a bit of advice or a helping hand,

but by setting an example that could only be an inspiration to anyone who is fortunate enough to know him. Outside of the fact that he has excelled as a performer at every facet of show business and is *one of our great living legends* [author's italics], his personal dedication to his fellow artists is a beautiful thing to behold. . . .

He is powerful, yet gentle. He is commanding, yet attentive. He is forceful, yet compassionate. When you talk, he listens—when he talks, everybody listens. If personal problems are being discussed, they are never his. If there is an inconvenience, it is never his. But when you need him, he is always there.

As the name of the recipient was about to be announced, Tex stood to walk over to Ernest Tubb. When the name "Tex Ritter" boomed over the PA system, the theater erupted in applause. Totally astonished, Tex turned from Ernest Tubb, and the applause followed him as he went onstage to express his surprise and appreciation and to embrace the plaque. His plaque, which erroneously listed the birthdate concocted by the old movie publicist, "January 12, 1907," summed up his Hall of Fame career:

> ALUMNUS UNIVERSITY OF TEXAS. ONE OF AMERICA'S MOST ILLUSTRIOUS AND VERSATILE STARS OF RADIO, TELEVISION, RECORDS, MOTION PICTURES, AND BROADWAY STAGE. UNTIRING PIONEER AND CHAMPION OF THE COUNTRY AND WESTERN MUSIC INDUSTRY. HIS DEVOTION TO HIS GOD, HIS FAMILY, AND HIS COUNTRY IS A CONTINUING INSPIRATION TO HIS COUNTLESS FRIENDS THROUGHOUT THE WORLD.

The first three members of the CMA Hall of Fame were deceased: Jimmie Rodgers (in 1933), Hank Williams (1952), and Fred Rose (1954). But Tex Ritter, at the age of fifty-nine, remained vigorous and in good voice. Although no more Broadway work appeared in his future, for the final decade of his life he stayed active in the other venues cited on his Hall of Fame plaque. Tex was a continuing presence on radio and television; he starred in two more motion pictures, appeared in another, and made a few other short features; his devotion to his God,

Music City, U.S.A.

The capital of Tennessee was founded in 1779 as a stockaded settlement beside the Cumberland River. Within five years Fort Nashborough was given the name Nashville. It became Tennessee's capital in 1843, and twelve years later the handsome State Capitol was completed on a prominent hill. In December 1864 one of the last major battles of the Civil War was fought in the area where Tex Ritter later would make his home.

By the twentieth century there were more than a dozen colleges and universities in Nashville, and the city boasted one of the finest park systems in the nation. From its inception during the 1920s, the Grand Ole Opry made Nashville a focal point of country music. In 1942 Opry star Roy Acuff and gifted songwriter Fred Rose formed Acuff-Rose Publications, which became a driving force in country music. During the years following World War II, Nashville became the home to more and more music publishing companies and recording facilities. The music industry began to center around the district southwest of downtown known as "Music Row," which became a mecca for country artists and tourists, and where the Country Music Hall of Fame would be built. By the 1960s, when Tex Ritter moved to town, the enormous popularity of the "Nashville Sound" completed the rise of Nashville as the "Capital of Country Music" and as "Music City, U.S.A."

his family, and his country became increasingly manifest; and he persistently championed the C & W music industry in a variety of ways, including endless personal appearances which seemed to range farther every year. The election of Tex Ritter to the CMA Hall of Fame solidified his position as a country music legend, a status that was increasingly confirmed with every passing year. After four decades of studying and collecting and singing and promoting western and folk music, Tex Ritter had become a living legend.

Tex was offered a lucrative job as co-host of the all-night show at Nashville's WSM, the 50,000-watt radio station which had created the Grand Ole Opry and which was one of the foundation stones of country music. *Opry Star Spotlight* had become an enormous hit since Ralph Emery had taken over the host's seat in 1957. Emery had a knack for making guests relaxed and comfortable, and a parade of country stars came to his show, often singing their latest hits, accompanying themselves on a guitar or

on the piano he kept in his studio. The music was good and the talk was rich, but in 1964 Emery left the show he had led to immense popularity. When the ratings dropped under Emery's successor, WSM executives felt that legendary country

Tex and Nashville Mayor Beverly Briley standing in front of the new Country Music Hall of Fame and Museum. As CMA president, Tex worked on plans for the building, while Mayor Briley donated the land.

Tex at center stage in the famous old Ryman Auditorium, built as a tabernacle in 1892 and home of the Grand Ole Opry *from 1943 to 1974. (Photo by Les Leverett.)*

Awards, and More Awards

An accurate gauge of a living legend is the number of awards he receives during his lifetime. The award for which Tex Ritter is most famous was his induction as the fifth member of the Country Music Hall of Fame. Later Tex received the CMA Founding President Award for his back-to-back terms as president, 1963-65. In 1962 he was awarded membership into the Aksarben (Nebraska) Western Hall of Fame at Omaha "for being a favorite Western entertainer of young and old alike."

Roy Acuff and Gene Autry were headliners for a testimonial dinner for Tex in 1966. Tex was voted Man of the Year by the Academy of Country Music and the Western Apparel Market. In 1969 Governor Preston Smith of Texas named Tex a "Most Notable Son and Ambassador of Good Will." Two years later he was admitted to the Nashville Songwriters Association Hall of Fame. And during nearly four decades of personal appearances, Tex was the gracious recipient of almost countless local awards and honors as he brought his music to his fans.

Bond already had opened an office for Vidor Publications in Nashville, and now Ritter himself was pulled toward "Music City, U. S. A."

His home and family were in California. But Tex always had gone where his work beckoned, and Dorothy and his sons were resigned to his long absences. Tom intended to study political science and pursue a law degree as his father had done; after finishing Hollywood High School, he would go on to study at the University of California at Berkeley and at the University of Southern California. From both parents John had inherited the gifts and instincts of an entertainer, and after graduation from Hollywood High he would earn a bachelor of fine arts degree at USC while moving toward a show business career. Considering these plans, the family decided to offer the Toluca Lake house for sale at a later date, while Tex moved to a Nashville hotel. Tom and John would continue their studies, and for the time being Dorothy would maintain her Los Angeles activities. She would visit Nashville periodically, and Tex would fly to California when his schedule permitted.

His schedule did not often permit. Tex worked *Opry Star Spotlight,* which ran weeknights from 11:00 P.M. until 5:00 in the morning. Grant Turner, veteran WSM announcer and widely admired as the "Voice of the Grand Ole Opry," agreed to run *Opry Star Spotlight* with Tex. Tex still slipped away whenever possible for personal appearances, sometimes touring from Thursday through Sunday.

After two months of the all-night show, Grant Turner decided to return to his customary early evening program. WSM persuaded Ralph Emery to come back to the show he had made famous. Emery initially felt misgivings about acquiring a co-star, much as Tex had experienced when he was

entertainer Tex Ritter might revive interest in *Opry Star Spotlight.*

During recent years Tex frequently had traveled to Nashville for CMA board meetings, as well as for guest appearances at the Grand Ole Opry. At the same time that work for Tex and other country entertainers was drying up in California, Nashville was throbbing with opportunity for C & W performers. Tex and Johnny

On May 29, 1969, Texas Governor Preston Smith (left) honored Bob Wills and Tex as outstanding native Texans.

During their show, Emery worked the controls, while Tex sat across a table from Ralph, exchanging banter into a microphone and smoking a pipe. Sometimes the travel-weary Ritter dozed off during the wee hours, and during one nap pipe embers set his shirt front to smoldering. Emery ribbed Tex about his cowboy movies and his right-wing politics, and Ritter fired back with his usual quick humor. The good-natured repartee was punctuated by C & W music, by call-ins from listeners, and by visits from performers. Emery described his partner's deep interest and feel for country music, and pointed out that Tex Ritter's "cowboy image went hand in hand with the tastes of the working people." The vast audience of *Opry Star Spotlight* responded warmly to America's Most Beloved Cowboy.

In addition to their broadcast partnership, Tex, lonely apart from his family, and Emery, unmarried at the time, became close companions. Dorothy flew to Nashville once a month, usually arriving on a red-eye in the middle of the all-night show. Tex would have her driven to the studio, and Emery described Ritter's "look of adolescent love" when Dorothy, bringing cookies for the broadcast team, would arrive.

Ritter worked with Ralph Emery for sixteen months, until the spring of 1966. He became a regular member of the Grand Ole Opry, first performing in the Ryman Auditorium as a regular on June 12, 1965. Tex was comfortable performing at the Grand Ole Opry, and association with the "Mother Church of Country Music"

teamed with Wild Bill Elliott and then Johnny Mack Brown. But the duo of Tex Ritter and Ralph Emery proved to be a memorable combination on *Opry Star Spotlight*. In his best-selling autobiography, *Memories*, Emery recalled standing in line in 1943 in a Nashville department store at the age of ten to get an autograph of America's Most Beloved Cowboy. Even though Emery had worked with a galaxy of country stars, he genuinely admired Tex for his versatility as a Broadway actor, hero of more than sixty movies, and longtime recording artist. "He was a mammoth man in physique and character," stated Emery, "a Gibraltar of a human whose heart was his largest asset."

A *Warm* Welcome

When Tex moved to Nashville in 1965, he took his clothing and performing costumes, his briefcases, his favorite guitar, and even a few hunting rifles to the Andrew Jackson Hotel. Late in October 1965, Dorothy came to Nashville to help look for a suitable new home and to attend the annual CMA convention, where Tex would deliver a speech as outgoing president.

At noon on October 22, Tex and Dorothy were returning to the Andrew Jackson in a taxi. The street in front of the hotel was blocked with firetrucks, fighting a blaze at the Andrew Jackson. With dismay Tex realized that smoke was billowing out of his window. Firefighters kept the damage confined primarily to the Ritter room, but everything inside was lost. Not only did Tex lose his wardrobe, briefcases, guns, and guitar, but Dorothy lost several suitcases of clothing, including the evening gown she had brought for the CMA banquet and a full-length mink coat.

With his famous sense of humor, Tex remarked that he still had two suits: one he had sent to be cleaned, and the one he was wearing. The hotel provided a new room, but Tex soon moved to an apartment.

Tex and Ralph Emery enjoyed themselves while presiding over WSM's popular Opry Star Spotlight. (Photo by Les Leverett.)

added further to his fame and prestige as a performer.

Beginning in 1965, Tex recorded at Capitol's Nashville studio, with Ken Nelson as producer. A successful 1966 album, *The Best of Tex Ritter*, featured original recordings of "High Noon," "Rye Whiskey," "Jealous Heart," "Boll Weevil," "Hillbilly Heaven," and other Ritter standards. For his next album, *Sweet Land of Liberty*, Tex recorded "This Land is Your Land," "Lincoln's Gettysburg Address," "Remember the Alamo," "The Pledge of Allegiance," "Old Glory," and other patriotic material for a country accelerating an unpopular war effort in Vietnam. A 1967 single, "Just Beyond the Moon," reached the Top Fifteen, and was followed by an inspirational album, *Just Beyond the Moon*, which enjoyed strong sales. His next album, *Bump Tiddle Dee Bum Bum*, was a collection of twelve songs—such as "In the Misty Moonlight" and "You Don't Know Me"—by Cindy Walker, considered by many as the greatest female songwriter in the history of country music. Released in February 1968, *Bump Tiddle Dee Bum Bum* was another successful Ritter LP.

"Incomparable Tex Ritter continues to sell, and this year was no exception, particularly on album sales," admired the October 19, 1968, issue of *Record World*. "This great man is the artist emeritus at Capitol, having been the first Country and Western artist for the label back in its infancy."

The "artist emeritus" managed to find his

Tex and Roy Acuff at the Grand Ole Opry *on June 12, 1965, during Ritter's first performance as a regular on the Opry. (Photo by Les Leverett.)*

Tex starred in the 1966 Nashville production, The Girl From Tobacco Row.

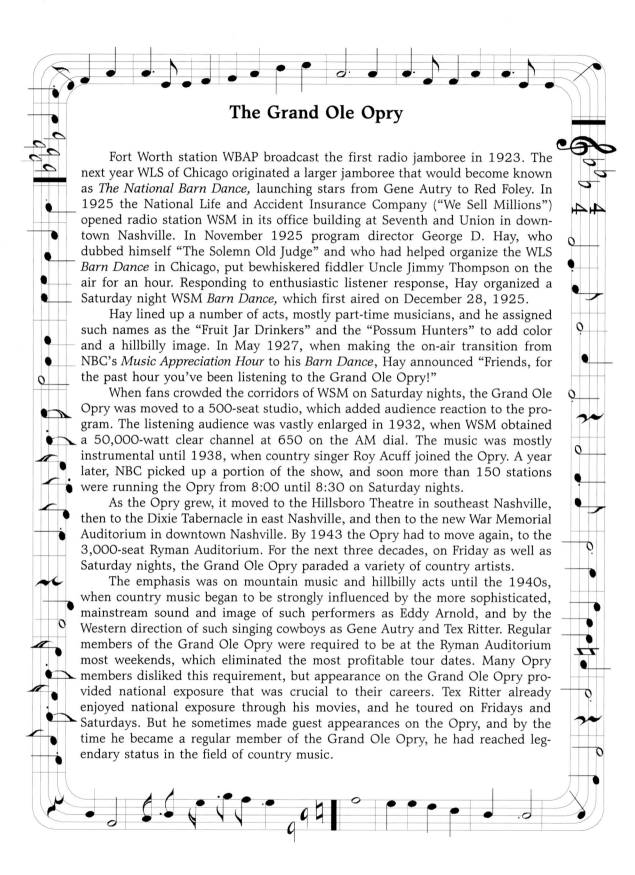

The Grand Ole Opry

Fort Worth station WBAP broadcast the first radio jamboree in 1923. The next year WLS of Chicago originated a larger jamboree that would become known as *The National Barn Dance,* launching stars from Gene Autry to Red Foley. In 1925 the National Life and Accident Insurance Company ("We Sell Millions") opened radio station WSM in its office building at Seventh and Union in downtown Nashville. In November 1925 program director George D. Hay, who dubbed himself "The Solemn Old Judge" and who had helped organize the WLS *Barn Dance* in Chicago, put bewhiskered fiddler Uncle Jimmy Thompson on the air for an hour. Responding to enthusiastic listener response, Hay organized a Saturday night WSM *Barn Dance,* which first aired on December 28, 1925.

Hay lined up a number of acts, mostly part-time musicians, and he assigned such names as the "Fruit Jar Drinkers" and the "Possum Hunters" to add color and a hillbilly image. In May 1927, when making the on-air transition from NBC's *Music Appreciation Hour* to his *Barn Dance*, Hay announced "Friends, for the past hour you've been listening to the Grand Ole Opry!"

When fans crowded the corridors of WSM on Saturday nights, the Grand Ole Opry was moved to a 500-seat studio, which added audience reaction to the program. The listening audience was vastly enlarged in 1932, when WSM obtained a 50,000-watt clear channel at 650 on the AM dial. The music was mostly instrumental until 1938, when country singer Roy Acuff joined the Opry. A year later, NBC picked up a portion of the show, and soon more than 150 stations were running the Opry from 8:00 until 8:30 on Saturday nights.

As the Opry grew, it moved to the Hillsboro Theatre in southeast Nashville, then to the Dixie Tabernacle in east Nashville, and then to the new War Memorial Auditorium in downtown Nashville. By 1943 the Opry had to move again, to the 3,000-seat Ryman Auditorium. For the next three decades, on Friday as well as Saturday nights, the Grand Ole Opry paraded a variety of country artists.

The emphasis was on mountain music and hillbilly acts until the 1940s, when country music began to be strongly influenced by the more sophisticated, mainstream sound and image of such performers as Eddy Arnold, and by the Western direction of such singing cowboys as Gene Autry and Tex Ritter. Regular members of the Grand Ole Opry were required to be at the Ryman Auditorium most weekends, which eliminated the most profitable tour dates. Many Opry members disliked this requirement, but appearance on the Grand Ole Opry provided national exposure that was crucial to their careers. Tex Ritter already enjoyed national exposure through his movies, and he toured on Fridays and Saturdays. But he sometimes made guest appearances on the Opry, and by the time he became a regular member of the Grand Ole Opry, he had reached legendary status in the field of country music.

way back before a movie camera. In 1966 Tex played his first starring role in a motion picture in more than two decades. *The Girl From Tobacco Row* was produced and directed by Ron Ormond, of Nashville's Ormond Productions. Portrayed as "probably filmdom's first Gospel Music drama," *The Girl From Tobacco Row* starred Tex, along with Ralph Emery and Ron Ormond. Tex played "a tobacco-growing rural preacher" and the songs were traditional gospel numbers that he loved: "Precious Memories," "The Church in the Wildwood," "Love Lifted Me," and "Softly and Tenderly."

Although *The Girl From Tobacco Row* was panned by critics and shunned by moviegoing audiences, Tex quickly was signed to star in *Nashville Rebel*. Co-starring were Waylon Jennings and Mary Frann (who later played Bob Newhart's wife on a long-running TV series), and also appearing were such country stars as Porter Wagoner, Loretta Lynn, Faron Young, Sonny James, Archie Campbell, and the Wilburn Brothers. The movie was something of a travelogue, showcasing Nashville and the Nashville Sound. One of the featured songs was the Ritter version of "Hillbilly Heaven," but the film suffered the same tepid reception as had *The Girl From Tobacco Row*.

The next year Tex made a cameo appearance in the movie *What Am I Bid?*, singing "I Never Got to Kiss the Girl." *What Am I Bid?* was an auction story starring Leroy Van Dyke, who had written and performed the hit novelty song, "Auctioneer." *What Am I Bid?* proved to be no better than *The Girl From Tobacco Row*, *Nashville Rebel*, or any of the other mediocre films which tried rather ineptly to capitalize on the swelling popularity of country music. But these movies were not worse than some of the singing cowboy films, and it certainly was good to see Tex playing himself on the big screen—one more proof of his status as a living legend.

Tex was in demand as a guest performer on a variety of television shows. He appeared, for example, on *The Porter Wagoner Show*, which was the most popular syndicated country program of the 1960s. In December 1967 Tex was on *The Mike Douglas Show*, discussing the evolution of Western movies with the host, and singing "The Wayward Wind," "A Working Man's Prayer," and "High Noon." In February 1968 he was a guest star on an NBC special on

Tex and Roy Acuff have just announced Bob Wills as the newest member of the CMA Hall of Fame, October 18, 1968.

Tex in 1973 on The Porter Wagoner Show, *which was syndicated in almost 100 markets. Shown with Tex are Porter, Dolly Parton, and the Wagonmasters.*

country music: a film clip of his 1937 movie, *Riders of the Rockies*, showed him singing "Home on the Range," then a segment of the Grand Ole Opry focused on his performance of "High Noon." When Tex visited his family in Los Angeles, he often appeared on Gene Autry's *Melody Ranch* radio program.

During his California visits, Tex worked nightclub dates to "earn some bread." As he had done for more than three decades, he continued to travel to a wide variety of personal appearances. In the course of his career, Tex not

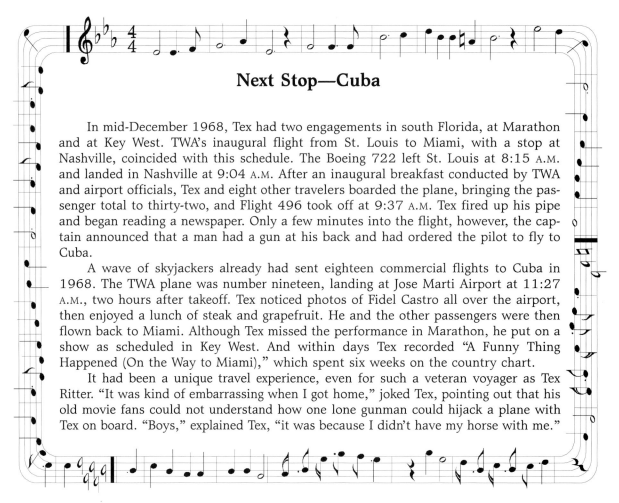

Next Stop—Cuba

In mid-December 1968, Tex had two engagements in south Florida, at Marathon and at Key West. TWA's inaugural flight from St. Louis to Miami, with a stop at Nashville, coincided with this schedule. The Boeing 722 left St. Louis at 8:15 A.M. and landed in Nashville at 9:04 A.M. After an inaugural breakfast conducted by TWA and airport officials, Tex and eight other travelers boarded the plane, bringing the passenger total to thirty-two, and Flight 496 took off at 9:37 A.M. Tex fired up his pipe and began reading a newspaper. Only a few minutes into the flight, however, the captain announced that a man had a gun at his back and had ordered the pilot to fly to Cuba.

A wave of skyjackers already had sent eighteen commercial flights to Cuba in 1968. The TWA plane was number nineteen, landing at Jose Marti Airport at 11:27 A.M., two hours after takeoff. Tex noticed photos of Fidel Castro all over the airport, then enjoyed a lunch of steak and grapefruit. He and the other passengers were then flown back to Miami. Although Tex missed the performance in Marathon, he put on a show as scheduled in Key West. And within days Tex recorded "A Funny Thing Happened (On the Way to Miami)," which spent six weeks on the country chart.

It had been a unique travel experience, even for such a veteran voyager as Tex Ritter. "It was kind of embarrassing when I got home," joked Tex, pointing out that his old movie fans could not understand how one lone gunman could hijack a plane with Tex on board. "Boys," explained Tex, "it was because I didn't have my horse with me."

only toured all fifty states, but made numerous foreign jaunts as well. He first toured overseas in 1952, to England and France. Tex returned to England five years later, and between scheduled appearances, he recorded six BBC radio shows, portraying the history of Texas in story and song. Tex enjoyed an enthusiastic following in England, because his movies had been released first-run in the British Isles during the 1930s and 1940s. There were extensive tours of England again in 1970 and in 1973, and during a parade in Plymouth, Tex was appointed Grand Marshal and rode with the Lord Mayor in a covered wagon. The *London Evening Star*, on March 20, 1970, commented on the old movie hero: "He was the singing cowboy with the white hat and the white horse who was always the good guy who won the fights and got the girl. He epitomized all that was good and right about the West. And that's a long way from 'Midnight Cowboy'."

The 1970 appearances were part of a promotional tour of twenty-one European cities in twenty-one days, arranged by Capitol for Tex, Buck Owens, and other recording stars. Tex averaged only two hours of sleep each night, but he and Dorothy managed to visit historical sites, particularly seeking out locations commemorating Martin Luther in Germany. Tex was especially well received in West Germany, where Tex Ritter movies had been exhibited in theaters during the 1950s (with German dialogue dubbed in, although the songs were left on the soundtracks in original form). Johnny Bond pointed out that the artists on this tour were only paid expenses by Capitol, and when Tex received a plaque in London on behalf of the entire troupe, he thought of the praise given by Winston Churchill to RAF pilots following the Battle of Britain. "To quote one of your noble countrymen," Tex said dryly, "never have so many come so far for so little."

Tex had headlined the cerebral palsy benefit for South Africa organized by Dorothy in 1957, and fifteen years later he headed a UNICEF (United Nations International Emergency Fund) tour with Connie Smith, Tom T. Hall, Wanda

Jackson, Freddy Weller, and other country artists. This fine troupe went to Australia, where they put on a television special, and to New Zealand, Japan and Hong Kong, journeying 36,000 miles in twenty-two days. In 1969 and 1970 Tex entertained troops in Vietnam. The 1969 trip was a month-long journey to the Orient, commencing with a flight to Japan, followed by four days in Taiwan and a stopover in Okinawa, before going into South Vietnam for two weeks. Tex entertained and visited military hospitals, and wherever he went he was protected by an armed escort. When he returned to South Vietnam the next year, he was accompanied by his son Tom.

Strongly supportive of the war effort, Tex felt a growing concern over war protests and flag burnings, as well as race riots, drug use, and other disturbances which wracked American society during the 1960s. Always outspoken in his convictions, late in 1969 Tex was approached by fellow conservatives who wanted him to run for the United States Senate in 1970. The incumbent, liberal Democrat Albert Gore, had served in the Senate for eighteen years, and the expected challenger, Republican Representative Dan Kuykendall of Memphis, announced in November 1969 that he had decided not to run against Gore. But Republicans intended to find someone to challenge Gore. In 1966, when Howard Baker was elected to the U.S. Senate from Tennessee, Republicans won their first statewide office since 1920. The Republican Party grew rapidly during the years after Tex moved to Tennessee, and by 1969 they made up half of the state's House of Representatives. Tex was told that he would face no serious challengers in the primary, and potential backers assured him that they would raise the necessary campaign funding.

For the past three years Tex had lobbied in the Senate and testified a dozen times before the Senate Judiciary Committee in an effort to secure air-play royalties for performing artists. (Writers and composers received standard royalties when records were played over the radio, but singers received nothing.) While lobbying for this cause, Tex had met half the members of the Senate. Tex Ritter certainly had the name recognition which is invaluable for a political

Tex wrote his own speeches and vigorously expounded his convictions during the 1970 Senate campaign.

candidate, although it should have occurred to someone that "Tex" might not be an attractive label for Tennessee voters. For Tex, it was an irresistible opportunity to indulge his lifetime fascination with politics. In January 1970, Tex announced that he was a candidate for the Republican nomination for the U.S. Senate.

Dorothy campaigned across the state with him, and so did Tom Ritter, who also worked

Tear the Screen Down!

The 1957 fundraising tour to build a cerebral palsy hospital in South Africa afforded Tex and other participants the opportunity to ride camels through Egyptian pyramids and to go on safari. Actor Don DeFore, who once had appeared in plays with Dorothy Ritter, recalled that Tex was the most popular of the entertainers, especially among the thousands of black laborers who worked in gold and diamond mines, "because they had seen practically all his movies."

Tex was so popular that when a movie villain would temporarily get the best of their hero, "they would tear the screen down." In the mining compounds where Ritter films were shown, a smooth concrete surface would be erected, then painted white, so that irate fans could not destroy the cement "screen."

behind the scenes as assistant to campaign manager Mark Brown. Although Tex wrote his own speeches, Dorothy and Tom helped with speechwriting, and they delivered speeches when Tex was not present. Roy Acuff headed a committee, "Citizens for Tex," and other entertainers pledged campaign contributions and promised to appear on behalf of their fellow performer. In April, Tex and Dorothy were guests at the White House when a country music show was staged for President and Mrs. Richard Nixon. Tex also took time off from his campaign to fly to Indianapolis to perform at a cerebral palsy benefit. Allied Artists TV packaged twenty Tex Ritter movies—the Monogram features, filmed from 1938 through 1941—to be shown on television while the star's name was in the news.

But Republican Congressman William Brock, who had been a member of the House of Representatives since 1961, announced on April 3, 1970, that he intended to run for the Senate. Brock was a multimillionaire from Chattanooga with long-established ties to the Republican Party in Tennessee, and he launched a smooth and well-financed campaign. Tex pushed himself relentlessly, catching most of his sleep in the back of a bus as he traveled from one speech to another. His show-business friends volunteered as promised: more than sixty artists performed at 140 rallies during the summer of 1970. Tex was optimistic, but his opponent continually reminded voters that the Texan had lived in Tennessee for merely five years. Pee Wee King told his biographer, Wade Hall, about an encounter with a typical voter while he was working a rally.

"Run him back to Texas," insisted the voter. "Where does this guy get off? Why does a Texan want to come over here and be governor [sic] of Tennessee? We ought to run him back to Texas."

"Do you know Tex?" tried Pee Wee.

"No," came the emphatic reply, "and I don't want to, either."

The attitude that Tex was a latter-day carpetbagger prevailed, along with Brock's superior financing and campaign expertise. In the primary election held in August, Brock totaled 161,009 votes to just 48,635 for Tex. Interviewed after the election, Tex pointed out an obvious factor: "Money? I think that's the

Tex, Dorothy, and Tom at a rally during his campaign for the Senate.

great tragedy of American politics today. I didn't have the kind of money that was required, and I didn't raise it."

Indeed, after he lost the election, the promised financial support failed to materialize, and Tex was forced to pay enormous campaign bills out of his own pocket. "I'll be singing 'The Boll Weevil' for the rest of my life just to pay for the campaign," Tex remarked ruefully—and accurately. But his irrepressible attitude manifested itself. "I rather enjoyed the campaigning and I'm not the kind of person who regrets many things. As you go through life disappointments are going to happen to you. I've faced them before and I don't let them worry me too much. I did what I could do. . . ."

Brock won the November election, defeating the incumbent Gore by a close margin. Following the August primary, Tom Ritter went to work on the gubernatorial campaign of Winfield Dunn, who became the first Republican governor of Tennessee in fifty years.

Governor Dunn was a neighbor of the Ritters, who had sold their California home in 1968 and moved to Brentwood, just south of Nashville. Adjacent to the west side of Franklin Road, the sprawling ranch-style house was located on six acres at the south entrance to Curtiswood Lane, the same street as the Tennessee Governor's Mansion and the home of Minnie Pearl, among other prominent neighbors. Dorothy was pleased to live in such a distinguished neighborhood, while Tex, with his keen interest in history, was gratified that General John Bell Hood and his Confederate Army had marched past the property in December 1864, during one of the last great clashes of the Civil War, the Battle of Nashville. Although John stayed at USC to work on his degree, Tom moved to Nashville to enter Vanderbilt Law School. Dorothy, of course, soon immersed herself in social and charitable activities in Nashville. Tex easily made himself at home in Nashville. In 1970, for example, he went to see the three-hour World War II movie, *Tora! Tora! Tora!*, at the Belmont Theater. Ignoring the "No Smoking" signs he puffed on his pipe throughout the film, and during the intermission Tex amiably strolled up and down the aisles, chatting with everyone.

Tex was not so amiable with an IRS agent who came to his Nashville home to press claims against the entertainer. The agent arrogantly questioned Tex for hours. When he finally left, Tex asked if his official duties had ended for the day. The agent said that he now was off-duty, whereupon Tex—drawing upon his fistic training under Charlie King—knocked him sprawling off

Ritter's Chuckwagon

Tex's neighbor, Minnie Pearl, had a fried chicken operation, and other stars backed other types of food franchises. Likewise, Tex, who often had invested in various enterprises, opened Tex Ritter's Chuckwagon in September 1969. Located at 21st and West End Avenue, the Chuckwagon specialized in hamburgers and was an immediate success. Tex often ambled in and introduced himself to customers: "I'm Tex Ritter, and I want to thank you for your business."

In 1969 Tex recorded "Chuckwagon Son of a Gun," written for him by Cindy Walker, and other songs which made up the album *Chuck Wagon Days*. Tex opened two more Chuckwagons in Nashville, but these restaurants did not enjoy the success of the first. Although Tex eventually pulled out of the restaurant business, he had the consolation of solid sales from *Chuck Wagon Days*.

the front stoop with one well-placed punch. The next day a hulking agent arrived to continue the investigation, but he assured Tex that everyone in the IRS office was elated that their disagreeable colleague had at last received his comeuppance.

Willie Nelson had left Nashville in 1972 for his native Texas, where he changed his image and sound to appeal to country rednecks and long-haired college students who were turning from rock music to C & W. In 1972 Willie staged the Dripping Springs Reunion, forerunner to his famous Fourth of July picnics. Performing at Dripping Springs, just

Tex got a taste of the restaurant business with his Chuckwagon.

Tex performing at a Cerebral Palsy Telethon in Nashville's Municipal Auditorium in March 1971. (Photo by Les Leverett.)

west of Austin, were Willie, Loretta Lynn, Roy Acuff, Waylon Jennings, Kris Kristofferson, Billy Joe Shaver—and Tex Ritter.

The next year, in early August at the Sheraton Peabody Hotel in Memphis, Tex was the featured attraction at the Second Annual Western Film Festival, a convention for B Western fans. Other former Western stars in attendance included Bob Steele, Lash LaRue, Max Terhune, Russell Hayden, Bob Baker—and Dorothy Fay. Such occasions allowed enthusiastic fans to mingle with the heroes and heroines of their childhood, while viewing the black and white films of years gone by. Tex enjoyed socializing with these ardent fans, who clearly regarded him as a living legend, and he presented a program about his life and career. But Bobby Fluker, who had seen Tex on three occasions since 1953, said that the old singing cowboy "looked so tired." Fluker emphasized to the author, "Tex looked like he could hardly put one boot in front of the other."

Tex was in a reflective mood when he was interviewed by Kathy Sawyer for the July 1973 issue of *Country Music* magazine. Probably the best and most extensive interview ever published about Tex, this informative piece covered almost every aspect of his career. Sawyer asked Tex, for example, about his famous schedule of personal appearances. "Well, I never did find it difficult at all, even at its worst. Naturally you'd lose a little sleep, but I always enjoyed it because you meet people in different towns and I enjoyed the stage more than the pictures—well maybe not the pictures, but maybe more than the television and radio—that's the part I liked the best because an audience does a little something to you. There's a chemistry there that the others don't have. I'm kind of a tourist.

"With people you can't get bored . . . my philosophy whenever I came to a new town was always that there were interesting things in this town, that there is beauty here," he explained.

Sawyer closed the interview by asking Tex if there was anything he regretted not yet having done. "Well," he mused, "I don't think anyone is ever satisfied with his accomplishments." Tex apparently thought about his age: "Some of the greatest accomplishments in the world have been performed by old men, so you're never washed up. You can always accomplish some-

Tex and Roy Clark on one of Ritter's last duck hunts. (Photo by Les Leverett.)

thing. But you'll never do it if you retire and just sit."

Tex had absolutely no intention of retiring. He helped prepare a remarkable album that Capitol would label *Tex Ritter, An American Legend.* The album consisted of thirty-one Ritter standards, from "Rye Whiskey" to "High Noon," on three LP records. Each song was preceded by a narrated reminiscence, with Tex recounting details about the origin or production of the most important numbers of his long recording career. This autobiographical album is invaluable for understanding the life and music of Tex Ritter.

At the end of the album Tex capsulized his professional career, carefully mentioning people who had helped him along the way: his parents, Oscar Fox, J. Frank Dobie, Ed Finney, Dorothy Fay, his sons, Johnny Mercer, Lee Gillette, Ken Nelson, and his friends in Texas, New York, Hollywood, Nashville, and "all across the country."

"It's been a great career that I've had—mostly the friends," he mused reflectively and with great deliberation. "Old friends are about all there is in life, I suppose—old friends, old books, old wine. I trust you'll find some enjoyment out of these songs."

December 1973 was a busy month for Tex. He appeared on the Grand Ole Opry each weekend, playing to appreciative crowds at the Ryman Auditorium (the Opry would move to its new home, the Grand Ole Opry House, early in 1974). On December 14 Tex and a CMA dele-

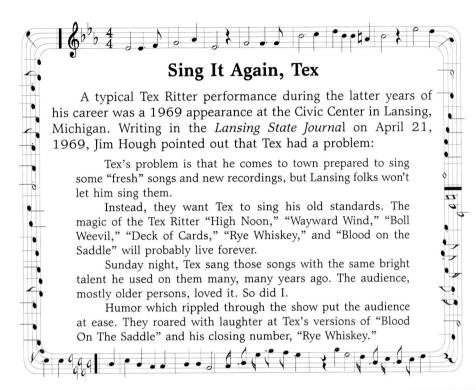

Sing It Again, Tex

A typical Tex Ritter performance during the latter years of his career was a 1969 appearance at the Civic Center in Lansing, Michigan. Writing in the *Lansing State Journal* on April 21, 1969, Jim Hough pointed out that Tex had a problem:

> Tex's problem is that he comes to town prepared to sing some "fresh" songs and new recordings, but Lansing folks won't let him sing them.
>
> Instead, they want Tex to sing his old standards. The magic of the Tex Ritter "High Noon," "Wayward Wind," "Boll Weevil," "Deck of Cards," "Rye Whiskey," and "Blood on the Saddle" will probably live forever.
>
> Sunday night, Tex sang those songs with the same bright talent he used on them many, many years ago. The audience, mostly older persons, loved it. So did I.
>
> Humor which rippled through the show put the audience at ease. They roared with laughter at Tex's versions of "Blood On The Saddle" and his closing number, "Rye Whiskey."

gation led by Jo Walker were at the White House to present President Nixon with a copy of the album, *Thank You, Mr. President*. Produced by the Country Music Association, the album featured hits such as "Coal Miner's Daughter" and "Battle of New Orleans," interspersed with excerpts from President Nixon's speeches and narrated by Tex. Only two albums were made up: one was given to the president, while the other would reside in the CMA Hall of Fame.

On December 6, Tex and Johnny Bond met at the Hilltop Studios to record two duets for a Bond album. After cutting "Sadie Was a Lady" and "Git Off My Horse," Bond reported that Tex had everyone in the studio "in stitches." On Tuesday, December 20, Tex drove through a heavy snowstorm to the Jack Clemments Studio for the last of more than 160 recording sessions. With his old friend, Joe Allison, working as producer, Tex cut two sides: "He Who Is Without Sin (Let Him Judge Me)" and "The Americans," a praise of America written by a Canadian journalist. During a time when his country was wracked by turmoil, Tex felt strongly about this material, and it was fitting that his final record would be a patriotic narration.

Eight days later, on Friday, December 28, Tex

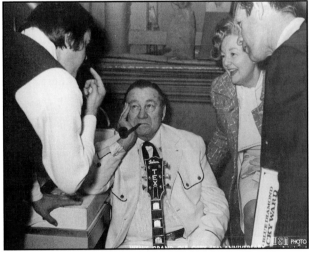

Tex and Dorothy listening to Tom T. Hall at the 47th anniversary of the Grand Ole Opry in October 1973. Tex is holding his customized Gibson J200 guitar. (Photo by Les Leverett.)

recited "The Americans" onstage at the Grand Ole Opry, bringing the audience to its feet with spontaneous applause at this moving narration. Backstage were producers of *W. W. and the Dixie Dance Kings,* a movie soon to be filmed in and around Nashville and starring Burt Reynolds. Strongly impressed by Ritter's performance and stage presence, the producers promptly offered Tex a role. Tex accepted, and was told that a script would soon be mailed to him. Sadly, Tex did not have the time remaining to play the part, and Ned Beatty would fill his role.

John Ritter flew to Nashville from California for the holiday, and the family enjoyed Christmas together. After Christmas Tex was interviewed by Ralph Emery for his nationally syndicated radio show. Tex and Ralph discussed David Akeman, the Grand Ole Opry performer known as Stringbean who, along with his wife, had recently been robbed and murdered. The interview then turned to

Ritter's movie career, and Tex described the technique of riding off into the sunset, with a turn in the saddle for a wave of farewell. When Emery ended the interview, Tex uttered his last words for broadcast, *"Adios, amigo."*

Tex flew to Denver for a New Year's Eve show at a country music club in nearby Littleton. In Denver, Tex bought a new hat and two Western shirts. He played to a packed house in Littleton, then immediately headed for the airport so that he could spend a few days at home before flying to another engagement at the end of the week.

The Ritter family was together for Christmas 1973.

New Star in Hillbilly Heaven

The new year began auspiciously for Tex Ritter. Although a winter storm blanketed Nashville with snow and ice, Tex flew in from Colorado, then settled down at home with Dorothy and Tom to watch the 1974 New Year's Day bowl games on TV. Throughout the day he received calls from Capitol officials about the enthusiastic response to "The Americans," recorded only a week and a half earlier and just released as a single record. He was told that distributors also were clamoring for *Tex Ritter, An American Legend*, the recently released autobiographical album of three LP records with introductory remarks by Tex about thirty-one of his most memorable songs.

Encouraged by the capacity New Year's Eve crowd he had recently enjoyed in Colorado, Tex was eager for his upcoming trip to Philadelphia, where he would play three nights at the Bijou Dinner Theater. Tex planned to fly to Philadelphia on Friday, January 4, while the band came on a bus. Shortly after returning from Philadelphia, Tex was looking forward to his annual duck hunting trip, with Tom T. Hall, Les Leverett, Grand Ole Opry manager Bud Wendell, and a couple of other friends.

On Wednesday afternoon, January 2, 1974, Red O'Donnell of the *Nashville Banner* was writing advance copy for Friday's "Movies on TV." Noticing that *High Noon* was scheduled for Friday night, O'Donnell dialed the Ritter home to talk with Tex about what had become his most famous song. Tex answered, "cheerful and cordial as per normal." After talking about "Do Not Forsake Me," O'Donnell noted that Tex would have a birthday in ten more days. O'Donnell wished Tex a happy birthday, then inquired if he contemplated retirement.

"No retirement plans, whatsoever," Tex replied. "We gotta work, you know. Long as the folks want to buy tickets to see me, I'll be up there on that stage trying to entertain them."

Tex made a few more optimistic remarks about his future, then responded to O'Donnell's query about his health.

"I believe a person—regardless of his or her age—is better off if he or she keeps active. Oh, I get a few colds every now and then, and I snort a little, but the snorting is more or less a habit. It just might be my attention-getter," Tex added prophetically. After a few more remarks, Tex thanked O'Donnell for calling. O'Donnell's interview was published the next day in the *Banner*.

The same day, January 2, Tex learned that one of his band members, Jack Watkins, had been arrested on a warrant for nonpayment of alimony. Watkins had been placed in the Nashville Metropolitan Jail on Tuesday night. Late Wednesday afternoon Tex, accompanied by his son Tom, braved icy streets to drive to the Metro Jail.

Tex and Tom entered the facility about 5:30 P.M. and inquired about paying bail for the release of Watkins. Lt. Johnny Brewer came out to greet his famous visitor. Tex announced it was his first visit to the jail. He was given a tour, then Tex and Tom were escorted to Brewer's office while Watkins was being processed for release. Tex, of course, thoroughly enjoyed the new experience, laughing and joking with Brewer and other jail employees while smoking a pipe.

At about 6:20 P.M., Tom saw his father, who was sitting in a chair, suddenly clutch at his chest and slump down. "He got real white all over," reported Brewer, "and we grabbed an oxygen mask and put it on him." The police rushed Tex to the emergency room at Baptist Hospital, where he soon was pronounced dead of a massive coronary. Tex had gained considerable weight through the years, and he had begun to suffer from emphysema. In ten days he would have celebrated his sixty-ninth birthday.

Tributes immediately began to pour in. "He was a great man, a great patriot," said Johnny Cash. "The people of America have lost a hero," declared Governor Winfield Dunn, a neighbor of the Ritters. "Tennessee lost one of its most distinguished citizens," he continued, "and America has lost a patriot."

"I had the privilege of introducing him last Saturday night on the Opry," said a saddened Roy Acuff. "I used all the kind words I could think of then, but they weren't nearly enough."

Perhaps no one offered a more fitting tribute than Tennessee Congressman Richard Fulton: "Tex was a big man with lots of love—love for his beautiful wife, love for his children, love for his friends, love for all of life, love for his country, love for his God. Some people take more from life than they give. Tex gave more than he took."

Tex lay in state at Nashville's Roesch-Patton Funeral Home in a walnut-stained coffin. A stream of mourners filed by on Thursday. Funeral services were conducted on Friday at the First Presbyterian Church, a lovely, white-columned edifice on a hill not far south of the Ritter home. A long stream of limousines crept slowly past ice-laden trees to the church. Governor Winfield Dunn, Senator Howard Baker, and Eddy Arnold were among many prominent figures who jammed the pews. Pallbearers were

Brentwood's First Presbyterian Church, where Tex Ritter's Nashville funeral was held. (Photo by Karon O'Neal.)

Acuff, Joe Allison, Mark Bates, Johnny Bond, Ralph Emery, Fowler Hollobaugh, Jr., George Richey, and Bud Wendell, while a long list of honorary pallbearers included Governor Dunn and Senator Baker. Following the funeral the body was flown to Texas for interment.

Several years earlier Tex had selected a burial site at Oak Bluff Cemetery in Port Neches, near Nederland, Texas. The cemetery offered a beautiful view of the Neches River, as it flowed toward the nearby Gulf of Mexico. Tex would be buried there on Monday, January 7, following services at Nederland's First United Methodist Church, where he once had sung in the choir and performed warmly remembered solos.

Dr. John Gray, Tex's roommate at the University of Texas, was president of Lamar

The Answer

"I've always had deep religious feelings," stated Tex repeatedly, remembering his upbringing in rural churches, his deep enjoyment of old hymns, and his lifelong faith. When asked what were his favorite books, he listed first the Bible. "I've always tried to live a Christian life."

"The church has been a great influence in my life, and in the life of this country." Tex felt that a return to religion was the solution to America's growing drug problem. "I think to fight this battle we're going to have to have a spiritual awakening. We have to turn to God. We have to turn to religion again and be a churchgoing people."

Tex reflected upon these beliefs for *Country Crossroads*, a weekly program of the Southern Baptist Radio and Television Commission. As though reminding himself of the core of his faith, he emphatically declared, "We're going to have to rediscover that Christ is the answer."

John, Dorothy, and Tom mourning Tex. (Photo by Les Leverett.)

Near Tex Ritter's grave is a Texas historical marker. (Photo by the author.)

Tex Ritter's final resting place at Oak Bluff Memorial Park in Port Neches, near his old home in Nederland. (Photo by the author.)

University, located only a few blocks from the old South Park High School building where the two adolescent students had been debate partners. During a brief eulogy, Dr. Gray reminisced about their school days together. "He was a kind man, who never turned a deaf ear to others," asserted Dr. Gray. "He gave generously of himself without fanfare."

Close to 1,000 people jammed the First United Methodist Church, which comfortably seated 600. Ola McCauley of Houston, Lucille Power of Beaumont, and Booty Ritter of Nederland were present for their brother's farewell. At least 1,000 mourners were at the cemetery, many waving little Texas flags. There was a boot-shaped floral wreath, complete with

spur. Another arrangement was shaped like a guitar, with sheet music of "The Old Rugged Cross" attached. Masonic graveside services were conducted. Texas Jim Cooper, faithful president of the Tex Ritter Fan Club, shook Dorothy Ritter's hand and whispered words of comfort.

Tex left his entire estate to Dorothy and his sons through a handwritten will. The former law student had written out his wishes on the front and back sides of a sheet of office stationery, and the document was successfully probated by County Court Judge Shelton Lutton of Nashville.

Dorothy stayed active in civic affairs and served for years as goodwill ambassador to the Grand Ole Opry. Tom Ritter soon finished his law degree from Vanderbilt, an accomplishment which Tex had anticipated with enormous satisfaction. While Tom fulfilled his father's academic goal, John Ritter followed Tex as a celebrated show business personality. John portrayed a series of charming, humorous characters in a variety of movie and TV roles, and gained vast popularity as the star of the comedy series *Three's Company* on television. The success of his sons provided a legacy that would have deeply gratified Tex Ritter.

For years after his death, an annual "Tex Ritter Roundup" was staged by Texas Jim Cooper in Carrollton, Texas, north of Dallas. Cooper was a young man from Carrollton who met Tex at a 1963 show in San Antonio.

Cooper idolized Tex, and started a fan club. Tex had enjoyed a number of fan clubs since his movie days, but none were ever run with the devotion employed by Texas Jim Cooper. In addition to the Tex Ritter Roundups and regular newsletters, Cooper sent out a constant stream of articles to various publications.

A number of Tex Ritter albums were released in the years following his death: *High Noon* (1983), *Lady Killin' Cowboy* (1985), *Singin' in the Saddle* (1986), *Greatest Hits* (1990), *Country Music Hall of Fame* (1991), *Capitol's Collectors Series* (1992). These albums feature Tex Ritter's standards, including the folk music and cowboy songs that he collected and performed—and loved—all his life. His recording of "Blood on the Saddle," emanating from an animated grizzly bear, was heard by countless visitors to Disney World in Florida. Tex Ritter's performances also lived on in videotapes of his movies, including a packaged collection of ten films, mostly his early singing cowboy movies. Many of his other films are available through video catalogues. Although these black and white B Westerns seem rather crude and silly today, Tex onscreen radiates the sheer joy of performing in movies. He was in his prime, tall and handsome and exuberant. The viewer sees a C & W Hall of Famer singing and picking—and whooping and yelping, just as he had learned from J. Frank Dobie and John A. Lomax and old-time cowboys in Texas.

Tex Ritter also is perpetuated in museums, initially at the CMA Hall of Fame, and later in Texas. His family turned over a vast collection of memorabilia to Tommie Ritter Smith, a relative from Carthage, who, as director of the Panola County Chamber of Commerce, wanted to open a Tex Ritter Museum in the star's home county. Although she had no background in museum work, Tommie plunged into the project with indefatigable effort. In 1993 she converted the upper floor of the spacious Chamber of Commerce building in Carthage into a museum bursting with the costumes, photographs, movie posters, record albums, awards, books, and countless other artifacts of the life of Tex Ritter. She loaned part of her collection to Tex Ritter exhibits at the Windmill Museum in Nederland's Tex Ritter Park and the Gulf Coast Museum in nearby Port Arthur.

Another loan came in 1996, to the Grand

Housed in the upper floor of the Panola County Chamber of Commerce, the Tex Ritter Museum is a treasure trove of Ritter memorabilia.

Texas Jim Cooper, devoted president of the Tex Ritter Fan Club, presents sheet music from High Noon *to the director of the Windmill Museum in Nederland's Tex Ritter Park.*

Ole Opry Museum in Opryland USA. On July 18, 1997, the Tex Ritter exhibit was opened with extensive media coverage and a large crowd in attendance. Tommie Ritter Smith headed a sizable crowd from Panola County, and these Texans mingled with Grand Ole Opry stars and numerous friends from Tex Ritter's past. Tex's sons, John and Tom, were on hand to acknowledge the award (since suffering a stroke in 1987, Dorothy Ritter has been confined to a California nursing facility). That evening, at the Friday night performance of the Grand Ole Opry, John and Tom Ritter were greeted with thunderous applause when they came onstage as their father's award was announced. John Ritter then introduced another native of Panola County, Linda Davis, and the lovely singer capped Tex Ritter Day at Opryland with a show-stopping performance.

Opryland Museum, July 18, 1997. Tommie Ritter Smith, curator of the Tex Ritter Museum, enjoys a kiss on the cheek from John Ritter, while his brother, Tom, looks on approvingly.

Throughout the day and evening Tex Ritter was praised, with tributes at the ceremonies, and with the informal reminiscences of his old friends and colleagues. The tributes and praise were offered by men and women who genuinely admired the legendary entertainer. But the most moving and fitting tribute to Tex Ritter was inadvertently uttered by Tex himself, during a thoughtful and carefully written address he delivered at the Country Music Association Awards Banquet in 1973, less than three months before he died:

> Every breath of every man who has ever breathed has brought me here. I am the sum total of every smile and every tear. I hope I never forget that. For we are in fact, you know, a part of each other. A part of all which has come and gone. Both the good and the bad. Love and hate belong to no one but are shared by us all, and the wise reap from their visit while the fools wait their return.
>
> But while we live in the present and help shape the future . . . let us accept the fact that the past is hallowed ground and the shrines of the past almost sacred. It is through such shrines as the Country Music Hall of Fame that the future is reflected . . . for all things which shall be have been. The Hall of Fame stands for something different to each one of us . . . but to all of us it is an echo of the strength on which this great country of ours was built. The strength of the common man. The strength which will enable this nation to survive.
>
> I would suggest to you that the most vivid picture we have of our country is contained in the songs of the common man . . . and those songs are country songs. Would you look with me for a moment at country music? It has become a multi-million dollar industry and if anyone doubts that statement just look around you tonight. No more is country considered a synonym for illiteracy . . . more a synonym for truth. And country music has been ever present in the day by day building of this country. As America huffed and puffed . . . sweat and bled . . . cursed and prayed . . . loved and hated . . . all the time growing . . . our music was ever present. Man has always compulsively tried to put his heart outside himself in his songs . . . and our country was pioneered with a song. As the pioneers found their way across the rivers and the ridges . . . into hid-

Dorothy Ritter looking on proudly at the 1975 unveiling of Thomas Hart Benton's mural, The Sources of Country Music, *at the CMA Hall of Fame. The artist was approached by Tex with the mural idea he and Joe Allison had conceived, and for which they helped raise support. Fittingly, the mural was dedicated to the memory of Tex. (Photo by Les Leverett.)*

Tex leading the audience in singing "Happy Birthday" at the 48th anniversary of the Opry in October 1973. When Tex addressed the gathering, the depth of his feelings would provide a moving epitaph. (Photo by Les Leverett.)

den valleys . . . their songs were the voice of a people seeking themselves.

Our songs fought our wars . . . found joy in peace . . . glory in birth . . . sadness in death . . . triumph in God . . . and always echoed that which was taking place. As a result our songs are the most accurate record history has. Is it any wonder, therefore, that the Country Music Hall of Fame has become the national shrine that it is . . . for our songs built it. In reality the heart of America beats there. And I feel one of the most important . . . perhaps the most important display there is the American flag which flies over our Hall of Fame every day.

I mean no slight for the beautiful things in it nor the great names which are found there. Names like Jimmie Rodgers, Fred Rose, Hank Williams, Roy Acuff, Ernest Tubb, Eddy Arnold, Jim Denny, George D. Hay, Uncle Dave Macon, Red Foley, Joe Frank, Jim Reeves, Steve Sholes, Bob Wills, Gene Autry, A. P. Carter and the Carter Family, Bill Monroe, Art Satherly, Jimmie Davis, and, of course, the newest members of the Hall of Fame, Patsy Cline and Chet

Atkins . . . for it is people like these who make us realize that country music is that American flag. And even as our headlines cry out about the wrongs of the world, let us thank God for our music. Changes do have to take place in all walks of life if we are to understand each other . . . if we are to grow . . . if we are to make this a better world for ourselves and our children and our children's children. And the answer is in our music. Simple, basic truth . . . from the heart to the heart . . . that's what it's all about. We seem to better understand each other in song. A song by its very construction leaves no room for shadings or sham. And the country song seems to be the most direct for the country writer knows no other way. His songs reflect the hopes and dreams of everyone as well as everyone's fears and failures. And his songs are a common meeting ground. His songs are not unlike the mirror held before the dirty-faced little boy which causes him to wash that face. And maybe, just maybe, if the whole world would listen to our country songs there'd be a whole lot of face-washing going on.

If I have sounded patriotic tonight, I meant to. If I have sounded proud to be a part of country music, I also meant to do that. If I have sounded God-loving and God-fearing, that was intended also. But mostly, I have intended to try and share with you what country music and our Country Music Hall of Fame means to me . . . and I thank you for listening.

The Films of Tex Ritter

Grand National

Song of the Gringo (1936)
Headin' for the Rio Grande (1936)
Arizona Days (1937)
Trouble in Texas (1937)
Hittin' the Trail (1937)
Sing, Cowboy Sing (1937)
Riders of the Rockies (1937)
Mystery of the Hooded Horseman (1937)
Tex Rides With the Boy Scouts (1937)
Frontier Town (1938)
Rollin' Plains (1938)
Utah Trail (1938)

Monogram

Starlight Over Texas (1938)
Where the Buffalo Roam (1938)
Song of the Buckaroo (1938)
Sundown on the Prairie (1939)
Rollin' Westward (1939)
Down the Wyoming Trail (1939)
The Man From Texas (1939)
Riders of the Frontier (1939)
Roll, Wagons, Roll (1939)
Westbound Stage (1940)
Rhythm of the Rio Grande (1940)
Pals of the Silver Sage (1940)
Cowboy From Sundown (1940)
The Golden Trail (1940)
Rainbow Over the Range (1940)
Arizona Frontier (1940)
Take Me Back to Oklahoma (1940)
Rollin' Home To Texas (1940)
Ridin' the Cherokee Trail (1941)
The Pioneers (1941)

Columbia

King of Dodge City (1941)
Roaring Frontiers (1941)
The Lone Star Vigilantes (1942)
Bullets for Bandits (1942)
North of the Rockies (1942)
The Devil's Trail (1942)
Prairie Gunsmoke (1942)
Vengeance of the West (1942)
Cowboy Canteen (1944)

Universal

Deep in the Heart of Texas (1942)
Little Joe, The Wrangler (1942)
The Old Chisholm Trail (1942)
Tenting Tonight on the Old Camp Ground (1943)
Cheyenne Roundup (1943)
Raiders of the San Joaquin (1943)
The Lone Star Trail (1943)
Frontier Badmen (1943)
Arizona Trail (1943)
Marshal of Gunsmoke (1944)
Oklahoma Raiders (1944)

PRC

Gangsters of the Frontier (1944)
Dead or Alive (1944)
The Whispering Skull (1944)
Marked for Murder (1945)
Enemy of the Law (1945)
Three in the Saddle (1945)
Frontier Fugitives (1945)
Flaming Bullets (1945)

Miscellaneous

Holiday Rhythm (1950)
High Noon (1952)
The Marshal's Daughter (1953)

Wichita (1955)
Apache Ambush (1955)
The First Badman (1955)
Down Liberty Road (1956)

Trooper Hook (1957)
The Girl From Tobacco Row (1966)
Nashville Rebel (1966)
What Am I Bid? (1967)

Tex Ritter Discography

American Record Corporation

New York (October 31, 1932)
The Cowboy's Christmas Ball (Unissued)

New York (March 15,1933)
A-Ridin' Old Paint (Unissued)
Everyday in the Saddle (Unissued)
Goodbye Old Paint
Rye Whiskey, Rye Whiskey

New York (April 14, 1933)
A-Ridin' Old Paint
Everyday in the Saddle

Decca Records

New York (January 21, 1935)
Sam Hall
Get Along Little Dogies

New York (February 5, 1935)
Thirty Three Years in Prison
Lady Killin' Cowboy
I'm a Do-Right Cowboy
Bill the Bar Fly

Chicago (October 16, 1935)
Nobody's Darling But Mine
My Brown Eyed Texas Rose
Boots and Saddles
The Oregon Trail

Chicago (April 17, 1936)
Answer to Nobody's Darling But Mine
A Melody From the Sky
The Hills of Old Wyoming
We'll Rest at the End of the Trail

Los Angeles (December 2, 1936)
High, Wide and Handsome
Headin' For the Rio Grande
Out on the Lone Prairie
Arizona Days
Jailhouse Lament
My Sweet Chiquita (Unissued)

Los Angeles (March 17, 1937)
Hittin' the Trail
I'm a Natural Born Cowboy
Ride, Ride, Ride
Ridin' Down the Trail to Albuquerque
Sing, Cowboy, Sing
Down the Colorado Trail

Los Angeles (January 4, 1939)
(Although unbilled, it is thought that the Sons
of the Pioneers accompanied Tex)
When It's Lamplighting Time in the Valley
Singin' in the Valley
Sundown on the Prairie
Ai Viva Tequila

Capitol Records

Los Angeles (June 11, 1942)
(Johnny Mercer was the first producer of Ritter sessions)
Jingle, Jangle, Jingle
Someone
Goodbye, My Little Cherokee
I've Done the Best I Could

Los Angeles (November 23, 1943)
There's a New Moon Over My Shoulder
Have I Stayed Away Too Long
I'm Wasting My Tears On You
There's a Gold Star in Her Window

Los Angeles (September 20, 1944)
Jealous Heart
I'm Gonna Leave You Like I Found You
We Live in Two Different Worlds
How Was I to Know (Unissued)

Hollywood (April 30, 1945)
San Antonio Rose
Try Me One More Time
Green Grow the Lilacs (Unissued)

Hollywood (May 1, 1945)
(Paul Sells Orchestra)
Boll Weevil
Rounded Up in Glory
You Two Timed Me One Time Too Often
Blood on the Saddle

Hollywood (May 7, 1945)
(Merle Travis and Orchestra)
The Old Chisholm Trail
Bad Brahma Bull
Rye Whiskey
Billy the Kid
Texas Rangers

Hollywood (May 9, 1945)
I Love My Rooster
Froggie Went A-Courtin'
The Wreck of the Number Nine (Unissued)

Hollywood (May 15, 1945)
(Wesley Tuttle and Orchestra)
Green Grow the Lilacs

Hollywood (May 18, 1945)
(New producer, Lee Gillette)
Night Herding Song
The Phantom White Stallion of Skull Valley
The Pony Express (Unissued)

Los Angeles (July 27, 1945)
Some Sweet Day
Christmas Carols By the Old Corral
Love Me Now

Los Angeles (July 28, 1945)
The Wreck of the Number Nine
The Pony Express

Los Angeles (July 31, 1946)
Teach Me to Forget
Have I Told You Lately That I Love You
When You Leave Don't Slam the Door
I Was Out of My Mind

Los Angeles (August 9, 1946)
From Now On
One Little Tear Drop Too Late
Ninety Nine Years Is a Long Time (Unissued)
Poor Unwanted Heart (Unissued)

Los Angeles (October 16, 1946)
Fort Worth Jail
Ninety Nine Years Is a Long Time
I Don't Want You Anymore
I Told My Heart (Unissued)
I'll Forget If You'll Forgive (Unissued)

Los Angeles (December 11, 1946)
(With the Dinning Sisters)
Cool Water
Trouble in Mind
The Roving Gambler (Unissued)

Los Angeles (December 13, 1946)
(With the Dinning Sisters)
Down in the Valley
You Are My Sunshine

Los Angeles (January 16, 1947)
My Heart's As Cold As An Empty Jug
Double Dealin' Darlin'
Toodle-Loo My Darlin'
I Cannot Tell a Lie (Unissued)

Los Angeles (February 25, 1947)
Bats In Your Belfry
Cattle Call
The Last Mile
The Prisoner's Song

Los Angeles (July 15, 1947)
Don't Make Me Sorry
I Can't Get My Foot Off the Rail

Los Angeles (1947)
(An Eddie Kirk recording with recitation by Tex)
The Gods Were Angry With Me

Los Angeles (December 23, 1947)
Coffee Pot
I've Had Enough of Your Two Timin'
Never Mind My Tears
Waitin' and Worryin' (Unissued)

Los Angeles (December 29, 1947)
Animal Fair
Cactus Jackson Had A Ranch
I Was Born a Hundred Years Ago
Thank You

Los Angeles (December 30, 1947)
Pecos Bill
Egg-A-Bread
Merry Christmas Polka
Dallas Darlin'
Tenaha, Timpson, Bobo and Blair
Rock and Rye
I Just Called to Say Goodbye (Unissued)

Los Angeles (December 31, 1947)
The Grass Grew All Around
The Big Rock Candy Mountains

Hollywood (January 15, 1948)
Skybird (Parts 1, 2, 3, 4 and 4B) (The five Skybird sides were never issued)

Montgomery, Alabama (March 25, 1948)
Deck of Cards (Recitation)

Hollywood (June 25, 1948)
The Pledge of Allegiance (Recitations)
Lincoln's Gettysburg Address

Charlotte, N.C. (March 28, 1949)
Jesus Loves Me

I'll Be a Sunbeam
Yankee Doodle
She'll Be Comin' Round the Mountain

Los Angeles (January 6, 1950)
The Eyes of Texas (Unissued)

Los Angeles (January 19, 1950)
Nobody's Fool
Boogie Woogie Cowboy
He's a Cowboy Auctioneer

Los Angeles (May 19, 1950)
Two Little Hands/Jesus Loves the Little Children
Little Feet Be Careful/Away in a Manger
I'll Be a Sunbeam
Jesus Loves Me

Los Angeles (May 22, 1950)
I've Got Five Dollars and It's Saturday Night
Coal Smoke, Valve Oil, and Steam
The Fiery Bear
Boiled Crayfish at Te Maurice

Los Angeles (June 6, 1950)
A Beautiful Life
Thief on the Cross
Jesus Loves Me
Rock of Ages, Hide Thou Me (Unissued)
Give the World a Smile (Unissued)
Chicken, My Chicken (Unissued)
The Picnic Song (Unissued)
The Cricket Song (Unissued)
If You Whistle (Unissued)

Los Angeles (September 20, 1950)
Stay Away From My Heart
Wearin' Out Your Walkin' Shoes
Big Blue Diamonds
Onward Christian Soldiers
Daddy's Last Letter
From the World of Love (Unissued)
Three Handed Women (Unissued)
Blast Your Hide (Unissued)

Los Angeles (September 26, 1950)
(New producer, Ken Nelson)
The Great American Eagle

Los Angeles (January 3, 1951)
You're Always Brand New
There's No One to Cry Over Me

My Bucket's Been Fixed
If I Could Steal You From Somebody Else

Los Angeles (April 3, 1951)
Blue Tail, The Red Fox
The Noise Song

Los Angeles (August 13, 1951)
Rock All the Babies to Sleep
Tennessee Blues
Mr. Buzzard
Carbon the Copy Cat

Los Angeles (January 16, 1952)
As Long as the River Flows On
When My Blue Moon Turns to Gold

Los Angeles (February 22, 1952)
(With the Oklahoma Sweethearts)
The Letter Edged in Black
There Shall Be Showers of Blessing
When It's Springtime in the Rockies (Unissued)
When It's Lamplighting Time in the Valley
(Unissued)

Los Angeles (February 25, 1952)
Go On, Get Out
The Hills of Pride (Unissued)

Los Angeles (May 9, 1952)
Everybody Likes a Little Lovin'
Talk Gobbler Talk (Unissued)

Los Angeles (May 14, 1952)
High Noon (drums later overdubbed)
Love You as Big as Texas

Los Angeles (January 16, 1953)
My Woman Ain't Pretty
Buffalo Dream

Los Angeles (February 9, 1953)
The Marshal's Daughter
The San Antone Story

Los Angeles (March 31, 1953)
One Misty Moisty Morning
Muskrat
Little Wendy Why Why

Los Angeles (August 27, 1953)
Let Me Go, Devil!
The Long Black Rifle

Los Angeles (December 3, 1953)
Lord, Send an Angel
The Red Deck of Cards

Los Angeles (February 18, 1954)
Brave Man
Turn Around, Boy
Has Anybody Seen My Kitty
Two Little Magic Words
The Touch of the Master's Hand

Los Angeles (May 18, 1954)
Lovely Veil of White
The Best Time of All
Your Heart and My Heart Are One (Unissued)

Los Angeles (May 19, 1954)
Is There a Santa Claus

Los Angeles (August 18, 1954)
Prairie Home
The Bandit
Old Tex Kringle

Los Angeles (October 5, 1954)
(Lee Gillette, producer)
A Whale of a Tale
High on a Mountain Top

Los Angeles (December 27, 1954)
(Lee Gillette, producer)
Pick Up After You
Happy Hands
It Doesn't Hurt to Be Polite

Los Angeles (April 11, 1955)
(Lee Gillette, producer)
Wichita
September Song
Cha Cha Cha (Unissued)

Los Angeles (August 15, 1955)
(Ken Nelson, producer)
Gunsmoke
Remember the Alamo

Los Angeles (December 21, 1955)
These Hands
The Last Frontier

Los Angeles (January 25, 1956)
If Jesus Came to Your House

Hollywood (April 16, 1956)
The Searchers
The Wayward Wind

Hollywood (August 16, 1956)
Green Grow the Lilacs
The Last Wagon
The History Song
Paul Bunyon Love

Hollywood (October 15, 1956)
He Is There

Hollywood (January 15, 1957)
(Lee Gillette, producer)
I Leaned on a Man
Children and Fools

Hollywood (June 5, 1957)
Trooper Hook, Part I
Trooper Hook, Part II
The Wind and the Tree

Hollywood (October 11, 1957)
Here Was a Man
It Came Upon A Midnight Clear

Hollywood (May 27, 1958)
I Look for a Love
Jealous Heart
Burning Sand

Hollywood (June 25, 1958)
Psalm 1—His Leaf shall Not Wither
Psalm 8—How Excellent Is Thy Name
Psalm 15—Who Shall Dwell in the Holy Hill
Psalm 19—O Lord, My Strength and
    My Redeemer
Psalm 23—The Lord Is my Shepherd
Psalm 121—The Lord Is Thy Keeper
Psalm 137—We Hanged Our Harps
    Upon Willows

Hollywood (July 1, 1958)
Psalm 24—Lift Up Your Heads, O Ye Gates
Psalm 30—I Shall Never Be Moved
Psalm 42—My Soul Thirsts For God
Psalm 43—O Send Out Thy Light
Psalm 98—Let the Sea Roar
Psalm 100—His Mercy Is Everlasting
Psalm 130—My Soul Doth Thirst
Psalm 150—Praise the Lord

Hollywood (May 5, 1959)
Conversation With a Gun
Rye Whiskey

Hollywood (September 10, 1959)
Deck of Cards

Hollywood (November 4, 1959)
Billy the Kid
Boll Weevil
Blood on the Saddle

Hollywood (November 10, 1959)
Streets of Laredo
Bury Me Not On the Lone Prairie
Sam Hall
The Face on the Barroom Floor

Hollywood (March 9, 1960)
The Vanishing American
The Gun, the Gold, and the Girl

Hollywood (February 1, 1961)
Lord, Let Thy Grace Surround Me
The Hope That Shall Sustain Me
The Sacred Guest
Salvation, O the Joyful Sound

Hollywood (February 2, 1961)
Grace Has Set Me Free
A Paradise Below
Help Me, O Lord
The Everlasting Song

Hollywood (February 3, 1961)
Awake My Charity
A Wicked World
I Dreamed of a Hillbilly Heaven
The Path of Sorrow
Let Me Freely Yield

Hollywood (June 26, 1961)
Crawdad Song
High Noon

Hollywood (July 24, 1961)
Have I Stayed Away Too Long
Jingle, Jangle, Jingle
We Live in Two Different Worlds
Deck of Cards

Hollywood (July 25, 1961)
There's a New Moon over My Shoulder
Pledge of Allegiance
Jealous Heart
Ol' Shorty
Green Grow the Lilacs
Love Me Now
Lonely Soldier Boy

Hollywood (September 14, 1961)
Strange Little Melody

Hollywood (March 26, 1962)
(With Stan Kenton Orchestra)
Cool Water
September Song

Hollywood (March 29, 1962)
(With Stan Kenton Orchestra)
Home on the Range
Red River Valley
The Green Leaves of Summer
Empty Saddles

Hollywood (March 30, 1962)
Cimarron
Wagon Wheels
The Last Roundup
High Noon
Boots and Saddles
The Bandit of Brazil

Hollywood (July 27, 1962)
(With Hank Thompson)
The Cowboy's Prayer

Hollywood (August 29, 1962)
Coo-Se-Coo
Cookson Hills

Mexico City (November 11, 1962)
(With Ralph Carmichael conducting)
Cielito Lindo
Yo Vendo Unos Ojos Negros
Alla En El Rancho Grande

Mexico City (December 1, 1962)
(With Ralph Carmichael conducting)
Adelita
Guadalajara
La Cucaracha

Mexico City (December 2, 1962)
(With Ralph Carmichael conducting a Mexican Orchestra)
El Abandonado
Lo Que Digo
Poor Lonesome Cowboy
Las Golondrinas

Mexico City (December 3, 1962)
The Border Affair

Hollywood (June 11, 1963)
The Will
La Cucaracha
The Gods Were Angry With Me

Hollywood (November 27, 1963)
Dark Days in Dallas (Unissued)

Hollywood (February 26, 1964)
That Son of a Saginaw Fisherman
The Gallows Pole

Hollywood (May 19, 1964)
My Darling Lola Lee
Papa Too
Just Down the Road

Hollywood (May 20, 1964)
Blue for the Emerald Isle
Big Brother
She Loved This House

Hollywood (May 21, 1964)
Railroad Life
Walk Big
The Fool's Paradise

Hollywood (June 16, 1964)
You Wild Colorado
Gimmee Some
The Fool's Paradise

Hollywood (December 29, 1964)
Branded (Unissued)
A Long Steel Road (Unissued)

Nashville (June 10, 1965)
(Ken Nelson, producer)
Bummin' Around
Take Him Fishing

Nashville (December 21, 1965)
Custody
The Men in My Little Girl's Life

Nashville (May 12, 1966)
Daddy's Last Letter
Mommy, Daddy, Tell Me

Nashville (June 9, 1966)
Remember Us

Nashville (July 29, 1966)
Deck of Cards

Nashville (September 27, 1966)
The Day for Decision

Nashville (September 28, 1966)
A Letter to Mrs. Bixby
A Message From the Alamo
History Repeats Itself
The Pledge of Allegiance
Old Glory

Nashville (September 29, 1966)
America Our Land
This Land Is Your Land
Remember the Alamo

Nashville (September 30, 1966)
A Letter to My Sons
Lincoln's Gettysburg Address
Lincoln's Farewell Address

Nashville (November 21, 1966)
Just Beyond the Moon
Greedy Old Dog

Nashville (April 26, 1967)
Trouble in the Amen Corner
The Wall of Silas Stone
Here Was a Man

Nashville (May 2, 1967)
Old Doc Brown
Beyond the Sunset
He Died Like a Man

Nashville (May 3, 1967)
Supper Time
The Touch of the Master's Hand
H. E. V. N.

Nashville (June 12, 1967)
A Working Man's Prayer
The Reverend Mr. Black

Nashville (November 2, 1967)
(Kelso Herston, new producer)
Blue Canadian Rockies
Distant Drums
You Don't Know Me

Nashville (November 8, 1967)
Two Glasses, Joe
The Wind and the Tree
Hey, Mr. Bluebird

Nashville (November 14, 1967)
China Doll
I Just Can't Get Away
Down in Old Matamoros

Nashville (November 16, 1967)
Bump Tiddle Dee Bum Bum
Jim, I Wore a Tie Today
In the Misty Moisty Moonlight

Nashville (February 2, 1968)
The Long Tall Shadow
The Blizzard
Stranger in Boothill

Nashville (February 9, 1968)
Dusty Skies
Texas

Nashville (February 28, 1968)
The Everlasting Hill of Oklahoma
Me and Tennessee
Conversation With a Gun
The Governor and the Kid

Nashville (July 5, 1968)
Me and Tennessee (Overdub)
The Governor and the Kid (Overdub)

Nashville (December 17, 1968)
*A Funny Thing Happened (On the
    Way to Miami)*

Nashville (May 6, 1969)
Growin' Up
Omaha

Nashville (June 24, 1969)
A-Ridin' Old Paint
Red River Valley
The Old Chisholm Trail

Nashville (June 25, 1969)
Home on the Range
A Cowboy's Prayer
Get Along Little Dogies

Nashville (June 26, 1969)
Chuckwagon Son of a Gun
Rounded Up in Glory
The Border Affair
Every Day in the Saddle

Nashville (October 6, 1969)
Wand'rin' Star

Nashville (March 4, 1970)
(George Richey, producer)
God Bless America Again
Green Green Valley
I Love You Now

Nashville (March 5, 1970)
My Elusive Dreams
Detroit City
Papa
Mama Tried (Unissued)

Nashville (April 10, 1970)
Okie From Muskogee
Legend of Shenandoah
Po' Folks
Make Friends

Nashville (April 11, 1970)
Drink Up and Go Home
Time (Unissued)
Jeremiah Jones
The Girl Who Carries the Torch for Me
(Unissued)

Nashville (November 11, 1970)
Legend of Shenandoah (Overdub)

Nashville (March 9, 1971)
Through the Years
MacArthur's Hand
One Heaven of a Woman

Nashville (March 10, 1971)
Fall Away
Looking Back
The Best Times of All

Nashville (April 1, 1971)
Battle Hymn of Lt. Calley (Unissued)
Restless Man (Unissued)
Obituary (Unissued)

Nashville (May 6, 1971)
One Heaven of a Woman (Overdub)
Fall Away (Ovedub)

Nashville (December 20, 1971)
(Joe Allison, producer)
Lorena
Little Peanut Shell
Lucy Let Your Love Light Shine

Nashville (December 21, 1971)
Bourbon Man
Charleston Cotton Mill

Nashville (February 28, 1972)
I Don't Believe I'll Fall in Love Today
Take Him Fishing
The Keeper of the Key

Nashville (February 29, 1972)
Love Me Now
Green Grow the Lilacs
You Will Have to Pay

Nashville (March 1, 1972)
The Wind of Oklahoma
Sweet Bird of Youth
Froggie Went A-Courtin'

Nashville (September 8, 1972)
Comin' After Jinny

Nashville (December 27, 1972)
One Night for Willie
This Ain't Mexico
Willie the Wandering Gypsy

Nashville (December 20, 1973)
The Americans
He Who Is Without Sin

Bibliography

Recordings and Movies

Of primary importance in researching the life of an entertainer is the study of his or her performances. I enjoyed access to most of Tex Ritter's LP albums through the record library of KGAS Radio and the collection of the Tex Ritter Museum, both located in Carthage, Texas. In addition to the musical sounds that may be studied on albums, album covers usually list the backup musicians, as well as information about the principal artist. A particularly significant album is *Tex Ritter, An American Legend,* consisting of thirty-one songs on three LP records, with explanatory remarks and reminiscences by Tex preceding each song.

The Tex Ritter Museum in Carthage, Texas, also afforded access to miscellaneous audio and video cassettes in their holdings, including audio recordings of Tex performing on the town square in Carthage. Especially useful was the video cassette compiled by the Grand Ole Opry Museum, nearly an hour of Tex Ritter's television appearances, each performance lasting only a few minutes.

I located twenty-seven Tex Ritter movies on video, including a packaged set of ten on five tapes. I viewed these movies repeatedly, especially studying the star's acting and singing techniques, along with his fighting and horsemanship, and the stunt work. *The Tex Ritter Story* is a documentary on video which profiles the entertainer's career, featuring film clips and songs. The following list indicates the Western movies I obtained on video for this project:

Song of the Gringo (1936)
Headin' for Trouble (1936)
Arizona Days (1937)
Trouble in Texas (1937)
Hittin' the Trail (1937)
Sing, Cowboy Sing (1937)
Riders of the Rockies (1937)
Mystery of the Hooded Horseman (1937)
Tex Rides With the Boy Scouts (1937)
Frontier Town (1938)
Rollin' Plains (1938)
Utah Trail (1938)
Starlight Over Texas (1938)
Where the Buffalo Roam (1938)
Down the Wyoming Trail (1939)
The Man From Texas (1939)
Roll, Wagons, Roll (1939)
Take Me Back to Oklahoma (1940)
Gangsters of the Frontier (1944)
Dead or Alive (1944)
Marked for Murder (1945)
Enemy of the Law (1945)
Three in the Saddle (1945)
Frontier Fugitives (1945)
Flaming Bullets (1945)
High Noon (1952)
The Marshal's Daughter (1953)

Scrapbooks, Files, and Newspaper Clippings

Tex Ritter's family donated most of his belongings to Tommie Ritter Smith of Carthage, with the intention that Tommie would create a Tex Ritter Museum. The collection includes everything from Ritter's guitars and saddles and costumes to his books and albums and pho-

146

tos. When Tommie asked me to write this biography, she permitted me to examine everything in the museum.

There are scrapbooks and file folders and boxes of materials that I kept in my office for months. I studied such items as publicity releases, fan club publications, magazine articles, and newspaper clippings. These clippings often were undated, and a great many did not even indicate the name of the newspaper or city, but the information and quotes they yielded were useful. Although these museum materials are uncatalogued, they constitute an invaluable resource for studying the life of Tex Ritter.

Photographs

If a picture is worth a thousand words, this book is far richer because of the photograph collection housed at the Tex Ritter Museum. There are hundreds of publicity stills and snapshots, mostly 8x10 glossies, although some of the snapshots are smaller photos. Many of these photographs were taken by the noted Nashville photographer Les Leverett, who graciously gave his permission to use his images. A few other images were obtained elsewhere, and my wife and I photographed a few objects and places that seemed significant.

Books

Berry, Margaret C. *The University of Texas, A Pictorial Account of Its First Century.* Austin: University of Texas Press, 1980.

Blum, Daniel. *A Pictorial History of the American Theatre.* New York: Grosset & Dunlap, Publishers, 1950.

Bond, Johnny. *The Tex Ritter Story.* New York: Chappell Music Company, 1976.

Bordman, Gerald. *The Oxford Companion to American Theatre.* New York: Oxford University Press, 1992.

Canutt, Yakima, with Oliver Drake. *Stunt Man, The Autobiography of Yakima Canutt.* Norman: The University of Oklahoma Press, 1997.

Cary, Diana Serra. *The Hollywood Posse.* Norman: The University of Oklahoma Press, 1996.

Cooper, Texas Jim. *Tex Ritter, The Inside Story.* Carrollton, Texas: Longhorn Productions, 1979.

Cusic, Don. *Eddy Arnold, I'll Hold You In My Heart.* Nashville, Tennessee: Rutledge Hill Press, 1997.

Davidson, Marshall B. *New York, A Pictorial History.* New York: Charles Scribner's Sons, 1977.

Dunning, John. *Tune in Yesterday, The Ultimate Encyclopedia of Old-Time Radio, 1925-1976.* Englewood Cliffs, New Jersey: Prentice-Hall, Inc., 1976.

Emery, Ralph, with Tom Carter. *Memories, The Autobiography of Ralph Emery.* Boston: G. K. Hall & Co., 1992.

Eremo, Judio, ed. *Country Musicians.* New York: Grove Press, 1987.

Erlewine, Michael, Vladimir Bogdanov, Chris Woodstra, Stephen Thomas Erlewine, eds. *All Music Guide to Country.* San Francisco: Miller Freeman Books, 1997.

Escott, Colin, with George Merritt and William MacEwen. *Hank Williams, The Biography.* Boston: Little, Brown and Company, 1994.

Everson, William K. *A Pictorial History of the Western Film.* New York: The Citadel Press, 1969.

Fernett, Gene. *Poverty Row.* Satellite Beach, Florida: Coral Reef Publications, Inc., 1973.

Finler, Joel W. *The Hollywood Story.* New York: Crown Publishers, Inc., 1988.

Fredriksson, Kristine. *American Rodeo, From Buffalo Bill to Big Business.* College Station: Texas A & M Univeristy Press, 1985.

Garfield, Brian. *Western Films, A Complete Guide.* New York: Rawson Associates, 1982.

Gentry, Linnell. *A History and Encyclopedia of Country, Western and Gospel Music.* St. Clair Shores, Michigan: Scholarly Press, Inc., 1972.

Hall, Wade. *Hell-Bent for Music, The Life of Pee Wee King.* Lexington, Kentucky: The University Press of Kentucky, 1996.

Hardy, Phil. *The Western.* New York: William Morrow and Company, Inc., 1983.

Hemphill, Paul. *The Nashville Sound: Bright Lights and Country Music.* New York: Simon and Schuster, 1970.

Hintz, H. F. *Horses in the Movies.* New York: A. S. Barnes & Company, Inc., 1979.

Hirschhorn, Clive. *The Universal Story.* New York: Crown Publishers, Inc., 1983.

Holland, Ted. *B Western Actors Encyclopedia.* Jefferson, North Carolina: McFarland & Company, Inc., 1989.

Jennings, Waylon, with Lennie Kaye. *Waylon, An Autobiography.* New York: Warner Books, Inc., 1996.

Kingsbury, Paul, Alan Axelrod and Susan Costello, eds. *The Country Music Foundation. Country, The Music and the Musicians, From the Beginning to the '90s.* New York: Abbeville Press, 1988.

Logsdon, Guy. *High Noon—Tex Ritter.* N.p., 1991.

Lomax, John A. *Songs of the Cattle Trail and Cow Camps.* New York: Duell, Sloan and Pearce, 1919.

Malone, Bill C. *Country Music, U. S. A.* Austin: University of Texas Press, 1985.

McCloud, Barry, and contributing writers. *Definitive Country, The Ultimate Encyclopedia of Country Music and Its Performers.* New York: The Berkley Publishing Group, 1995.

Moore, Thurston, ed. *Pictorial History of Country Music, Vol. 3.* Denver, Colorado: Heather Enterprises, Inc., 1970.

Nassour, Ellis. *Honky Tonk Angel, The Intimate Story of Patsy Cline.* New York: St. Morton's Press, 1994.

Nelson, Susie. *Willie Nelson, Heart Worn Memories.* Austin, Texas: Eakin Press, 1987.

Ringgold, Gene. *The Films of Rita Hayworth.* Secaucus, New Jersey: The Citadel Press, 1974.

Rothel, David. *The Singing Cowboys.* New York: A. S. Barnes & Company, Inc., 1978.

Schlappi, Elizabeth. *Roy Acuff, The Smoky Mountain Boy.* Gretna, Louisiana: Pelican Publishing Company, 1997.

Tinkle, Lon. *An American Original, The Life of J. Frank Dobie.* Boston: Little, Brown and Company, 1978.

Tiomkin, Dimitri. *Please Don't Hate Me.* Garden City, New York: Doubleday & Company, Inc., 1959.

Torrence, Bruce T. *Hollywood: The First Hundred Years.* New York: Zoetrope, 1982.

Townsend, Charles R. *San Antonio Rose, The Life and Music of Bob Wills.* Urbana, Illinois: University of Illinois Press, 1976.

Tuska, Jon. *The Filming of the West.* Garden City, New York: Doubleday & Company, Inc., 1976.

West, Richard. *Television Westerns, Major and Minor Series, 1946-1978.* Jefferson, North Carolina: McFarland & Company, Inc., Publishers, 1987.

Whitburn, Joel. *Top Country Singles, 1944-1993.* Menomonee Falls, Wisconsin: Record Research, Inc., 1994.

Willoughby, Larry. *Austin, A Historical Portrait.* Norfolk, Virginia: The Donning Company, Publishers, 1981.

———. *Texas Rhythm, Texas Rhyme.* Austin: Texas Monthly Press, 1984.

Zinman, David. *50 From the 50's, Vintage Films From America's Mid-Century.* New Rochelle, New York: Arlington House, Publishers, 1979.

Articles

"*Billboard* Salutes Tex Ritter and His 40 Years in Show Business." *Billboard* (December 7, 1968), 43-48.

Comber, Chris. "The Tex Ritter Story." *Country Music Review* (August 1972), 21-24.

Cooper, Texas Jim. "The Comeback Trail." *The Dallas Times Herald Sunday Magazine* (October 23, 1966), 15-16.

———. "Tex Ritter." *Trails West Magazine*, Exclusive Edition (June 9, 1979).

———. "Tex Ritter." *True West* (April 1972), 38-41.

———. "Tex Ritter, The Best Loved Singing Cowboy." *Remember When* (1971), 3-8.

———. "Tex Ritter, His Songs & Personality Expressed The Ethos Of Our West." *Films in Review* (April 1970), 204-216.

———. "Tex Ritter, My Favorite Entertainer." *KGBS Country* (June 1968), 30-35.

———. "Tex Ritter's Going Strong." *Alcalde*, The Univeristy of Texas Alumni Magazine (July 1972), 16.

Long, Allen. "Tex Ritter: Cowboy Legend." *Record Collector's Journal* (September 1975), 7.

Mallory, Randy. "Where Country Meets Western." *Texas Highways* (June 1995), 22-25.

McDonald, Archie P. "B Westerns of the 1930s: Singing Cowboys and Others." *Journal of the American Studies Association of Texas.* Vol. XII (1981), 3-7.

O'Donnell, Red. "'High Noon' Query Starts Last Tex Ritter Interview." *Nashville Banner* (January 3, 1974), 1,8.

Parks, Jack. "Hollywood's Singing Cowboys: They Packed Guitars As Well As Six-Shooters." *Country Music* (July 1973), 34-38.

Paxman, Bob. "Tex Ritter still riding high in Nashville." *Country Weekly* (August 26, 1997), 50-52.

Pugh, John T. "Tex Ritter: From Sagebrush to Senator." *Music City News* (July 1970), 4, 25.

Ritter, John, and Jerry Buck. "I'm Proud of My Brother." *Redbook* (November 1987), 76-77.

Sawyer, Kathy. "An Interview With Tex Ritter, Champion of the West." *Country Music* (July 1973), 24-32.

Smith, M. P. "The Ritter Family." *Western Film Collector* (March 1973), 14-27.

Stewart, Richard. "Tex Ritter—Good Guy to the End." *Beaumont Enterprise-Journal* (February 4, 1979), E-1.

"Tex Ritter." Fourth Annual Golden Boot Awards Program (August 15, 1986), 6.

"Tex Ritter Dead at 67." *Billboard* (January 12, 1974), 6.

"Tex Ritter Exhibit Draws Big Crowd." *C & W Variety* (September-October 1997), 4-5.

"Tex Ritter at Monogram, 1938-39." *Yesterday's Saturdays* (June 1977), 1-10.

Thompson, Jerry. "Tex Ritter Plans To Start Food Franchise." *The Nashville Tennessean* (January 15, 1969), 16.

Wheeler, Bill A. "Nudie the Tailor." *Country Music Review* (March/April 1965), 40-41.

Miscellaneous

Cactus, The. Published by the Students of the University of Texas. 1923-1927.

Campaign book on "Song of the Gringo." Hollywood: Grand National Studio, 1936.

Cariker, Earl. Interviews with Essie Bayers and Grace Gray, on audiotape. 1988.

Cariker, Earl, and Donnie Pitchford. Videotaped interviews with Omar Thomas and Howard Hardin, and footage of Murvaul townsite. 1988.

Country Crossroads Scrapbook, Tex Ritter. Fort Worth, Texas: Southern Baptist Radio and Television Commission, n.d.

The Fabulous Johnny Cash Spectacular. Program for 1964 television special. Duluth, Minnesota: Tele-Vue Publications, Inc., 1964.

Johnson, Robert Lee. *The Devil's Trail*. Movie script. Columbia Picture Corp., September 1941.

"Just . . .Tex." Promotional pamphlet from the Acuff-Rose Artist Corp., designed by the Charlie Lamb Corp., Nashville.

Panola County Birth Record Book, Volume I. Panola County Courthouse, Carthage, Texas.

Program for the Fourth Annual Golden Boot Awards of The Motion Picture and Television Fund, held on August 15, 1986, at the Warner Center Marriott Hotel, Woodland Hills, California.

Ritter, John. Reminiscences of his father, on videotape. October 19, 1989.

Ritter, Tex. Address before Country Music Association Awards Banquet, October, 1973. Fort Worth, Texas: Southern Baptist Radio and Television Commission.

Ritter, Woodward Maurice. Transcript, South Park High School, Beaumont, Texas, 1920-22 (includes credits from Carthage High School, 1918-20).

Ritter, Woodward Maurice. Transcript, University of Texas, 1922-27.

Spindletop, The. Published by the Seniors, South Park High School. Vols. V and VI (1921, 1922).

Stars of RANCH PARTY on Tour, souvenir picture program.

Stovepipe Hat, Program.

Tex Ritter Capitol Record Hits, Song Folio. New York: Tex Ritter Music Pubications, Inc., 1948.

Tex Ritter Show, The. Advertising folio.

Tex Ritter Song Folio With Scenes From Columbia Pictures.

Tex Ritter's Death and Funeral. File at Tex Ritter Museum, Carthage, Texas.

Ward, Luci. *Vengeance Of The West*. Movie script. Columbia Pictures Corp., March 1942.

Index